AUTOB...
VO...

PICTURES IN THE HALLWAY

Each volume in the evocative and richly entertaining autobiography of Sean O'Casey is essential reading for a proper appreciation of this major Irish dramatist whose plays were among the most exciting developments in modern drama.

Born in the back streets of Dublin, suffering from weak and diseased eyes, he lived in poverty and physical hardship for many years. In his late teens he became a manual labourer and after working on the roads or in the docks from five in the morning to six at night he would spend his evenings helping the cause of the Gaelic League and Sinn Fein. He became Secretary of the Irish Citizen Army and a founder member of the Irish Labour Party. Although his first published work was in 1907, not until the success of *Juno and the Paycock* in 1925 did he give up manual work and become a full-time writer.

Sean O'Casey wrote his autobiography in six volumes over more than two decades, recreating in Volume 1 the days of his Dublin childhood. Volume 2 tells of his coming to manhood and includes episodes later used by the playwright in *Red Roses for Me*.

The photograph, 'Hubrand Bridge' by Evelyn Hofer, reproduced on the cover, is from *Dublin: A Portrait* by V. S. Pritchett and Evelyn Hofer, published by The Bodley Head.

By the same author in Pan Books

AUTOBIOGRAPHY (VOLUME 1):
I KNOCK AT THE DOOR

AUTOBIOGRAPHY
VOLUME 2

PICTURES IN THE HALLWAY

SEAN O'CASEY

UNABRIDGED

PAN BOOKS LTD : LONDON

First published 1963 in a three-volume edition
of the Autobiographies in St Martin's Library series
by Macmillan and Company Ltd.
First published 1971 in this form by Pan Books Ltd,
33 Tothill Street, London, S.W.1

ISBN 0 330 02717 4

*Printed in Great Britain by
Richard Clay (The Chaucer Press), Ltd, Bungay, Suffolk*

CONTENTS

PICTURES IN THE HALLWAY

Time flies over us, but leaves its shadow behind

To the memory of the Rev E. M. Griffin, BD, MA, one-time Rector of St Barnabas, Dublin. A fine scholar; a man of a many-branched kindness, whose sensitive hand was the first to give the clasp of friendship to the author.

A COFFIN COMES TO IRELAND

AN OCTOBER sky was black over the whole of Dublin; not a single star had travelled into the darkness: and a bitter rain was pelting down on the silent streets. The rain had the still and un-resisting city to itself. No one was out to feel it, and it seemed to pelt down harder in rage because there wasn't a soul out to shiver under its coldness and its sting. Even the heavy-coated and oil-caped police were hidden back in the shelter of the deepest door-ways, uneasily dozing the night hours away, lulled into drowsi-ness by the slashing rain's pelting murmur falling on the spray-swept pavements. Everyone else was fast asleep in bed. Safe and sound oul' Dublin swept itself to sleep, well watched over by God and His Blessed Mother, assisted by the glorious company of the apostles, the goodly fellowship of the prophets, and the noble army of martyrs; each man, woman, and child having as well a guardian angel leaning over the bed, watching, with a well-cocked eye, the charge left in his care; so safe and sound and well oul' Dublin slept. Sound she was in sleep, and safe she felt, for God was there, and they were here, and the night was passing silently away, and soberly, except for the rain dancing a savage dance all over the city on the patient pavements. Behind heavy silken curtains, in happy-looking beds, slept the nicely night-gowned; behind tattered and tumbled curtains, on muddled mattresses, gowned in paltry calico or faded flannelette, slept the sisters and brothers of the nicely nightgowned. But the poor Protestants turned up their noses at the guardian angels, for they didn't believe in them, and felt sure and safer stuck in the arms of Jesus, their rock of ages and their morning star.

Between two narrow sheets, thickly ribbed with patches, under the eyes of God, among the prophets, apostles, and martyrs, in the midst of the valley of sleep, slept Johnny in his skin, for he had neither calico nor flannelette to decorate his rest. Under a few old coats and several big squares of buff felt, showing the inky im-print of the *Daily Express*, pinched by Archie from the stereo-typers' room, Johnny lay snug, for the fire of the day lay half awake still in the grate and the room was still warm; while his mother slept in the little room opposite, in a fast sleep, too tired to feel cold, finding in sleep the one glamour of a hard day.

The fire was the one thing that Mrs Casside kept going without fail. It was the one thing, she said, that made a house a home. Without a mother, she'd say, a home isn't much; without a fire, it's less. The poor must walk in the light of God and in the light of their fire. A full belly in a fireless room felt frosty; an empty belly beside a fine fire felt fuller. A bright fire, she said, in a poor home is the shadow of God's smile.

Johnny opened his sleepy eyes with difficulty, and saw over opposite the dull glow of the fading embers in the dusty grate. The fire was slowly dying, and the room was growing a little chillier, so Johnny's hand groped around the bed and pulled the *Daily Express* blanket closer round his naked shoulders; pulled it nice and tight around him, and closed his heavy eyes, while he dimly heard the rain pouring down outside and beating on the window-pane.

—Pity, he murmured, that a fire had to die down, to grow cold, to pass away, to change from dancing flame to throublesome dust an' ashes: like us, he thought, like ourselves, like every man; in everyone, the Sunday school says, sooner or later, the flame dies down to dust an' ashes. But me Ma says, he went on thinking slower and slower, me Ma says th' oul' Sunday school says a lot it shouldn't think, an', an' it's time, time enough to think o' dyin' down to dust an' ashes when you're old an' blind an' deaf an' dumb an' bothered.

As he tried to slide back into a warm and steady sleep, he heard a stir out in the rain-soaked, shivery streets, coming nearer and nearer till the stir was heard in the house, and nearer, till the stir was heard in his own room. Through his heavy-hanging lids, the shadowy glimpse of a dark form, like his mother, and another, like his brother, Archie, moving stealthily about the room, slid like a sly dream into his sleepy mind, and low, far-away murmurs told him they were talking together. He saw the tiny glow that still lingered in the fire suddenly darken down and disappear, and he felt faintly that his mother had flung a shovel of coal on to the fire. He waited in a drowsy stillness, watching and listening, till he saw bright flames rising steadily from the fire that had darkened down, and, in the midst of the rising flames, the dark form of his mother fixing the kettle firmly down on the top of the flaming coal.

—Tea, thought Johnny; she's going to make tea, so something must be up.

He raised himself up on his elbow, rubbed his eyes, looked over at his mother who was now putting some cups and saucers on the table; while Archie was tugging on his trousers standing by the old horsehair sofa which was a stately seat by day and Archie's narrow and nettlesome bed by night.

Now Johnny heard the patter of feet in the street mingling with the patter of the rain upon the pavements, and the sound of voices crossing and recrossing each other, crying Stop Press, Stop Press! He could hear the hasty Archie cursing querulously that a fella could never get his trousers on quick when he wanted to, and his mother muttering, half to herself, We'll get to know all about it soon enough; and the noise of windows and doors opening, and the murmur of the kettle singing her song, panting it out, panting it out, and she sitting in the midst of the flames rising from the red glow of the fire.

—What's wrong, mother? asked Johnny, his sleep falling from him, his eyes opening wider, his ears hearing heartily the sounds in the room and the sounds outside in the street.

—You lie down, you lie down, replied his mother, an' go asleep again.

—Why've you lit th' fire, an' why've you made tea? inquired Johnny.

—Poor Parnell's dead, said Archie, busy with his boots.

—It may be only a rumour, murmured his mother.

—We'll soon know for certain when we get a paper, muttered Archie.

Parnell! What had this man done that all the people were so upset about him, one way or another? The mention of his name always gave rise to a boo or a cheer. The Roman Catholics who wouldn't let a word be said against him a while ago, now couldn't pick out words villainous enough to describe him; while the Protestants who were always ashamed of him, now found grace and dignity in the man the Roman Catholics had put beyond the pale.

Well, they could all breathe in peace now that he was dead. His Ma said his Da often said that the first chance the priests ever got, they'd down Parnell. And here he was now, down among the dead men.

The pattering of the feet went on in the streets outside, mingling with the patter of the rain on the pavements. Archie, safe now with his breeches and his boots on, whipped up his cap, and hurried out to try to get a copy of the Stop Press telling that a golden bowl was broken, a silver cord loosened, and a wheel broken at a mighty cistern.

For fiddling with a woman or something, the Catholics had turned away from him. Kitty O'Shea it was who had brought the anger of the righteous overmuch upon him. Johnny, one day, had hadda row with Kelly over him, sticking up for Parnell when Kelly shouted Parnell was a bad bugger, an' no right-minded Irish kid 'id mention his name. He had answered Kelly, saying that Parnell was a mighty man of valour, and acquainted with thruth; and Kelly had chanted,

> *We'll hang oul' Parnell on a sour apple three,*
> *We'll hang oul' Parnell on a sour apple three,*
> *We'll hang oul' Parnell on a sour apple three,*
>   *As we go marchin' along!*

And he had chanted back,

> *We'll hang oul' Tim Healy on a sour apple three,*
> *We'll hang oul' Tim Healy on a sour apple three,*
> *We'll hang oul' Tim Healy on a sour apple three,*
>   *As we go marchin' along!*

Then Kelly had spat on him, and he had made for Kelly with eyes flaming, teeth bared, fists clenched, to diminish him, down him, and utterly destroy him out th' land o' Canaan; but Kelly ran for his life, stopping a safe distance off to throw a stone; and they had fought a great battle, with stones, each aiming at the other's head, till a policeman appearing round the corner, they hooked it off to get outa reach of the horney's hand.

Now Parnell was dead, and they were crying it in the streets; and fear came upon them that the one man they had was gone. A great thing had been taken, and a lot of little things had been left. They'd have to go now through the valley of the shadow of life alone; face their enemies alone; fight their enemies alone; and they divided, and moved by every wind, unstable as water. The pillar of fire that had led them so long and so bravely and so brightly had died out; and they were all in the dark, like the Protestant bishops.

Johnny's mother had wet the tea, and was sitting thoughtfully by the fire, waiting for Archie to come back with the Stop Press. Johnny was well awake now, and could fully hear the patter of the feet on the street outside and the more musical patter of the rain falling on the pavement. Something exciting had happened, and he wasn't going to be left out of it. Besides, getting up gave him a further chance of reading the grand adventures of Frank Reade Jr, the Professor, Barney and Pompey, with their electric car in the unknown jungles of Central Africa. So he slid from the bed and began to put on his trousers. When he was dressed, he sat down by the fire on the opposite side to his mother, flung himself into the middle of the jungle, and waited, with his mother, for Archie to come back with the Stop Press.

His mother looked at him for a moment or two, then she got silently up and put another cup and saucer on the table.

—You might as well have a cup with us, she murmured. It won't do you much harm to lose a little sleep on a night like this.

Johnny's mind was in the midst of the jungle, and his heart was gladdened by the warmth of the fire, when the door opened and in came Archie, wearing a solemn face, the glistening rain-drops gathered thick on the hair his cap hadn't covered, and with a paper snugly sheltered under the breast of his coat.

He went over, sat down by the fire, and opened the paper slowly.

—It's thrue, he said, it's too thrue – Parnell's gone from us for ever.

Johnny could hardly help tittering. He knew in his heart that Archie was forcing sorrow into his face; that he didn't care if Parnells died every day of the week; for often and often Johnny had heard him run Parnell down, for no one who didn't do that could stay very long working for the *Daily Express* and *The Warder*, whose weekly cartoons for years had been a generous denial of anything good, or semi-good, or damnmy-semi-good in Parnell or his policy; for the owners of the papers were begotten of the whorus of England, through MacMourrough of the curses, the time the Normans came over the sea to set up a new civilization where none was; blessed by the holy Pope, they came, with horse and sword and lance and shield and a sthrong desire for thrue religion to be fostered among the holy heathen Irish.

—In Brighton, when the clock was sthrikin' twelve, said Archie, he passed away. Give me love to me colleagues an' to th' Irish race, were th' last words he utthered in this world. He said he'd be with us on Saturday an' he's keepin' his word: he's comin' back to us on that very day – in a coffin. Archie crumbled up the paper viciously. The dastards have done it to him: in room 15, they slew th' man that made them. That's where it was done; that's where Parnell was sacrificed by Healy an' his pack o' conceited

Catholic curs. In room 15, they sthruck him down undher ordhers from that spidery-minded, Bible-basted bastard, Gladstone!

There, thought Johnny, th' pack gathered to down their Leader. They sat up all night so that they might be there first thing when the door opened. Their hearts were warm for the work. A pig grunted, a dog snarled, a fox barked, a wolf howled, and a rat squealed, waiting for the door to be opened. They were in a state of grace; Parnell wasn't. They were the ten or twenty righteous men who would deliver the Nation from God's and the Catholic bishops' wrath. Parnell had forfeited the right to lead the holy men of the holy island of scuts and schemers. Besides giving an untidy look to Kitty O'Shea, the man had gone too far in other ways. Didn't he say in America that, None of us, whether we be in Ireland or America, or wherever we may be, will be justified till we have destroyed the last link which keeps Ireland bound to England; and didn't the large towns and small towns and great cities vie with each other to show him honour? Didn't Governors of States knock each other down going to receive him, in the dint of their hurry to get there first? Didn't armed soldiers line the streets he passed through, firing salvoes of artillery when his carriage came in sight; and didn't Congress make him come to speak to its members, and let them hear the message his heart had for Ireland and the world? Was there e'er an Englishman ever got that in the Land of the Stars and Stripes? Salvoes of artillery they got, right enough, and musket-fire at Bunker's Hill, York-town, and Saratoga; but that was a welcome that they didn't want.

But the O'Briens, the Dillons, and the Healys, mudmen, mad-men, badmen, bedmen, deadmen, spedmen, spudmen, dudmen, poked on by the bishops, were dead set on making an end of him, so that they might keep a tight hold on the people they were groom-ing down for an insect seculorum life; for it was plain that Parnell was turning the people aside from the bishops that maketh them poor, and were striving to make their homes their own, and to plant and to mow and to reap and to sow in safety; forgetting that the real seeds to be sown were eternal seeds, and not just those that sprang up this season and died down the next; seeds that were likely to be trampled down, dug up, and scattered abroad in the medley of the plan of campaign; while in the distance, the Right Honourable Ewart Gladstone, with his big ear on his big head, cocked to hear what was going on, sat with his most honourable, most respectable, and most moral bum glued to the impregnable rock of Holy Scripture; sat on, and waited for the Irish swine-hearts to do unto Parnell as they wouldn't that others should do unto them, so that he could satisfy the Nonconformist conscience after the impudence of Parnell shoving his white and slender finger into the solid, cold, glittering eye of plump biblical piety fashioned in the new annunciation of the Westminster Confession. Then there was the scandal the good Catholics felt had been given to the multitude of saints who had made her what she was and is and is to be; and in the heat of it all, whom did they hear calling over the banisters of the top story of heaven but St Patrick himself, and he yelling at them out of a

Exordium Purgatorius Patricius

to stir themselves, and dhrain out this bad dhrop which had fallen into Ireland's pool of perfect virtue, so that I may have a little ayse where I now am, afther toilin' an moilin' for yous, day in an' day out, for years, prayin' on the cowld top o' Croagh Pathrick for yous till I was near black in th' face; for, if yous don't do the needful, it's all up with me labour of huntin' yous into a state o' grace, unequalled in any other so-an'-so land th' wide world over; an' yous ought to know, since I didn't let it go with Oisin, son o' Finn, son o' Coole, I'm not going to let it go with Parnell, an' so make a show of meself before all the grinnin' foreign canonized bowseys gathered round me, here, waitin' for a chance to laugh outright an' inright, all of them glaumin' to see something that'll put a sthrain on perpetual piety for me Irish flock; an' a guffaw from them 'id be a poor thing for me to hear an' have to bear, considerin' th' pains an' penances o' Mount Slemish, an' then, afther I had slipped home, comin' back, sailin' over the sea, over th' boundin' wave, to bring th' thruth to Ire-land, that was full o' Dhruids bendin' their knees to th' sun, thin-kin' it to be somethin' above the ordinary because it went down every mornin' an' rose up every night; seekin' weary an' wasteful knowledge outa th' movement of stars an' comets, the nature of all earthly things, instead of confinin' their seekin' an' searchin' to the undherstandin' of things unseen, not made with hands, eternal in th' heavens; with me landin' first in Wicklow, an' dhriven out again be th' ignorant thicks; and' afther bearin' divers hard things pleasantly for your sakes, didn't I light the Paschal fire on th' hill o' Slane, right undher th' eyes o' Leary, King o' Taraxum, which when the king saw, he swore a mighty oath be the elements, an' sent for his high Arch-dhruids, sayin' to them, looka here, me fine fellas, yous 'ud betther find out who it is is after kindlin' a fire on the hill o' Slane, goin' again' the law of none to be lit for the time while th' fire on Tara flames; an' th' high Dhruids answerin' him, sayin', O great king o' th' Leinster-men, none of us know from Adam who has done this thing, but we warn you, if the fire on Slane isn't put out before the people have a chance o' seein' it, you an' your kingdom'll be *non est* an' done in for ever.

An' th' king, in a fit o' fury, hastened off at high speed in his chariot o' gold, followed be his chiefs in their chariots of silver, followed be their warriors in their chariots of bronze, right up to where I was and me companions were; the king, in a rage, jumpin' down from his chariot before it had stopped, near breakin' his neck with the sudden jolt he got, an' hard put to it he was to keep a look of dignity on him, an' he staggerin'; but when they came up, all they could see was a little herd o' deer singin' a psalm round th' fire; so when I saw that his heat had cooled a thrifle, I changed meself an' me comrades back into our own fair forms again; but no sooner was I lookin' as per usual, when the threacherous oul' varmint flung back his philibustherin' arm to fling his fella-damnable spear to let the daylight through a holy saint; but lo and behold, when the spear was tossed, it stopped short in its flight, came to the ground upright on its butt, fornent me, an' started to execute a Kerry dance round the fire, bowin' low to your humble every time it passed, murmurin' to me, *laus* to youo, *laus* to youo, an' then the king, the chieftains, and the warriors fell flat on their faces, sayin' this is a great doing, and it is marvellous in our eyes; an' when I thought they had been long enough on their faces, I told them, sayin' yous can get up, now, an' thry to behave like decent people; an' with that, they got up, hangin' their heads for shame, so that I took pity on them, an' said to the spear buckin' about in th' Kerry dance, off with you now, an' get back to where you came from. The spear stopped dancin', and afther givin' me a low bow, throtted back to where the king was, an' settled itself neatly in his hand again. Didn't I pluck the shamrock, shovin' it undher their poor ignorant noses so that they could get a good idea of the Holy Thrinity afther a short discourse. Didn't I go fairin' east an' fairin' west, an' fairin' south, endurin' many thrials an' various vexations, shapin' yous for th' joys o' heaven, regardless o' cost, thrimmin' yous into a state of grace that won an everlastin' ordher o' merit from GHQ up here; givin' cause for jealousy to the English cowled an' mitred boyos roamin' round here who scraped into canonization by the skin of their teeth, let in outa pity that any counthry 'ud be left out of representation in th' city o' Zion, which wouldn't be good democracy, an' might give rise to a misunderstandin'; rememberin', too, all the sthrange an' wondherful miracles that were done be me of changin' bees into butther an' butther back again into bees; hookin' a cloud with me crozier outa the sky, an' turnin' it into wolsey blankets for th' deservin' poor; turnin' a corn-cub into a curate, a bell-wether into a bee-sheep, a chosen chance into a chesty church, a porbeagle into a prayer, a penance into a pokerface, a pagan into a pursebearer, the rights of man into the benefit of clergy, an act of attrition into an *auto-da-fé*, a hell-incised poverty into a *gloria in excelsis* destitution, the lure o' life into a set o' rosemary beads, gatherin' th' joy o' the world round a cross; an' now yous want to spoil it all, an' to bring these glories to a timely end, to mar the merit of a creeping host descending down to heaven, makin' what is bitther sweet, an' what is heavy light an' easy to bear. Ye backsliders! seekin' security o' tenure when yous ought to be savin' your souls, followin' Parnell when yous ought to be followin' me, rushin' with money for the plan o' campaign, while your fathers in God sweat in an effort to collect their dues. There's no use in yous shoutin' at me that if yous as much as put a coat of whitewash on your walls th' rent goes up; let it; yous have heaven. I'm not listenin'; I want yous to listen to me, an' whisht about th' fear of wearin' decent clothes in case th' landlord 'ud see yous; let him; for the Lord is no respecter of persons, an' has a mitt outsthretched out for him in rags as well as for him in plushy broadcloth; so listen, an' keep quiet an' be still, an' ordher yourselves rightly to what I'm sayin', before the sanctified English bowseys here get to know I'm growin' hoarse sthrivin' to keep the members of me flock from throwin' off th' thraces of godly conthrol, an' sing silent about your livin' an' sleepin' an' dyin' undher one coverin', an' the' quarter acre's clause killin' thousands, an' that women are dyin' o' starvation with babies at their dhried-up breasts; for yous should be well used to these things be now, and, mind yous, while yous are watchin' your little homes gettin' levelled be th' crowbar brigade, or lyin' with your childher on the hard frosty road undher a red-berried rowan three, be night or be day, dyin' of hunger or perishin' o' cold, your last breath blessin' God for everything, yous'll all be slowly floatin' up here to me, unbeknown to yourselves, till yous are near enough for me to haul yous in be th' hand, the scruff o' th' neck, or th' sate of your throusers; only, when yous do come up, thry to act like civilized beings; don't shove, don't push, don't all thry to get in front, an' sweep, like rowdies into the New Jerusalem, but, number off, form fours, an' march tidily, as if yous' were all used to these things, an' that it was no novelty for yous to be in high-grade quarters, an' so show th' English saints up here, th' lowest o' them, esquires, that St Patrick's children can enther into eternal bliss without gettin' excited about it.

An', once for all, let me hear no more o' someone diggin' a grave outside of a poor landlord's door; or of some decent Catholic rent-agent havin' to walk well bent forward to keep himself from suddenly sittin' down be the weight o' buckshot poured into his innocent backside; or of hapless men stealin' about in th' moon-light, bent on business, with a mean musket stickin' its nose through the brambles an' briars of a hedge, waitin' for something to turn up, sendin' me flyin' for a dark corner to hide in, till th' explosion was over; an' don't have me comin' to this windy nook again, for it's not a warnin' yous'll get next time, but a blast that'll send yous all sluicin' down to th' lowest channels o' hell, where yous'll have all eternity an' a day or two longer to regret that ye ever laid a hand on another person's property; rollin' round like porpoises, yous'll be, in a sea o' fire, surgin', singein', scourgin', scorchin', scarifyin', skinnin', waves o' fire gorgin' themselves on every part of your bodies so that every ear, every eye, every mouth, every nose, an' every arse'll be penethrated be flames, each as sharp as a loony surgeon's knife, red hot, an' plungin' deep wherever its point turns; an' then it'll be no use bawlin' out to St Patrick, Oh, St Patrick, jewel o' th' Gaels, lift me up outa this, for th' love o' God; for there'll be no liftin' up or out, but only a deeper shovin' down each time a minute of a second passes, if yous don't listen to the counsel of your pastors an' th' witherin' advice of the grand oul' man, Gladstone, kissin' th' hand o' Mariar Curehelli for luck, when he was shocked by hearin' Parnell sayin' in his icy way, afther bein' asked what he thought of the great William, I think of Mr Gladstone and of the English people what I always thought of them; they will do what we can make them do; an' the English awkward squad up here with their ears cocked, listenin' to every word, thinkin' themselves God's own household guards, an' never tired o' whisperin' that their form o' government might be inthroduced here with some advantage to keep things goin' straight; so on yous go, now, holdin' on to th' grand name yous have outa all th' glories of our past spare life, seen in th' lovely ruins scattered about from one end o' th' counthry to th' other, showin' your disconcern for anything in th' nature of a worldly vantage; an' don't let a few goboys sthruttin' round spoil it all be thryin' to keep a mad an' miserable sinner as a leader of the holy Irish people. So arise today through th' sthrength of th' love o' cherubim, in obedience to angels, an' down Parnell; in th' service of archangels, in th' hope o' resurrection to meet with a good greetin', an' down Parnell; in th' prayers o' pathriachs in predictions of prophets, in preachings of apostles, rise up today, an' down Parnell; in faiths of confessors, in innocence of holy virgins, an' in deeds o' righteous men, rise up today, an' down Parnell! Get a holt of that oul' balls, Tim Healy, who's as good as yous can get at th' moment, an' lift him into th' place of honour; take him, an' yous'll be safe in takin' heed of what I'm sayin' here over the cowld banisthers of heaven, in imminent danger of catchin' a chill, for the gauzy clothes supplied by th' commissariat department here's nice enough for ceremonial occasions, but a bit of a delusion when you leave the cosy corners.

We're just closin' down here, now; th' time be th' heavenly clock is exactly one-thousandth part of a second past the first hour of eternity, an' we're closin' down. God night, everybody, God night.

Johnny roused himself from his book, and saw Archie take down from the wall a fine crayon drawing done by Michael some years before, which had won him a bob from his Da, a fine crayon drawing of Charles Stewart Parnell, his bold, black-bearded, cold, Irish, menacing face that hid a wild, unwearying, tumultuous love for Ireland.

Archie reverently placed the picture on the table beside his cup of tea, while Johnny drank his, sitting close to the fire, feeling the presence of a calamity he couldn't fully understand. A large lot of crape, remaining safely in the big box after his Da's death, was brought forth by their mother, who cut some of it into strips, hemming the edges, and these sombre scarves were wound round and round the picture of Parnell. Then, on a white piece of cardboard, Archie, in beautifully-formed letters, wrote down, Give My Love To My Colleagues And To The Irish Race, afterwards fixing it firmly to the bottom of the frame. Pulling over the little table as close to the window as it could go, he placed the picture on it, safely propped up by several volumes of Merle d'Aubigné's

History of the Reformation; and there stood Parnell, gazing out over the dim street, as bravely and defiantly as he would ever look out upon anything again.

—There he is now, said Archie, with defiant sorrow in his voice, lookin' out on the people who first denied, an' then bethrayed him.

—It's sore they'll miss him, before many days are over, said his mother; an' we may be sure, if there's such things as rewards goin', there's one for him, wherever he is.

—What did he die of? asked Johnny.

—Sorra one knows, said Archie. All we know is that he's lyin' face down in a coffin, unlike any coffin ever seen be anyone.

—It's half past three, Archie, said Mrs Casside, glancing at the alarm clock, an' you've just time to get to your work, without puttin' yourself to a gallop.

Archie wound a brown muffler round his neck; put on a thick old ulster-coat; donned again his peaked hat with its two ear-flaps, kept up by being tied over the top; looked at the picture again for a second; saluted smartly, and murmured, Ireland's uncrowned King comes back in a coffin, an' half-dead Ireland now lies close beside him.

Then Archie went out into the darkness and the rain to do his work for the *Daily Express* and *The Warder*, in their dispatch and publishing office, where he toiled from four o'clock in the morning till six in the evening, for fifteen bob a week and a free copy of the *Express*, daily, and another free copy of *The Warder* when the week was nearing its end.

After Johnny had finished his tea, his mother got him to bed again, while she sat staring into the fire, her chin cupped in her hand, and a puzzled, weary look in her black eyes.

Johnny closed his eyes and dozed, opened them again slowly; saw the wet grey dawn creeping in through the window, closed them once more, to open them on what he would see when the coffin came to Ireland.

The brown coffin came along, the box that held all Ireland had, sailing, like a drab boat, over a tossing sea of heads, falling, rising, and sinking again, polished by the falling rain; flanked on the one hand by the dirty dribbling railway station, and by the fat and heavy-pillared front of St Andrew's Church on the other; but few were going in to bow before the altar, or mutter a prayer for the repose of a pining soul in purgatory; for all were here, all were here, gazing at the brown coffin sailing along, like a drab boat, over a sea of tossing heads, falling, rising, and sinking again, polished by the falling rain, silent, the coffin went on, in the midst of the rolling drumbeat of the Dead March.

Ireland's uncrowned King is gone.

And a wail came from a voice in the crowd, keening, We shall lie down in sorrow, and arise sorrowing in the face of the morning; there is none left to guide us in the midst of our sorrow; sorrow shall follow us in all our ways; and our face shall never wear the veil of gladness. We shall never rejoice again as a strong man rejoiceth; for our Leader has vanished out of our sight.

No damask, silk, or brocade threw beauty into the moving, silent throng; no rich banners, heavy with heraldry hatched a thousand years ago; not a single jewelled order flashed from a single breast, rising and falling with the dark rolling drumbeat of the Dead March; no bishops, posing as sorrow and salvation, in purple and gold vestments, marched with the mourning people; many green banners, shrouded with crape, flapped clumsily in the wet wind, touched tenderly, here and there, with the flag of the United States and the flag of France, floated over the heads of the stricken host, retreating with its dead to the place that would now be his home for ever.

An Ireland came into view, an Ireland shaped like a hearse, with a jet-black sky overhead, like a pall, tinged with a broad border of violet and purple where the sun had set for ever, silvered gently by the light of many cold and silent stars; and in the midst of the jet-black sky, the pure white, set face of the dead chief rested, his ears shut dead to the wailing valour. Our uncrowned King of Ireland's gone.

A moving mass of lone white faces strained with anger, tight with fear, loose with grief, great grief, wandered round and round where the whiter face lay, set like a dimming pearl in the jet-black sky, violet-rimmed where the sun had set for ever, silvered softly by the dozing stars, sinking deeper into the darkness soon to for ever hide the wan hope of Ireland waning.

Out of the east came a sound of cheering.

Joy is theirs, cried a voice from the wailing; overflowing joy, for they feel safe now, and their sun is rising; their table is spread and their wine is circling; lift your heads and you'll hear them cheering:

The English!

THERE THEY were all on the bed, nicely folded and smoothed out, laid ready for Archie. Johnny counted them again: the black tights, red satin slippers ornamented with gilt buckles, white silk shirt heavy with gold embroidery, round fluffy velvet cap with a feather encircling it, and the long, gorgeous crimson velvet cloak, to furnish him out for the character of King Richard the Third.

Johnny, himself, looked gay and glorious in black tights, crinkled a lot, for they were a little too big for him; black silk shoes, stuffed with paper to make them stay on his feet, each shoe bossed with a pretty red rose, the rose of Lancaster; and a lovely black velvet coat, dazzled with silver, lined with blue silk and slashed in the wide sleeves with fluffy diamond shapes of white silk to give him a look of the imprisoned King Henry the Sixth, mortal foe of the hunchbacked Duke of Gloucester. It had all been arranged that Archie and Johnny should give the prison scene where the poor King is murdered by the Duke determined to let nothing stand between him and the crown.

The scene, with one or two from *Conn the Shaughraun*, and a Minstrel Show, in which Archie was to sit in the right-hand corner making jokes and rattling the bones, was to be given at a charity concert to be held in the Coffee Palace, Townshend Street, a few nights later on. His mother had gone against it, giving out that that sort of thing was altogether too much for a boy of Johnny's age. She would have conquered, too, if Archie hadn't been the only one bringing in the wherewithal to keep the little home together. Johnny, too, had to be kind to Archie, and careful not to say anything that would offend, for, as well as keeping him, he gave Johnny tuppence a week, a treasure that gave him the power to buy *The Boys of London and New York* and a further volume of *Deadwood Dick* or *Frank Reade Jr, and his Electric Airship*. So Johnny cleaned Archie's boots with a cake of Cooney's Paste Blacking taken out of its oiled green paper, and pressed into an old tin to keep it soft; ran errands for him; and generally laboured to please and serve his brother in every possible way. All the same, Johnny didn't like him, and did these things because there was no way out of it. When he was old enough to go to work, it would all come to a sudden end. Then, when he was told to go there or come here, or do this or do that, he'd say I'm goin' to be your servant no longer; you're big an' able enough to do all these things yourself. Just now he had to wear the handcuffs. So Johnny waited for time to bring him out of the land of Egypt and out of the house of bondage, to march straight into the land of Canaan,

Caanan, sweet Canaan, I'm bound for the land of Caanan,
Caanan is a happy place, so I'm bound for the land of Caanan.

Oh, it wasn't Canaan that should be beating into his mind, but all that Henry had to say to Gloucester:

Ay, my good lord: My lord, I should say rather;
'Tis sin to flatther, 'good' was little better:
'Good Gloster' and 'good devil' were alike,
And both prepostherous; therefore, not 'good lord'.

He wished Archie would put in an appearance, to go over in costume the parts they had to play. He was more than minutes behind time already. He hoped nothing had gone wrong with the scheme. He had toiled and toiled over his part, saying it to his mother a hundred times, getting her to tell him, as well as she could, what the hard words meant; seeking out Ella when his mother failed, and getting her to give him the right sound and way of speaking them. He had learned the part from one of three volumes of the *Works of Shakespeare* won as a prize by Ella when she was a student in Marlborough House Teachers' Training College. Big and stately books they were, packed with pictures of battles, castles, and marching armies; kings, queens, knights, and esquires in robes today and in armour tomorrow, shouting their soldiers on to the attack, or saying a last lone word before poor life gave out; of mighty men of valour joining this king and reneging that one; of a king gaining a crown and of a king losing it; of kings and knights rushing on their foes and of kings and captains flying frantic from them; of a frightened man, with a naked sword in his hand, meeting a roaring lion in a city street; of men on a bare and bony heath sheltering each other from lashing rain, stormy wind, and noble lightning turning the jet-black sky into a deadly dawn of a day of wrath; of murderers slaying men, women, and children, with many other pictures of stirring and delectable things that happened before order, fair-play, and civility took root in the world.

Johnny moved about restlessly, sitting down and standing up, murmuring his part softly to himself,

So flies the reckless shepherd from the wolf;
So first the harmless sheep doth yield his fleece,
And next his throat unto the butcher's knife.

Johnny wandered to the door, and looked anxiously up and down the street, watching and waiting for Archie.

—Oh, come in owre that an' don't be standin' at the door, he heard his mother call out sharply; what'll the people passin' think of you in that extraordinary get-up? Come in an' play with the things in the basket, an' keep quiet till Archie comes.

The basket his mother meant was a huge thing, quarter as big as a small room, brought to Johnny's place in an ass and cart driven by Archie and Tommie Talton, who wanted it out of the way for a few days to make room for a spread his family was giving in honour of his sister's wedding. Neither Mother nor Ella liked the idea of Archie getting too pally with these acting folk who were little bether than heathens and publicans, if you opened your eyes to the truth. And Ella had heard from a friend that Talton's sister had been married years and years ago; and what they really wanted was to get the stuff away safe from the bailiffs, who were expected to come down on them any minute for money they owed. Ella's friend said, too, that Tommie Talton and Bill were just two mouldy down-at-heels mummers who snatched up a few frayed shillings a week by cod-acting in the Mechanics, a well-soiled, tumble-me-down theatre in Abbey Street, where no fairly respectable man or woman would dare to be seen.

Tommie Talton looked respectable enough. He was a long lanky young man of twenty-four, with a pale perky face, heavily pockmarked. His small head was covered with bunches of golden-brown curly hair. His eyes were pale grey and so big that they seemed to take a long time to shut or open whenever he blinked. A tiny golden moustache lined his upper lip. He was gone in the knees, and though his feet where wide apart when he walked, his knees nearly knocked together. He wore a dark-blue suit, thin, and so bright with brushing that he shone in the sun like a knight in armour. A jerry hat was perched rakishly on the side of his head, pressing down on a golden curl that foamed out from under the rim of the hat and fell down over his ear. He walked with a saucy sway, like a knock-kneed sailor just beginning to get used to the roll of a ship. Johnny had liked him the moment he had seen him perched on top of the basket, with Archie carefully leading the little ass. Besides, he had brought in the basket treasures that the kings who rejoiced when they saw His Star in the east, and came to worship Him it shone over, might have carried in their caravan when they journeyed to the town of Bethlehem.

Only a day or so ago Johnny had nothing; now he had more than all the toys of all the boys in all the streets, even if they were gathered together into one big heap.

He thought of the toys he had had since he could remember: a little cart painted red and blue, a drum, a big bender kite of green an' yellow paper, with a blue tail, made by Archie when he was in a good humour, a Union Jack, a little bigger than his hand, got for answering Bible questions correctly, transfers, lots of regimental badges sent him by Tom and Michael. That was about all; oh, no, there was the half of the Noah's Ark he got the time he an' Archie were in the one bed sufferin' from scarlet fever, Archie gettin' the other half of the Ark. That same time, Michael an' Ella were down with it too, an' his mother put Tom in the same bed with Michael who had it the worst, so that Tom might get it too, an' she could nurse them all at the one time. An' she nursed them all without help from a single soul, though Tom escaped it, and had a gay time because he couldn't go to work, and got paid for doing nothing. When they were well, men had put them into the streets while they took away all the bedding and lighted sulphur in the rooms, pasting paper over the cracks in the doors to keep the cure from gettin' lost.

What's this comes after, bush an officer? bush an officer, bush an officer? Oh yes,

> The bird that hath been limed in a bush,
> With trembling wings misdoubteth every bush;
> And I, the hapless male to one sweet bird,
> Have now the fatal object in my eye,
> Where my poor young was lim'd, was caught, and kill'd.

Johnny fingered fondly the lovely things in the basket. It was filled with the costumes for *Macbeth*, *King Henry the Sixth*, *Richard the Third*, *The Shaughraun*, *The Colleen Bawn*, *The Octoroon*, and other plays; with swords, shields, daggers, cutlasses, halberds, lances, armour, kepis, shakos, pistols, clergymen's robes and soldiers' uniforms, and silk, satin, sateen, dimity, and damask costumes in great an' wonderful variety.

Today he was a King, tomorrow he could be a Bishop, and the next day a Colonel. What other boy in the whole vicinity could come near him in all the glorious things that he possessed? If he was only a little older, or a little taller even, he could wear all these things well, without his mother havin' to put tucks in them to keep from thrippin' up an' makin' a holy show of himself before people ready to laugh from the crow to the cock to the last star's enthry into the night sky.

What a pity they hadn't chosen a bit outa *Conn the Shaughraun* insteada pouncin' on Shakespeare's stiff stuff. If they only knew, Boucicault was the boyo to choose. What did Tommie Talton say when they were takin' tea an' tinned salmon, the time the basket came, and Johnny's Ma had piped out of her that Johnny's Da always held by Shakespeare as the greatest writer of all time; an' Ella backed her up with a huh an' a sniff at the mention of Boucicault. This is what Tommie Talton said in the face of their fright an' their fury:

> *Shakespeare was a great choice: but Dion Boucicault was really quite as great a choice as Shakespeare. Shakespeare's good in bits; but for colour and stir, give me Boucicault!*

There they were stuck, an' couldn't say a single word in con-thradiction; for Tommie Talton had known the theatre since he was a chiselur, an' neither Ma nor Ella had never as much as put a nose inside a theatre since they were born except to see a Shakespeare play. Ay, an' Archie capped it all be tellin' them that Tommie's brother, Bill, was the greatest Conn the Shaughraun that ever walked the boards. In a way, Johnny felt sorry over his Ma an' Ella makin' such sillies of themselves be displayin' their ignorance of things far beyond their understanding.

So wasn't it a sthrange pity that those in charge of the comin' event hadn't chose more o' Boucicault an' less o' Shakespeare? He'd be at home in the part of the priest in *Conn the Shaughraun*. Hadn't he done a good bit of it in front of Talton, with Archie as Corry Kinchella, the villain; an' hadn't Tommie Talton said, *Be God, that's wondherful for a chiselur like you!* How could anyone beat this:

FATHER DOLAN: *I'd rather see her tumble down in death an' hear the sods fallin' on her coffin, than speak the holy words that would make her your wife; for now I know, Corry Kinchella, that it was by your means and to serve this end that my darling boy, her lover, was denounced and convicted.*

C. KINCHELLA: *'Tis false!*
FATHER DOLAN: *'Tis thrue. But the thruth is locked in my soul*
(he points finger at heaven), *an' heaven keeps the key!*

But that's not what I ought to be thinkin' of, but the part I have
to play. When the time comes, I won't know a word.

He pulled over two chairs, nailed together underneath by a
baton, with semicircular pieces to form arms, the whole covered
with a crimson cloth; and sat down in it, thinking.

Let me think, now. Yes, Archie says,

> *Thy son I kill'd for his presumption*

and I say

> *Hadst thou been kill'd when first thou didst presume,*
> *Thou hadst not liv'd to kill a son of mine.*
> *Men for their sons', wives for their husbands' fate,*
> *An' orphans for their parents' timeless death,*
> *Shall rue the hour that ever thou wast born.*
> *The owl shrieked at thy birth, an evil sign;*
> *The night-crow cried, aboding luckless time;*
> *Dogs howl'd, an' hideous tempest shook down trees;*
> *The raven rook'd her on the chimney's top;*
> *An' chatthering pies in dismal discord sung.*
> *Teeth hadst thou in thy head when thou wast born,*
> *To signify thou cam'st to bite the world.*

An' afther gettin' up from the chair before the last few lines,
Archie runs me through with

> *I'll hear no more; die, prophet, in thy speech.*

I'll have to tell him to be careful of that lunge, for he ripped me
coat a little, once before. An' I'll have to learn to fall betther. It's
all very well for Talton to say, just let yourself go. I did that once,
an' nearly broke me neck.

Oh, here's Archie, now, at last, thanks be to God!

Johnny heard Archie go into the other room where his tea was
waiting for him. Even if he took his tea first, Johnny knew Archie
wouldn't be long, for in anything new he was always bursting to
be in the middle of it. So he gave a last look-over and a last pat to
the pompous garments, nicely folded and smoothed out and laid
ready for Archie to compose himself into the part of the hump-
backed Duke of Gloucester. They were all there, waiting, beaming

out their beauty through the gathering dusk. So Johnny sat down beside them, and waited, murmuring over the words of his part to himself, and listening to the cheers he imagined the audience would give when the scene had ended.

The gentle dusk crept away and dismal darkness sat in her place. But Archie did not come, and Johnny's heart was troubled. Let not your heart be troubled, neither let it be afraid. A ray from a street lamp sidled in through the window and laid a sad light on the pompous clothing, nicely folded and smoothed out, lying lonely on the bed. Everything was quiet; even silence lay sleepy in the room; and Johnny's bowels ached with disappointment.

—Johnny, Johnny, are you there? his mother called from the other room. Take your gay get-up off, and come an' take your tea.

He sat on for a moment; then he took off the black velvet, the blue silk, and the silver, and went on into the other room.

There was Archie, close to the fire, reading the pink-coloured *Evening Telegraph*, saying no word, taking notice of no one.

Johnny sat silent, sipping his tea.

When he had read the paper, Archie got up, brushed his hair before a little glass hanging on the wall, lighted his pipe from a spill thrust into the fire, put on his hat and coat, and went out without a word.

—He's in one of his tanthrums, said his mother, as she sighed, because the whole thing's been put off on accounta the death of the Duke o' Clarence.

—It's a shame, she went on sighing again, as she sipped her tea, it's a shame that the young prince died, for they say he was the best beloved son of his sorrowin' mother, and a prime favourite with the poor old Queen.

ROYAL RISIDENCE

JOHNNY'S MOTHER had brushed and brushed his clothes, had darned some holes in his stockings, had bought him a cheap pair of yellow shoes; had fixed a new white collar round his neck, had spit a lot on his hair, calling the spit gob-oil, and brushed his hair till the skin on his skull stung; had put a tiny square of well-washed rag, carefully hemmed, into his pocket, warning him to use it whenever he felt the need to snuffle; planted his sailor's cap tastefully on his head, had slipped a dee into his pocket, telling him not to buy anything foolish with it; adding that pennies weren't easily come by; and, standing a little distance away from him, had said, I think you'll do all right now. The night before she had made him wash himself all over from hot water in a basin, so that he would be clean and presentable when his Uncle Tom came to bring him to see Kilmainham Jail.

—Your Uncle Tom's Crimean comrade has said that he may bring you with him, an' it's a chance that you won't get again in a lifetime to see the jail.

His Uncle Tom had come to time, and after promising Johnny's mother that he wouldn't let the boy see anything that might keep him awake at night, had taken the boy's hand and led him forth to see the sight of a jail where men who did wickedly were kept safe away from the temptation of doing anything worse than they had done before.

Johnny was proud of his uncle because he had fought in the Crimean War where a sabre-cut had sliced an arm from the shoulder to the elbow, where often, after a night's sleep beside his horse, his uncle's hair had been frozen to the ground; and Nurse Nightingale had bandaged the wound up with her own hand in the hospital at Scutari. Ay, an' his uncle, too, was a member of the Purple Lodge of the Orange Ordher, a great thing to be; though his Ma said his Da said that it was just as foolish to duck your head before a picture of King Billy as to duck it before the picture of a saint.

Johnny thrust his chest out, and walked swift beside the lanky figure of his uncle, glancing now and again at the soft dark-brown eyes, the wide mouth sthretchin' nearly from ear to ear, and the snow-white hair tumbling over his ears and falling over his forehead.

Away in a tram from Nelson's Pillar they went for miles an' miles, having first managed Cork Hill where the two tram horses were helped by another, called a pulley-up, that waited there to link itself in front of any tram wanting to mount the Hill; along Thomas Street, Uncle Tom pointing out St Catherine's Church, where, he said, Robert Emmet had been hung, drawn, and quartered for rebellion against England.

—Is it a Roman Catholic church? asked Johnny.

—No, no, said Uncle Tom; it's a Protestant one.

—You'd think they'd hang a Roman Catholic rebel outside a Roman Catholic church, said Johnny.

—But poor Emmet was a Protestant, Johnny,

—Now, that's funny, said Johnny, for I remember the night of the illuminations, the conductor of the thram we were in, singing about someone called Wolfe Tone, an' me Ma told me he was a Protestant too.

—Ay was he, said Uncle Tom, an' Parnell an' Grattan an' Napper Tandy too.

—They all seemed to have been Protestants, murmured Johnny, relapsing into thoughtful silence for some moments. What's dhrawn an' quarthered? he asked suddenly.

—Oh, said his uncle, when a man's hanged, they cut off his head and divide him up into four parts.

—An' was that what was done to poor Robert Emmet?

—It musta been when he was sentenced to it.

—Why was Robert Emmet a rebel, Uncle?

—Oh, I suppose he didn't like to have the English here.

—What English, Uncle? I've never seen any English knockin' about.

—The soldiers, Johnny, the English soldiers.

—What, is it Tom an' Mick you mean?

—No, no; not Tom or Mick; they're not English – they're Irish.

—But they're soldiers, aren't they?

—Yes, yes; I know they're soldiers.

—They're Irish soldiers, then, Uncle, that's what they are. Aren't they, Uncle? Same as you were when you fought in the Crimea.

—No, no, no; not Irish soldiers.

—Well, what sort of soldiers are they?

—English, English soldiers, really.

—Then Emmet musta wanted to get them outa the counthry, as well as the others, if they're English soldiers. But Mick an' Tom an' you are Irish, so how could you be English soldiers?

—We're Irish, but we join the Army to fight for England, see?

—But, why fight for England, Uncle?

—Simply because England's our counthry, that's all.

—Me Ma says me Da said it isn't, but that Ireland's our counthry; an' he was a scholar, an' knew nearly, nearly everything, almost; so it isn't, you see.

Uncle Tom stroked his chin, glanced at Johnny with his big soft eyes, and looked puzzled.

—Isn't what, what isn't what? he asked.

—That England's not our counthry at all, and that everyone here's Irish.

—Well, so they are, said Uncle Tom.

—Well, went on Johnny, if Mick an' Tom are Irish, how can they be English soldiers?

—Because they fight for England; can't you understand?

—But why do they, an' why did you fight for England, Uncle?

—I had to, hadn't I?

—How had you?

—Because I was in the English Army, amn't I afther tellin' you! said his uncle, a little impatiently.

—Yes, but who made you, Uncle?

—Who made me what?

—Fight for England?

—Good God, boy, don't you know your Bible? And Uncle Tom took a fat-headed pipe from his pocket, and was about to stick it in his mouth when he remembered he couldn't smoke in a tram, so he put it back again. Johnny felt that his uncle was puzzled, and a little cross because he was puzzled. So he sat silent, and for a few moments looked out of the tram window, thinking how hard it was to get anything out of the grown-ups unless they had a book in their hand. He wanted to know these things; he felt he must know. He glanced at his uncle's kind face. He had heard that long ago, and Tom a young man, that he had been a policeman, wearing comical clothes, sky-blue cut-away coat, top hat, and white duck trousers; that he hated pulling anyone; that when he did, and they came near the station, his uncle would push the prisoner from him and say, For God's sake go home and have a rest, and come out again when you've had a sound sleep; and that all the oul' fellas an' oul' ones called out after him when he passed, God bless you, God bless Mr Hall who wouldn't harm anybody, so that, in the end, he had to leave the police.

—Where in the Bible does it say, Uncle, that the Irish must fight for the English?

—In the seventeenth verse o' the second chapter o' the first o' Pether, it says, Fear God, honour the king, so there you are, Johnny; we can't get out of it. Me father before me learned it; I learned it; and you're learning it now.

—An' whoever doesn't is a very wicked person, and is bound to go to hell, isn't he?

—Very wicked and bound to go to hell, echoed Uncle Tom.

Johnny thought for a moment, watching the horses' heads nodding as they strained forward to pull the heavy tram along.

—Me Ma says me Da said that Parnell was anything but a wicked man, Uncle.

—Parnell a wicked man? 'course he wasn't. Who said he was?

—Why didn't he fight for England, Uncle, then?

The fat-headed pipe came again out of Uncle Tom's pocket, who looked at it longingly, then put it back again.

—What are you goin' to buy with the penny your mother gave you, when we get outa the thram? he asked Johnny.

—Oh, just jawsticker of a sponge cake or something – why didn't he, Uncle?

—Why didn't he who?

—Why didn't Parnell fight for England an' not go again' the Queen?

—I wouldn't say that Parnell went again' her.

—Oh yes, he did, said Johnny deliberately; for me Ma heard me Da sayin' once that Parnell paid no regard to the Queen; and would sooner rot in jail than obey any law made be her, an' that he worked, night an' day, to circumvent them because, he said, English law was robbery. An' Georgie Middleton told me he had a terrible row with his father because Georgie stuck up for Parnell, and his oul' fella was afraid of him, and slunk out to get dhrunk and came home cryin'.

—Georgie shouldn't go against his father be sticking up for Parnell.

—But why shouldn't he stick up for him, Uncle, when you say that Parnell wasn't a wicked man?

—Because Georgie Middleton's a Protestant, that's the why, Johnny.

—Yes, but Parnell you said was a Protestant too, so why shouldn't a Protestant stick up for another Protestant?

—Oh, you're too young yet to understand things, replied Uncle Tom with a little irritation. When you're older, you'll know what's right and what's wrong.

—Grown up, like you, Uncle?

—Grown up, like me, Johnny.

—When I'm like you, I'll understand everything, won't I?

—Yes, yes; then these things won't be a bother to you any more.

—But he was grown up, wasn't he?

—He, who?

—Parnell an' the Queen, and all them who went about arguing the toss; they didn't know, for when I was ever so little, I heard some of them shoutin' at me Da on accounta what he was sayin', an' he laughin' at them, an' makin' them more angry an' shout louder than ever.

Uncle Tom looked out of a side window to see rightly where they were. We're just there, he said; an' looka here, Johnny, while we're in the jail, say nothin' about Parnell, nor anything you think your poor Da used to say either.

—For why?

—Oh, there's no why about it – you've just got to do what you're told.

—Here we are, he added, as the tram slowed down amid a bright jingle of bells swinging from the horses' necks.

—The jail – right ahead, isn't it? he asked the conductor.

—Right ahead an' a little to the left, said the conductor; is the young fella's father one o' the boys?

—No, no, no; not anything like that, said Uncle Tom, as he swung off the tram and helped Johnny down, though Johnny didn't want his help, for he could spring off the tram a far sight sprightlier than stiff oul' Uncle Tom.

They hurried up Bow Lane into the heart of Kilmainham where everything made the place look as if it were doing a ragged and middle-aged minuet.

—There, said Johnny's uncle, pointing a thumb to the right, is Swift's Hospital that the Dean o' St Pathrick's got built for the lunatics; and there to the right again, when they had got a little farther on, is the Royal Hospital, where hundhreds of oul' men who fought for Queen an' counthry are kept safe in perfect peace; and, soon, we'll see the jail, so, when you're talkin' to your friends, you'll be able to boast about the wonderful things you've seen today.

There it was. A great, sombre, silent stone building, sitting like a toad watching the place doing its ragged middle-aged minuet. A city of cells. A place where silence is a piercing wail; where discipline is an urgent order from heaven; where a word of goodwill is as far away as the right hand of God; where the wildest wind never blows a withered leaf over the wall; where a black sky is as kind as a blue sky; where a hand-clasp would be low treason; where a warder's vanished frown creates a carnival; where there's a place for everything, and everything in its improper place; where a haphazard song can never be sung; where the bread of life is always stale; where God is worshipped warily; and where loneliness is a frightened, hunted thing.

His uncle pulled his coat open showing the Crimea medal shining on his waistcoat, with two bars striding across the coloured ribbon. They went through the iron gateway leading to the main door of the jail, the ready way in and the tardy way out, a heavy thick iron gate set deep, desperately deep, into solid stone, with a panel of five scorpions wriggling round each other carved out of the stone that formed the fanlight that gave no light to the poisoned city of Zion inside. As Johnny and his uncle came near, the heavy thing swung open, and a warder stood there, with the Crimea medal glittering on his breast, and a hand stretched out to greet Tom, who seized it and held it for a long time.

—Come along in, Tom, me son, and your young friend, said the warder. You're welcome, he's welcome, you're both as welcome as the rooty call blowing for dinner.

They went inside to the courtyard, the heavy thing swung back again, and Johnny was installed as a freeman among the prisoners and captives.

They went into the central hall, and, standing on the flagged floor, gazed at the three tiers of cells, with narrow railed lobbies on the first and second floors, and a narrow steel stairway leading to each of them.

It's a great sight, said the warder, to see the prisoners coming in, in single file, step be step, hands straight be their sides, over a hundhred of them quiet an' meek, marching right, left, right, left, each turning into his own little shanty when he comes to it; with half a dozen warders standing on the alert, and the sound of the steel doors clanging to, like the sound of waves on a frozen sea, all shut up safely for the night, to read their Bible or stretch themselves down and count the days to come before the Governor dismisses them and wishes them godspeed. Here, me lad, he said, opening a cell door, have a decko at the nice little home we provide for them who can't keep their hands from pickin' an' stealin'; or think by the gathering together of the froward, they can overcome the submission they owe to our Sovereign Lady; forgetting that they have to reckon with the goodness of God who will always weaken the hands, blast the designs, and defeat the entherprises of her enemies. Go on in, me lad – no fear o' the door closing on them who are the friends of those sent by the Queen for the punishment of evildoers.

Johnny went a little way into the cell, with his heart beating. It was spick and span, the little stool scrubbed till it was shining like a dull diamond, and the floor spotless. A slop-pail stood to attention in a corner; over it a tiny shelf holding a piece of yellow soap and a black-covered Bible, showing that cleanliness was next to godliness; and a tiny grating to the side of the door, letting the air through to keep the cell fresh and wholesome; all, in the night, lighted up by a baby-tongued flicker of gas in a corner, the light that lighteth every man that cometh into the jail, the captive's little pillar of fire, the prisoner's light of the world, a light to them that sit in darkness, with this light, needing no light from the sun, lead kindly light, amid the encircling gloom, lead thou me on till the day break and the shadows flee away.

Johnny stepped back out of the cell, for he could hardly breathe in it, and he felt a warm sweat dewing his forehead. Stone and steel surrounding loneliness, pressing loneliness in on itself, with a black-coated Bible to keep it company, and a jaundiced eye looking out of the darkness. They peeped into the chapel with its plain benches in the nave for the jailbirds and the seats on the side for the guards; and dimly, in the distance, shrinking into an archway, the althar, having on it two candles, one on each side of a crucifix that stood on the top of a little domed cabinet where, the warder said, the priest kept his God all the secular days of the week and took him out for exercise on Sunday.

—Here's something to see, said the warder, showing a fairly-sized room, lighted with two arched windows, for this is the room where Parnell was kept when we had him prisoner here. A man, he went on, if ever there was one, a sowl man. The least little thing you done for him, it was always thank you, thank you, from him even when you opened the door before you locked him up for the night. A sowl man, I'm tellin' you, Tomas, an honour to do anything for him, he was that mannerly, even to us, mind you, that you'd fall over yourself in thryin' to please him; and never the icy glint in his eye, unless the name of some big bug in the opposite camp was mentioned; oh, be Jasus, then the flame in his eye 'ud freeze you, ay, man, an' shook hands when he was leaving, too; imagine that, Tom, shook hands with us that was busy holdin' him down, though no one in this world, ay, or in the next either, could really hold Parnell down; for even in here he was more dangerous than he was roamin' about outside, a deal more dangerous, for, with Parnell a prisoner, the Irish 'ud stop at nothin', ay, an' well he knew it – an' one of us, too, Tom, me boy.

—How one of us? asked Uncle Tom.

—Why, a Protestant, man, makin' him fair an' equally one of ourselves. Not fit to do anything for themselves, the Roman Catholics must have a Protestant to lead them. Looka at them now, an' Parnell gone! Gulpin' down the sacrament while they're tryin' to get at each other's throats; furiously tetherin' themselves to the roar o' ruin; twistin' into a tangle everything that poor Parnell had straightened out, with the hope of ever standing up against a single law that England likes to make gone for ever!

Johnny edged over to a window and looked out: there they were, a big gang of them, some with hand barrows, carrying stones, some with wheelbarrows, wheeling them away; and others, with great hammers, smiting huge stones into little pieces, each hammerer gruntin' as he brought his sledge down with a welt on the obstinate stone, while two warders, with carbines, watched well from a corner.

Earnest-lookin', evil-lookin', ugly-lookin' dials on the whole o' them, thought Johnny to himself.

—There, said their guide, pointing to a steel door opposite to Parnell's room, is the cell that Carey, the informer, lived in, afther he had turned Queen's evidence till he was taken down to Kingstown be three different journeys in three different cabs, an' put on board the liner, only to be shot dead when he came in sight of Port Elizabeth. But come on, now, an' see the best sight of all.

Tom's warder friend stopped by a cell door away by itself in a quiet part of the prison. He opened it, stepped back, stayed silent for a moment or two, then, bending over, said almost in a whisper, Gentlemen, the condemned cell.

Uncle Tom took off his hat, and when Johnny saw that, he took off his too; and they both tiptoed a little way into the condemned and silent cell: a little less like a cell, a little more like a room with its silent stool, silent table, little bigger than the stool, a cold fireplace, and a cold hearth.

—If only the walls could speak, murmured Uncle Tom, looking around and nodding his head wisely.

Johnny felt his heart tighten, and he wished he was well away out of it all; at play with Kelly or Burke or Shea; or tryin' to say something nice to Jennie Clitheroe. He'd look, an' wouldn't see; he'd listen, an' wouldn't hear; but would keep his mind fixed on pretty little Jennie Clitheroe. She had gone down to the counthry for a week. Wasn't it well for her! He had never been to the counthry yet. He had never been in a train – only watched them go by, leaning over the railway bridge in Dorset Street. Jennie was bringing back with her a bundle of yarrow stalks, and she'd give him some of them. He an' Jennie were to put nine of them under their pillows, and throw one over their left shoulders so that he'd dream of his future wife and she'd dream of her future husband. He knew who his future wife 'ud be, so he did, well: her name began with a J. And when he was throwin' the yarrow stalk over his shoulder, he'd say, sing-song like,

> Good morrow, good morrow, fair Yarrow,
> Thrice good morrow to thee!
> I hope, before this time tomorrow,
> You'll show my thrue love to me.

—He sat there on that very stool, the warder was saying, sayin' nothin', only murmurin' here as he did on his way to the gallows, Poor oul' Ireland, poor oul' Ireland. Brady, the best an' bravest of the Invincibles, never losin' an ounce o' weight the whole time, waitin' for the day, for the hour, for the last minute to come, for ever murmurin', Poor oul' Ireland, poor oul' Ireland. Underneath the flags outside, in one big grave lie the five of them, goin' to the grave without a word of who did it or how it was all done.

—A sinisther commination on any poor man's life, said Uncle Tom sadly.

—'Tis an' all, replied the warder, just as sadly; but fair in the square of a respectable life we've got to do, if we want to come to a faithful an' diminishin' end.

—Anywhere here, said Uncle Tom, suddenly, in a loud whisper to his friend, where we could thrance the youngster, an' go for a dhrink?

The warder hurried them down a corridor, at the end of which was a door. He opened this, and they all went into a room where there was a fire, with a bareheaded warder sitting beside it, smoking, his feet inside the fender. In the centre was a dirty-looking table and some hard chairs; a frying-pan, saucepan, kettle, and teapot stood on the hobs. On a rack along the wall hung some warders' caps, two carbines, and some batons were hanging from hooks in the rack.

The warder, seated by the fire, turned and looked, then turned away again, and went on smoking.

—We're leafin' the kidger here for a few seconds, said Tom's friend; he'll just sit quiet an' be in nobody's way.

—He's welcome, said the warder seated by the fire, and went on smoking.

Tom's friend settled a chair by the fire for Johnny, and when he was seated, hurried away with Uncle Tom. The bareheaded warder sat still, never once glancing at the boy, but went on smoking, smoking, and gazing into the fire.

Johnny sat tight in his chair, wishing that his uncle would come to bring him home. He'd force himself to forget seeing the condemned cell, and think, only think of going home again, home, going home again, homeward bound –

> *Homeward once more, homeward once more,*
> *The good ship is speeding for old Erin's shore;*
> *The exile's returning, no longer to roam,*
> *But to end his career in his own native home.*

The bareheaded warder sat on silently, staring into the fire, smoking. Johnny began to lilt softly, very softly, to himself:

> *His counthry he loved, an' for Ireland he bled,*
> *For which he was sentenced to hang until dead;*
> *The sentence was not carried out, if you please,*
> *Instead he was sentenced for years 'cross the seas.*
> *For twenty long years, the prime of his life,*
> *He was banish'd from children, his kindred, and wife.*
> *Oh, how his heart yearns as he stands on the shore,*
> *Awaiting the steamer bound homeward once more!*

The bareheaded warder turned, suddenly, to stare at Johnny.

—If I was you, he said, I wouldn't sing a song like that here.

Johnny hushed his murmuring song, and gazed at the staring warder, puffing fiercely at his pipe, and staring straight at him.

—No, me boy, he went on, such a song doesn't sound decent in such a place as this.

Then he turned his head away, and stared again straight into the fire, as if he had been sentenced to staring for the rest of his life: I'm an old bird alone, he said, after a long pause, an' just waiting for what we all must meet. My own an' only son did three years, an' then had to fly the counthry. He was a Fenian, an' I never knew. Then the missus died. Three long years me own an' only son did in jail, an' then had to fly the counthry.

Johnny's heart went out to the old man. How bitther it musta been to have had a son who done three years in jail.

—Maybe, he said, your son, in the counthry he's gone to, 'ill do away with the disgrace he brought on yous all here.

The bareheaded warder sat and sat silent for a long time staring away into the fire, an' puffin his pipe.

—I'm proud of me son, he said slowly, proud of him, an' ashamed of me son's father. I'm tellin' that to you, young boy, because you haven't yet been fortified be the world against the things good men do. He took the pipe out of his mouth and jerked the stem over his shoulder towards the door. Say nothin' to them two dismissioners when they come back of what I said to you, young boy. He slapped the mouth of his pipe against the palm of his hand to loosen up the tobacco in it. I was in the Crimea meself, but I never wear me medal; never since the day me boy was sentenced to three years' penal servitude. Mind you, I'm only saying that there's a lot lyin' soft undher an althar no nearer heaven than a lot of others lyin' hard undher the flagstones of a prison yard.

Johnny sat still, thinking, for he didn't quite know what the oul' fella meant. The ould head had sunk down deep into the breast, and the pipe was shakin' in the oul' mouth. Johnny watched it tremblin', give an upward jerk as the lips tried to close upon it, then slide down the breast of the blue coat, and fall, scattering the silken ashes over the hearth, while the old warder slumbered on, and the fire began to sink down into a dull glow.

Johnny glanced over again at the batons hanging from the hooks in the wall, like dried-up little dead men, the batons that battered the bowseys. There must be a lot o' bowseys in Ireland, for his Ma told him his Da had said that the police were never tired of batonin' the people. It was the only way that God could bless Ireland, for God moves in a mysterious way His wondhers to perform. Yet the sleepin' warder looked a kindly oul' man. Maybe he was too ould to use a baton properly any longer. Maybe this was the very man who had brought food to the Invincibles while they were waitin' for to go to the gallows. Only a few steps away, five of them, Brady, Curley, Fagan, Caffrey, and the boy Kelly, were lyin' low, dead arms round each other, in one common grave, the warders an' convicts walkin' over them, day afther day. Johnny shuddered, and drew his chair a little nearer to the dying fire. The Invincibles, the Invincibles.

The dusk was falling, the fire was burning low, and the old warder slept on, sunk back in his hard chair, his hoary old head bent down deep in the hard breast of his trim blue coat.

Johnny remembered the cross cut deep in the path a long way up the road from the main gate of the park; an' the mounted Constabulary, a constant glint of silver an' black, goin' up, goin' down the road ever since the time of the killin', the shinin' steel of the harness tinklin' to the gentle throt o' the horses, watchin' an' waitin', with carbine and sabre, for the worst to happen. But the great We are the Invincibles had been there before them. The cab crawling about, holding men with revolvers itching their hands. A jaunting-car waiting, waiting some distance away, the driver flicking the mare with a whip to keep her warm and taut, the day Burke jumped off his car to join Lord Cavendish walking his way to the Vice-Regal Lodge, full of plans to circumvent Parnell; putting his foot down firmly on foreign soil, his fine head full of the fact that he would do unto Ireland as he would that Ireland should do unto him, fresh from England, with a fresh heart and a fresh mind eager to plant and to sow and to reap and to mow and to be a firmer boyoy-oy, to show how things could be done and should be done and must be done if the four parts of the United Kingdom were to go hand in hand through this vale of tears, strong and hopeful, firm and faithful, fond and free, bringing a new era to Eire, a push afoot, a push ahead, and who will separate it? None. For ever. *Trio juncta in-aequalitas.*

There the two of them strolled along together, he and him, English and Irish, Lord and Commoner, boss temporary and servant permanent, Protestant and Catholic, warm-hearted Cavendish, cold-hearted Burke, open-faced Cavendish, dark-kissered Burke, the follower in front of the leader, follow me up to Carlow, listen to me, listen, me lord, a firm hand for Charlie, for Parnell is his name, me lord, Ireland is his station, Wicklow is his dwellin'-place, an' the jail his destination – that's the plan, that's the plan of campaign, me lord.

The sun was setting redly while the cab crawled about, the jaunting-car waited, and the selected Invincibles were slowly nearing the man in grey; the butler who polished John Bull's silver in the back yard, who made a wheel from Ireland's harp to break her bones; the Irish Catholic bodach was coming nearer so the Invincibles holding their knives hidden, untarnished by a tear of dew, nearer to the herculean Joe Brady and his companions, beside them; now, and their knives are deep in the man in grey who has suddenly left Ireland for ever. A second more, and Cavendish lay along him as sad and as still as the bonnie Earl o' Moray, his handsome head half hidden in the grass, lying quiet there till a coffin came to carry him home; beside the man in grey he lay, a memory now, covered soberly by a stately purple pall that the setting sun was slowly spreading over the sky, high above the rat and the lion as they lay in a desperate sleep together.

Johnny made a clatther by striking the fender with the toe of his boot, but the hoary-headed oul' fool slept on, his head bent down deep in the dark of his trim blue coat. He was sure that strange things strolled about in the dead of night in this queer place. The air was scorched with the thoughts of those who had suffered here. He knew that, for he couldn't keep Jennie in his mind for two solid seconds. Something was dragging his mind to dwell on things that had happened before he was born. Had he been a Roman Catholic, he'd ha' made the sign of the cross, but all he could say was, Jasus. Ay, Jasus help the Invincibles and the two men they slew. They were lying stretched out on the grass in the park and the cold night dew fallin'; while Skin-the-Goat was dhrivin' the cab as hard as the horse 'ud go out through the north circular road gate, and the car went gallopin', gallopin', gallopin' down the road through the fifteen acres, out through the Chapel-izod gate, scattherin' the kids in wanton fear playin' on the road, out into the thick of the counthry, gallopin' out gallopin' on past hedges of hazel an' holly, past woodbines and bramble bushes, gallopin' still, goin' a long and roundabout way to the dark little torturin' room in Dublin Castle where they were bullied and borne about in bewilderment, first to the Inns of Quay Police Court, on to Kilmainham, then through the con-demned cell to the last minute's walk before they were finished; an' Mr Mallon, Justice o' the Peace an' Commissioner o' Police, just to show there was no ill-feelin', shook each one of them be the hand, an' wished them well on their way to the Land o' the Leal, feelin' fit from what he had done to preserve truth an' justice, religion an' piety in the land where the Queen's writ ran; while Marwood, the hangman, Ireland's only guardian angel, danced round Brady, crowing that it was the grandest execution of the nine-teenth century, with the eye o' the world watchin'; while the big man stepped on, no flicker in his eye, no tremor in his limbs, no signal of fear in his face, no ear for the murmurin' of the prayers for the dyin', no crack in his voice as he went on through a gauntlet o' carbines, muttering the creed of the felon, poor oul' Ireland, poor oul' Ireland that was fadin' fast away from him; for it was time to be goin', goin' out of this sad place, goin' home before the heavy darkness came, an' he alone with the sleepin' warder who looked for all the world as if he, too, was sleepin' the sleep of the

dead, seemin' to say in his stillness that this was the only sleep
that had rest in a place like this is Tom's voice callin', in the corridor for me to come; and Johnny rose up and hurried out, leaving
the hoary-headed oul' man asleep by the dying fire in the dusk,
his head bent down deep in the dark of his trim blue coat.

THE HAWTHORN TREE

JOHNNY STOOD in the old waste field at the head of the street,
looking at the hawthorn tree. It was a big tree, and its broad
branches of rich white bloom were bending down so low that, if
he sprang up into the air, he could easily catch one. The waste
place was a tangle of weeds in a hurry to hide with their leaves
and timorous flowers the rubbish that many careless hands had
thrown about there. Scutch grass, docks and dandelions, daisies,
small and big, and a few poppies did their best to hide the ugly
things from the stately hawthorn tree who set off the weeds with
her ladylike look and her queenly perfume. Her scented message
of summer's arrival came pouring out of her blossoms, and went
streaming down the little narrow street. A spicy smell, thought
Johnny, like all the spicy breezes that blow from Ceylon's isle,
where every prospect pleases, and only man is vile. There were a
few vile boys, all the samey, allee savee, in Dublin's fair city, if
y'ask me, with wondherful chokers on them, too, like oul'
Hunther holin' his head up as if he shook hands with God the
very first thing in the mornin'.

There were other scents, too. There was another Big Tree at the
corner of the north circular road, but that had a scent of whiskey
an' beer flowin' out of it. This scent from God, that a scent from
the devil; for he had been told so once by a Leader of the Blue
Ribbon Army, the Ballyhooley Blue Ribbon Army, the Band of
Hope that lured innocent Protestant children into takin' a pledge
against ever wettin' their little lips with any kind o' beer brewed
from barley or rye or anything else that might show and shove
them into rioting and drunkenness, separating them from their
heavenly inheritance for ever. He had never worn the blue ribbon,
nor had he ever been presented with a coloured testimonial in
return for a pledge never to touch, taste, or handle it. He had a
bad character. He had been seen with people who, if they got the

chance, would simply dhrink Loch Erin dhry. He had, from time to time, and in one way or another, carried enough beer to float a good-sized ship. Anyone in the neighbourhood who wanted dhrink to be brought to them would look out for Johnny to go, get it, and carry it back to them. One thing he could do that was beyond the power of either Slogan or Hunter – tell with a single glance from his eye whether a jug or a can would hold half a gallon or only three pints of porther.

But he hated the smell of beer, and loved the smell of the hawthorn tree. The spice of Ireland, Ireland's hawthorn tree. And this grand tree was theirs. Right at the top of the little street it stood for everyone in the street to see it. The people of the street were always watching it, except in winter when it was bare and bony, cold and crooked. But the minute it budded, they took their eyes to it, and called it lovely.

Th' hawthorn tree's just beginnin' to bud, someone would say, just beginnin', and the news would go from one end of the street to the other. Th' hawthorn's buddin' at last. Did yeh hear? No; what? Why, the hawthorn tree's burstin' with buds; I seen Mrs Middleton a minute ago, and she says the hawthorn tree's thick with half-openin' leaves, so it is. And the first flower would send them into the centre of a new hope, for the praties were dug, the frost was all over, and the summer was comin' at last. And no cloud of foreboding came till autumn's dusky hand hung scarlet berries on the drowsy tree, and all the people, with their voices mingling, murmured, the long dreary nights, the reckless rain, the chilly sleet, the cowld winds, an' all the hathred in winther is comin' again.

Johnny turned his thoughts away from the thought of winter, and gazed again at the pearly-blossomed hawthorn tree. Here, some day, in the quietness of a summer evening, in a circle of peace, it would be good to sit here with curly-headed Jennie Clitheroe, nothing between them save the sweet scent from the blossoms above. It would be good, good, better, best, positive, comparative, superlative, an' God would see that it was good, and would no longer repent that He had made man in His own image.

If he wanted, now, he could easily climb up and break off a branch to bring the scent of the hawthorn tree right into his own home. But all the people round said it was unlucky to bring hawthorn into a house, all except his mother, who said that there was no difference between one tree and another; but, all the same, Johnny felt that his mother wouldn't like to see him landing in with a spray in his hand. It was all nonsense, she'd say, an' only a lively superstition; but you never can tell, and people catching sight of hawthorn in a house, felt uneasy, and were glad to get away out of it. So it was betther to humour them and leave the lovely branches where they were. Leave it there, leave it fair, and leave it lonely. Sacred to the good people, Kelly said; but he was only up a few years from the bog. They, the fairies, danced round it at night, he said, gay an' old an' careless, they danced round it the livelong night, and no matter how far away they were, they heard it moan whenever a branch was broken.

From under the shade of the hawthorn tree Johnny looked down the little street, and saw a stir in it. Down at the far end he saw what looked like little hills, one after the other, on each side of the narrow way. Women, opening doors and standing on the thresholds, were gazing about near where the little hills lay. I lift up mine eyes unto the hills.

Suddenly, he heard a call of Johnny Casside! Johnnie Casside! He turned his gaze to the right, and, a little way down the street, saw Ecret with hands cupped over his mouth to make his voice travel farther, calling, Johnnie Casside, your mother wants you!

Lower down still, he saw Kelly, with his hands cupped over his mouth, calling out louder than Ecret, Johnny Casside, Johnny Casside, your mother wants you quick! Th' dung-dodgers are here!

Johnny hated these dirt-hawks who came at stated times to empty out the petties and ashpits in the back yards of the people, filling the whole place with a stench that didn't disappear for a week. He sighed, and, leaving the shade of the hawthorn tree, hastened as slow as he could down the street to join his mother.

The whole street was full of vexation and annoyance. Women standing at their doors this side of the street were talking to women standing at their doors on the other side of the street, and murmuring against the confusion that had come upon them, upsetting all they had to do till this great fast of the purification had come to an end.

—Always comin' down on a body at an awkward time, was the king of the murmurs, managing to present themselves when the families were in the throes of doin' important things. If they didn't come on washin' day, they came when the clothes were flutterin' on the lines to dhry; an', if they didn't come then, they were knockin' at the door when the few white an' delicate coloured things a body had were bein' spread out to be carefully an' tenderly ironed.

—It 'ud vex th' heart of a saint, said Mrs Casside, over to Mrs Middleton, an' she standin' on the kerb in front of her hall door, comin' just when me two boys are home for a little leave. They'll come thrampin' in an' go thrampin' out, leaving the dirt of petty an' ashpit ground into the floor of the room an' the hall, an' the two boys expectin' everything to be spick an' span, an' a special ever-ready attention to them as a little compensation for the constant right turn an' quick march of the barrack square.

—It's a rare hard an' never-endin' fight we have, said Mrs Middleton from her door on the opposite side of the street, again' the dust an' dirt we gather around us in the course of our daily effort to keep things in ordher. Here I am, with the youngsters all ready, bar the puttin' on of their caps, to take them over to me sisther's I haven't seen for months, living on a green patch be the side of the Tenters' Fields, who'll be waitin' for our arrival, an' sthrainin' her ear for a knock at the door, the time she's gettin' ready a pile o' pancakes for the gorgin' of the kidgers she sees so seldom.

—An' the dark row that'll shine over the whole place, went on Mrs Casside, heedless of what Mrs Middleton had told her, if as much as a speck violates the tender crimson of the boys' tunics, issued undher a governmental decree of a spotless appearance, so that no scoffer may be given a chance to pass a rude remark about the untidiness of the Queen's proper army.

—Now, looka the poor Mulligans, said Mrs Middleton, meandering across the road to stand on the pavement a few feet from Mrs Casside, watching her trying to pry up the tacks that held the faded oilcloth to the floor, shoving an old knife-blade under the tack heads, and gently forcing them out so as not to make the oilcloth any worse than it was, looka the poor Mulligans, with their four chiselurs down with the measles, two o' them lyin' in the room the dung-dodgers'll have to pass through, with the doctor shakin' his head over one of them, an' the mother's soul-case worn out runnin' from one to the other, thryin' to ward off any dangerous thing that may be hoverin' over their little heads, while the dung-dodgers are busy filthifyin' the whole place, an' she only havin' two hands on her to tend the children an' clean up the mess when the dung-dodgers are gone, before she dare sit down in the shade of a little less to do.

—Well, we'll only have to give her a hand when we're a little free ourselves, said Mrs Casside, an' save the poor woman from suddenly dhroppin' outa her standin'.

—An', went on Mrs Middleton, looka Mrs Ecret, afther pain-tin' her hall door only yestherday, with a tin o' paint her boy providentially found – when no one was lookin', I suppose – an' varnishin' it well to finish it off, all afther comin' to grief with them tearin' their baskets of dirt against it, comin' an' goin' out, refusin' to wait till the door was decently dhry, an' leavin' it lookin' for all the world like the poor little maiden all forlorn who married the man all tatthered an' torn. Though I'd say sorra mend her, goin' about like the cock of the south because her hall door was the only one on the sthreet that had had a lick o' paint on it since Noah first saw the rainbow. But there's always a downfall in front of them who sthrive to ape the airs of the quality.

Mrs Casside gazed at the oilcloth she was lifting, and sighed resignedly.

—This is the last time I'll get this to stand the sthrain, she said. It's fare you well, me lady, the next time I thry to get it up. You're perfectly right, she added, turning towards Mrs Middleton, for it's a bad thing to allow yourself to crow over worldly possessions, for we brought nothing into the world, an' it's certain we can take nothing away.

—Only a good character, murmured Mrs Middleton, only a good character, an' God knows it's hard enough to take that away with us, either. Here's your Johnny, now, to help you, with a tiny sprig o' hawthorn in his hand. Don't let him bring it into the house, she said seriously, bending her head close to Mrs Casside, for it's the same may bring with it the very things we thry to keep at a distance.

—An' what does it bring into the house with it? asked Johnny.

—Things that toss in a golden glory to a distant eye, said his mother, and, at the touch of a human hand, turn to withering leaves whirling about in a turbulent wind.

—And, said Mrs Middleton, things that swing in a merry dance to a silver song that changes, quick as thought, to a dolorous sigh and a thing stretched out in a white-wide sheet in the midst of a keen an' the yellow flame from a single candle. So leave your little twig o' hawthorn on the window-sill outside, alanna.

—Ay, Johnny, said his mother, leave it there, for though it is only Roman Catholics who cherish such foolish fables, it's always safer to be on your guard.

Heaps of muck were appearing before the various houses in the street, growing bigger and bigger as the dung-dodgers added big basket after big basket of filth taken from the backsides of the houses. Each door would have a horrid hill outside of it till a cart came later on to carry them away. In and out, in and out of the houses went the dung-dodgers, carrying huge baskets on their backs filled with the slime and ashes of the families, their boots and clothes spattered with the mire that kept dropping from the baskets as they carried them out.

—Eh, you there, said one of the dung-dodgers who had stopped to light his pipe, over to the two talking women, Eh, you, quit your gostherin', and make ready for us, or we'll be with you before a thing's stirred.

Each of the women departed into her own house, and Johnny and his mother shifted their bits of furniture into safe corners, and tenderly rolled up their few precious yards of oilcloth and put it safely aside from the armoured feet of the dung-dodgers.

—Stay outside in the fresh air, said Mrs Casside to Johnny, till all the dirt is out, and then you can come in and help me to put the place to rights again.

Johnny went out to stand by the window-sill and fiddle with the spray of creamy hawthorn, all the while watching the dung-dodgers cleaning out his mother's place and Mrs Middleton's opposite, watched them bendin' low under the heavy load in each basket, then dumping it with a grunt on the rising heap in front of the door. Sometimes they would pause to straighten their backs and pass a few remarks to each other, before they went back for another load. One of them, a stocky man, with a squint in his right eye, paused, sucked at his dirty pipe, and glanced over crookedly at a comrade helping to empty out the house opposite.

—Did yeh take me advice an' go to the Queen's yestherday night? he called out.

—No, I didn', replied the other, a burly fella with a voice like a croakin' corncrake. I'm follyin' me own bent, an' I'm goin' tonight to Th' Bohemian Girl.

—You can have your Bohemian Girl for me, said the other scornfully, and he hoisted the empty basket on his back again. Give your humble servant The Lily o' Killarney, an' th' tenor warblin' I Come, I Come, Me Heart's Delight, with Danny Mann, the divil's darlin', hurlin' the Colleen Bawn off the rock into the wather, an' me boul' Myles na Coppaleen leppin' into th' night-dark lake to pull her out again. And he marched off to add another load to the heap of muck outside of Johnny's hall door.

Johnny waited there, fiddling with the spray of hawthorn, till ashpit and petty had been emptied, and the dung-dodgers had moved on to the next house; then he went back to give a hand to his mother to coax cleanliness back again to the soiled flooring of their home. With the aid of a neighbour's broom, they swept the crushed cinders and ashes and some of the slime from the flooring. Then Johnny poured hot water from a kettle into a bucket, while his mother used a blue-mottled soap that made her hands shrivel and sting, washed and rubbed, time and time again, to make the first cleanliness of the place come to life again.

So she toiled as all in the street did on the day of their purification, in the midst of a dense smell, shaken with tremors towards vomiting, hard and fast at it, all together, boys, cleansing the sanctuary of her home, breathing the breath of death into her nostrils, scrubbing the floor, knees bent, worshipping dirt, washing away the venom of poverty, persuaded that this was all in the day's work; Johnny emptying out the sullied water and bringing in the clean for her, then watching her working without the sign of a song from her, breathing hard, conjuring away the turmoil of dirt with the aid of fair water and the blue-mottled soap that made her quick-moving hands shrivel and sting.

The day was stretching close to the evening when the place felt fresh again, the oilcloth was laid, and the bits of furniture stood at ease in their old places. Johnny hurried off and came back with a glass of beer for his mother.

—Fine head it has, she said, as she sat and sipped it.

—G'on, you, she said to Johnny, giving him a chunk of bread and butter, an' get as much of the fresh air as you can.

Johnny hurried out, and away with him up the street, past all the mounds of mire, to eat his chunk of bread in peace beneath the scented shade of the hawthorn tree.

CAT 'N CAGE

TOM WAS home on leave, his number dry, a good-conduct badge on a sleeve; for he was no longer a rooky, but had passed through all drill with colours flying, and crossed gold guns shining a little way above a cuff told the tale that he was a first-class shot in his regiment. He and Archie and Johnny were on their way through the crisp air of an autumn day to the Cat 'n Cage for a drink –

beer for Tom and Archie, and ginger cordial or claret for the boul' Johnny. Along Dorset Street the three of them went, Archie and Johnny chucking out the chests and keeping well in trim with the military step of Tom, looking brave and fine and proud in the get-up of the 1st Battalion of the Royal Dublin Fusiliers: tunic as crimson as a new-blown poppy, long streaming black ribbons stretching down his back from the natty, square-pushing silk-edged Scots cap set jauntily on the side of his head, white gloves stuck neatly into his pipe-clayed belt, and a dear little cane, knobbed with the arms of his regiment, under his arm, a cane to be presented to Johnny as soon as Tom found it convenient to get another.

He had overstepped his leave by a day, and laughingly drew the picture of Captain Bacon's moustache bristling when he'd be brought on the mat before his officer for absence without leave.

—You'll lose your good-conduct badge, won't you? asked Archie.

—Not unless I get a regimental enthry, and that isn't likely, for I've got a clean sheet so far, and I'm in request for work in th' orderly room and that counts a hell of a lot. But, if I do aself, what about it?

And he laughed defiantly, thinking it great fun, and Johnny thought so too, when he heard Tom humming:

> *Around th' prison walls,*
> *There I've got a token;*
> *All around Victoria's walls, picking tarry oakum.*
> *The shot dhrill an' the shell —*
> *Mind, boys, what I say —*
> *It's a military prison for a soldier!*

While he was humming the last line of the tune, Tom whipped off the golden head of a dandelion, shooting out from a slit in the side walk opposite a bright-red brick building with the words on a wall telling everyone that this was Father Gaffney's Catholic School, built, his Ma said, to keep the Catholics as far away as possible from the Protestants, and leave them free to flourish in their errors, for as the Church of Jerusalem, Alexandria, and Antioch have erred, so also the Church of Rome hath erred not only in their living and manner of ceremonies, but also in matters of faith.

They stopped for a moment looking up the narrow street that ran like a narrow stream into the wide river of Dorset Street where they had lived for so long, and where the two elder ones had left for their first job.

—There, said Tom, pointing at the street with his cane, is where we lived for a long time, where the old man died, and where you, Johnny, ran around in petticoat and pinafore. Remember?

Remember? Ay, did he. From nine Innisfallen Parade he had run for the ounce o' cut Cavendish. He remembered, too, going out often with a white delft jam-jar in his hand to get thruppence-worth of threacle from Dunphy's o' Dorset Street, an' watching a dark, little, yellow-faced man, for all the world like a Chinaman, holding the jam-jar to a tap in a green tin barrel, watching the deft little yellow hand turning the tap to let the black sticky stuff flow down into the white jar, and then, like lightning, cutting off the dark sthream when enough had flowed for the money offered, and swiftly cutting with his thumb the threacle blossoming from the tap, and licking it off, before he handed the jam-jar back to Johnny with one hand, while he swept the three pennies into the till with the other.

A big, black, tarry canal-boat, filled with a cargo covered by a huge tarpaulin, was lying idly against the lock-gates, waiting for the lock to fill so that it might glide in and sink to a lower level. The sluice-gates were open, and the green water, laced with foam, tumbled through into the vast pit of the lock, adding its energy to the water that had poured in before, whirling madly about, and rising slowly to the level where the canal-boat lay, waiting for the lock to fill. The old nag that had heavily pulled the boat to where it was, cropped a few clumps of grass growing thickly near the railway wall, while the man who led him idly watched a loaded goods train that went lumbering by far away below. A sturdy, brown-bearded, dirty-faced man stood on the poop of the boat, gazing at the waters tumbling through the sluices of the lock, occasionally taking a cutty clay pipe from his mouth, and jetting a flying spit right into the heart of the green and white tumbling waters, seeming surprised and disappointed that the spit was so rapidly lost in the whirling cascade. A man on the boat, with a boat-hook in his hand, watched the spit disappear the moment it struck the water.

—We all go like that poor spit, he said to his comrade, a gathering together, a second or so in the mouth, a sudden jet of life, an' we're out of sight of all.

—Ay, indeed, said the brown-bearded man; casual spit or special spit – all gone together an' lost in a whirlin' medley.

—Oh, none of us is lost altogether, replied his comrade with the boat-hook, no, not altogether; no, not quite.

—No one's no more nor a dhrownded dhrop in a mill-sthream, went on the one with the beard, a dhrop there in th' dark, showin' no sign at all, an' a dhrop here with the sun on it shinin' for a second, an' then meetin' th' darkness of th' other one. I know you're here an' you know I'm here, an' that's about as far as it goes. But what th' hell are you to a Chinaman, or a Chinaman to me? He comes as I go, or I go as he comes, an' him nor me is no wiser of one another. You don't know even who may be havin' a pint in Leech's opposite while we're talkin' here.

—I don't, agreed the man with the boat-hook, but I know who's not havin' one, and that's more important to me.

The bearded man shoved the pipe into his pocket, hurried swiftly along the narrow gangway to the aft where he grasped the tiller, ready to guide the barge, for the lock was full; Tom, Archie, and Johnny leaned against the great arm of the lock gates, and pushed the arm open through a gurgle of rippling water, men on the opposite bank doing the same with the other arm. The man with the boat-hook fixed it in a part of the gate, and began to pull and shove the barge forward past the open gates. When the boat had passed through, these gates were pushed shut again, and sluices farther down were opened to empty the lock and let the boat sink to a lower level. Down and down she went, slowly; the men's legs disappearing first, then their waists, till only their heads could be seen peeping over the stone parapet of the lock, the bearded man jetting a last spit into a far-away clump of daisies before his head disappeared altogether.

—Eh, there, shouted Archie down to the bargemen when the boat was well down and safely caged between the dripping walls of the lock, where's your barque bound for? Is it to Yokohama you're settin' your course, or dim an' distant Valparaiso?

—Farther than ever you'll wandher, you pinched an' parched an' puckered worm, shouted the man with the boat-hook, while he shoved the barge along out of the lock into the farther stretch of the canal ahead.

Archie whipped out a handkerchief and waved it to the departing boat, as he chanted:

Oh, Shenandoah, I long to hear you,
Away, you rolling river;
Oh, Shenandoah, I long to hear you,
Away I've got to go 'cross the wide Missouri!

They turned away from the lock when the canal-boat had drifted away down to where the ships go down to the sea, and pass out, over the bar, to the rolling billows beyond; and so on to where there are cannibals, an' spicy smells that make the sailors faint, an' lilies on lakes big enough to hold a house up, an' palms so high that the highest tufts scratch the lower clouds, and where there are wild beasts wandering through the streets of towns at night, touching their snouts to windows shut tight and doors barred soundly; an' places, too, where men are as small as a three-year-old nipper, dangerous, for they can well hide in the long grasses and send a tiny arrow, touched with poison, into the guts of a passer-by so that he drops dead just as he feels the first faint prick of the barb entherin' his thin white skin, and is never found again and is lost for ever; maybe the only son of a poor woman waitin' for him to come back an' puttin' a light in the window so that he won't miss his way,

A light in the window shines brightly for me,
Her bold sailor lad who has gone far away;
His absence an' silence makes mother's heart yearn,
As brightly the light in the window doth burn,

so sure an' senseless is she that the wanderer will come back again, an' he, all the time, lying stiff, a flower forcin' itself out of his mouth maybe, the grasses climbin' over him, the night dew fallin' fast on him, gone home, gone for ever, gone to earth, gone to rest, gone to glory, gone to be with Christ which is far better.

Crossing over Tolka Bridge, they passed out of the town into a hedge-bordered road, the great northern road leading to Belfast and the Irish north where the loyal and trusty true-blue followers of King Billy lived and defended the Protestant Faith and all ceevil and releegious liberty.

The hedges were beaming with the scarlet clusters of haw and hip shining forth from the midst of the gold and brown leaves of the declining may and dog-rose. The hips were fat and luscious-looking, their scarlet more riotous-looking than the lesser and more modest red of the haws. Johnnie Magories, Johnny called the hips, and he pulled a rare big bunch of them, half of them a dazzling scarlet, and the rest that hadn't ripened yet, the colour of rich gold slashed with crimson, for his mother who liked to put them in a jug that had lost a handle, to brighten up the room a bit, she said, and make us feel a little less like what we are. The room was always a little different, she'd say, when it showed a sprig o' green or a bunch of berries. They brightened up a dull room as the stars, on a dark night, brightened up the sky. They carried their colours so quietly, she said, that they coaxed you to feel a little quieter yourself. And, if you thought of them at all, you knew they were as lovely as the richest roses the rich could buy. You never knew how often a linnet's wing had touched them, or how often they had held up a robin while he sang his share o' song when the sun was low and the other birds were sitting silent. In time, like the rest of us, she said, they'll lose their gay colour, will shrivel, and get tired, but they will have had their day, will have shone for an hour, and that is something.

A brisk breeze, spiced with the pungent smell of weeds afire in the fields, blew about them, gave speed to a lot of clouds drifting in a silky blue sky, swung the bunches of berries in a gentle dance, rustled the brown and yellow leaves strewn under their feet, and sent many others whirling and falling to join the others that fell before them. Several jaunting-cars went trotting by them, packed with young men wearing white-cuffed green jerseys and carrying hurleys. Most of them were singing as recklessly as they could,

> Oh, for a steed, a rushing steed,
> On the Curragh of Kildare,
> And Irish squadrons thrained to do what they
>   are willing to dare!
> A hundred yards, an' England's guards
> Dhrawn up to engage me there,
> Dhrawn up to engage me there!

A policeman halted, stiffened himself, and gazed fixedly at the cars trotting by. The hurlers gave a jeering cheer and waved their hurleys on high. The policeman watched them away into the distance, with a foolish grin on his gob.

—As long as they rest content with shouting, he said to Tom, we don't mind much.

But Tom, Archie, and Johnny, taking no notice, walked by, eyes front, for they didn't want to be seen talking to a policeman.

—The horney wanted us to take notice of him, said Johnny.

With a clever swish of his cane, Tom whipped off a bramble twig that was sticking itself out over the side walk.

—The less anyone has to do with harvey duffs an' horneys the better, he said: ready to swear a hole through an iron pot.

—Ambush their own mother into the arms of the hang-man, added Archie, if it meant a pat on the back from a head constable.

The blue of the sky had given way to the dimmy purple of the gathering twilight; the bright berries were hiding in the dusk; the trees were dark and drooping figures sleeping, yielding a densely drowsy welcome to the birds thrusting a way to a rest in the branches; the breeze still blew, but everything and every stir in the dusk grew quieter as the three of them went on their way to the Cat 'n Cage.

—Here we are at our home 'n destination, said Tom, whose mouth was watering for a drink.

They stopped before what was no more than a country cottage, with a small window at each side of a narrow door. A heavy, weather-soaked thatch covered the low roof. A low hedge sur-rounded a grass plot, separated by a path leading from the gate straight into the doorway. Along the grass plot, nearest to the hedge, sprawled clumps of neglected dahlias, still trying to carry soiled crimson and yellow blossoms, looking as if they, too, had been into the pub, had lowered a lot of drinks, and were just able to crawl out and lie around the border, or lean tipsily against the hedges. From two squat chimneys, one at each end of the roof, thin streams of delicate blue smoke rose unsteadily, stood straight for a moment, then staggered away into the higher air as if they, too, had had a merry time, and didn't quite know which way to go. The door had once been a bright green, but was now well faded and smeared with many dirty patches made by the rain, snow, and sun of many seasons. Swinging over the door was the sign of the house: a large square board, with a picture on it of a huge wicker cage holding a blackbird stiffly standing on a perch, while outside, with her nose close to the bars, and a thoughtful look in her eyes, sat a big black cat.

As the three of them walked up to the door, they saw shining through the dusty windows the gleam of blazing fires, singing out that there was a welcome and a fair snugness and a fine warmth to be found inside for all who came. Tom pushed the door open, and in he and Archie and Johnny passed into the warm beer 'n whiskey cosiness of the Cat 'n Cage.

The place was a bit dim from the smoke of several pipes and the smoke that was too tipsy to climb up the chimney, and, to Johnny, everything seemed to be floating about in a warm-smelling mist. Along the whole length of the room stretched the bar-counter of thick deal, once white, but now grimly stained with many porter stains and dirt carried in on the clothes of them who came in to take a rest and slake their thirst. At one end of the bar stood the three glorious beer-pulls, shaped like the spokes of a ship's wheel, made of glowing crimson porcelain and polished brass, having on the thicker parts of them lovely oval panels of gaily coloured shepherds and shepherdesses surrounded by their baaing sheep.

Four of the hurlers who had passed them on the cars were drinking by the counter near the beer-pulls, and a carman sat in a corner with a pint before him. The barman, a thick-necked man with bushy eyebrows and a partly-bald head, his big eyes, sleepy-looking, bent over the counter, listening to what the hurlers were saying.

When he saw Tom and his companions, he pulled himself slowly apart from the talking group and came over to them, sending a questioning look towards Tom as he came near, while the brisk gab of the hurlers suddenly ceased.

—Pint, said Tom to the questioning glance, glass o' plain, an' a small claret, warm for the boy, sweet.

The gay shepherds and shepherdesses tugged up the beer cheerfully, with a long, long pull an' a strong, strong pull, gaily, boys, make her go, and the pint and glass o' plain were handed to Tom and Archie, while a dandy-glass, half full of ruby liquor, was put into Johnny's eager hand.

Tom was a handsome fellow, and was swanking it a bit now before the hurlers. Five foot eleven in his socks, broad-chested, lithe of limb, ruddy-haired, a handsome ginger moustache sweeping his upper lip, grey eyes that sparkled when he was excited, genial, especially when he was drinking his beloved porter, a hater of quarrels, but a lover of an argument.

—Bet Mick has a sackful in him be now from the Jesuit he was to meet in the Cross Guns, he murmured, balancing the pint in his steady hand.

The hurlers were sending over quick, cross-grained glances at the redcoat, poising themselves in a little silent bunch beside the beerpulls, while the barman, pretending to take no notice, wiped some dirty glasses and hummed half softly to himself:

The fountain mingles with the river,
And the river with the ocean;
The winds of heaven mix for ever
With a sweet emotion.
Nothin' in th' worrld is single,
All things, be a law divine,
In one another's being mingle –
Why not I with thine?

Archie saw the black looks that the hurlers were bending on them, looks quickly given and quickly withdrawn, and he was nervous. Johnny, too, saw the looks, and saw Archie was nervous and that the hand holding the glass of plain trembled a little, saw him bending his head over towards Tom's.

—They're havin' a good gawk at us, he whispered.

—Eh? Who? asked Tom, for he was too full of himself to take notice of half-hidden scowls.

—Boyos, with the hurleys.

—Oh, said Tom, sending a swift glance to where the hurlers were, them? Gawks. Bog-trotters. Never seen anything higher than a haystack. Hayfoot, strawfoot fusiliers. Let them look their fill at one o' the old toughs. He lifted his glass level with his chin. Where it goes, he said, and gurgled down more than the half of his pint, leaving his fine moustache gleaming with a frothy dew. He pulled a handkerchief from his sleeve, and as he was wiping the frothy dew from his moustache, the door of the pub opened and in walked the boul' Mick, his pill-box cap set rakishly on the side of his small, tight head, looking like one o' God's guards in his superb crimson tunic, with its velvet blue-purple cuffs and collar, piped with yellow cord, skin-tight trousers, slashed with a wide scarlet stripe down each leg, and caught under his square-pushing boots with leathern straps to make them tighter still.

Tom looked at him as if he had seen an apparition.

—Jaysus, he ejaculated, I though you were to meet a Jesuit in the Cross Guns!

The Cross Guns: Johnny knew it well, near to the bridge of the same name, called Westmoreland Bridge by the loyal Irish and the more respectable Protestants, one of his brother's favourite pubs. He knew them all well, outside and in: Cross Guns; The Bleeding Horse, up behind the northern quays; The Big Tree in Dorset Street; Royal Oak in Parkgate Street, where the Invincibles had a last drink before going on to do in Cavendish and Burke;

The Jolly Topers in Finglas, a well-known bona-fide house;
Leech's beside Binn's Bridge; Galvin's in Capel Street; Bergin's in
Amiens Street; The Brian Boru nicely stuck in the way to or from
a burial in Glasnevin; Meredith's in Derrynane Parade could
hardly be counted, for it was only a shebeen where drink had to be
taken off the premises, unless someone stood at the door to keep
nix for fear a horney hove in sight round a corner, though here
they could always be sure of a few because Cissy, daughter of
Meredith, was sweet on Tom, in spite of the oul' fella grumblin'
that there was more goin' out than was comin' in, an' Cissy havin'
to help the family be workin' from eight till six for half a dollar a
week, in Williams & Woods cleanin' the fruit that came to the
place to make the jam; and last, but not least, Nagle's in Earl
Street, a rendezvous for all the post-office boys who had worked
with Tom and Mick before they joined the Army. Johnny knew
them all, had drunk ginger beer or claret in each of them; had
listened to the rare manly talk beatin' round the house like the
stirring wind or a bustling sea. And now he was in the Cat 'n Cage.
He was getting on and filling out his young life with wondhers.
Here he was in a pub miles from home, between two oul' swaddies,
havin' his share o' dhrink with the best of them. Few more years
an' he'd be workin', able to go his own way, swagger about the
streets, an' show Jennie Clitheroe the sort he was.

—Go on, boys, dhrink up an' have another, Mick was saying;
and, turning to the barman, added, same again here, mate.

The room wasn't large and the counter wasn't long; there was
little more than a hair's-breadth between the red-coated elbow of
Tom and the green-covered elbow of a hurler.

Red an' green, thought Johnny, red an' green are the colours of
oul' Ireland, an' an oul' ballad, sung be a one-eyed man mouchin'
along Dorset Street, came into his mind,

Green is the flag an' green are the fields of our sireland,
While the blood our sons have shed has tinged the green with red,
That's why red an' green are the colours of oul' Ireland.

Whenever a movement brought the red-coated elbow of the
soldier into touch with the green-covered one of the hurler, the
green-covered one would give the red-coated one a vicious shove
away, but, beyond a wondering backward glance, Tom took no
notice.

—Here's to the time, said a hurler suddenly, in a loud voice, raising his glass above his head, when there won't be an English soldier seen in our land from one end of it to the other!

The other hurlers clinked their glasses against his, and they all chanted,

Clink your glasses, clink,
Here's a toast for all to drink:
By every Irish Chief beneath a cairn,
Some day, without a doubt, we'll dhrive th' English soldier out
From every field an' glen an' town in Erin!

The door opened in the silence that followed the song, showing two tall Irish Constabulary men standing on the threshold, with their martial coats around them, the dusky bronze harp, with the crown over it, sleepy-looking on its oval bed of red cloth stuck in front of their round black caps, set to the side of their heads, a chin-strap keeping the cap in its perky angle, and their glossy black belts, with batons hanging from them, fencing their heavy coats into two long neat folds down the backs.

After dawdling at the door for a few moments, the two of them sidled up to the counter, Tom and his party moving up to their end of the counter, the hurlers moving closer up to theirs, so that the policemen had a little space at the counter between the backs of the soldiers on the left hand and the hurlers on the right one.

—Two Guinnesses, said one of them in an apologetic voice, for he knew that the barman and the hurlers knew they were supposed to be out patrolling the roads, and far away from the sight or even the thought of a drink.

The barman, all attention to these gods o' the Irish countryside, hurried the bottles of stout to the policemen, who moved over nearer to Tom and his comrades, who moved farther away still when they felt the touch of the peelers.

Quarrelsome Mick couldn't let well enough alone; couldn't let the silence sing its song of peace.

—If y'ask Mick, he said, when the redcoats weren't dhriven out o' Ireland when Parnell was high an' mighty, they'll hardly do it now he's down among the dead men.

Then Tom had to go one better – he was always weak enough to follow on where Mick led.

—Who was it threw Parnell to the English wolves? he asked in a voice meant for the hard of hearing. Was it the English redcoats done it?

—A sowl man, he was, chimed in Archie, lifting the people from their knees by the scruff of their necks. An' what did he get for it?

—A home in a coffin, said Mick, and a roomy grave in the famine plot in Glasnevin.

—Ay, said Tom, taking great gulps out of the beer, an' in their mangy hearts the priests an' people sang a Te Deum when they found he was dead.

—An' I'll go bail, said Mick, there were a few hurlers' hands helpin' to pack him into his coffin.

A hurler whirled round on his heel, his face tense, his eyes blazing.

—No hand here helped him into his coffin, he shouted, his face flaming in the black gap between the two Constabulary men.

—The whole bang lot o' them, said Tom, taking no notice of the hurler, deserted their Leader in his time o' need.

—Th' Irish always down a great man, said Archie, while they cling to a clyura as they did to Sheamus the shit at the battle o' the Boyne.

—Here, here, now, said the barman, shoving his gob over the counter in Archie's direction, there's to be no bad language heard here, for this is a highly respectable house, fully approved of be the magisthrates an' the parish priest.

—Now, boys, now, murmured one of the policmen, talk it over easy. This is a free counthry where everyone has a right to his own opinion.

—Looka Swift MacNeill, said Tom, now more excited than ever, but still keeping his back to policemen and hurlers, when he shouted at the Dublin meetin' of the National League, God forbid that the man who led us through darkness an' difficulty should be deserted be us – an' he the first to vote for the betrayal of his Leader to the English.

—An' he a Dublin man, too, said Mick; Dublin went awhoring when she bred that bastard who betrayed Parnell!

—Easy, easy, murmured the other constable.

The barman again leaned his gob over the counter, gently shoving a constable a little aside with his head to get nearer to Mick.

—Isn't it afther sayin' I am, he said, that no other language, other than that in common uttherance, is to be used in this respectable house?

—No bad language, no bad language, murmured a constable.

All, except the police, were getting very excited. The police were uneasy, and couldn't, rightly, without loss of dignity, slink out of the discussion now. So there the two of them lounged over the counter, trying to look undisturbed, stuck in the middle of the hubbub like a pair of crows among a group of coloured jays.

—An' what about Healy, said Mick, bitther an' brave with envy, swearin' at the same meetin' that he'd never, never desert the chief who had led Ireland so far forward; an' all the time, the Banthry bowsey, itchin' to make an end o' Parnell, even if he had to make an end of Ireland at the same time! Tim Healy, the biggest snake Pathrick left behind him! Healy's your hero now: muck that Parnell made into a man; the guck in the silken gown; England's fosther-brother! An' where's Ireland now? In Glasnevin. An' what's Ireland now? A mingy plot of grass in Glasnevin with th' name o' Parnell fadin' away on it out undher the frost an' the rain!

—Let the poor man rest, said a constable; he's dead, isn't he? So let the poor man rest.

—Who's dead, who's dead? asked a hurler fiercely, turning to face the constable.

—Parnell, replied the constable, softly and slyly, so let the poor man rest in peace.

—You an' your like 'ud like him to be dead, said the hurler, we all know that; but Parnell's more alive than ever he was! Rest in peace! That's what you and the political pathrols among the clergy'd like too. But Parnell'll never rest till the swarm of thraitors that hounded him to his death and flung Ireland's power into England's lap are stretched out cold, unremembered be a single soul that's left to lift a hand for Ireland!

The carman, sitting in the corner, suddenly jumped up and slid over to where the talk was, wiping the drains of beer from his lips, his green-gone bowler hat balanced on the back of his head, a stained clay pipe waving in his left hand, like a conductor's wand, his dull eyes trying to force a gleam into them, and the corners of his big mouth twitching.

—It's sick I'm gettin', he said, listening to the whole of yous. If he'd ha' loved his counthry, he'd ha' known he wasn't fit to lead us when he committed himself with Kitty O'Shea!

—Who wasn't fit to lead us? cried a hurler, turning savagely on the car-driver.

—He wasn't.

—Who wasn't?

—Parnell, if you'd like to know.

—Is it Parnell who united the whole nation together, who coaxed the Fenians to follow him, who forced the Church to toe the line, is it him I hear you saying wasn't the man who was fit to lead us?

—Amn't I afther tellin' you, persisted the car-driver, that all that happened before Parnell committed himself with Kitty O'Shea.

—Jasus, said the hurler, with the sound of agony in his voice and the look of agony on his face, is it listenin' to an Irishman I am when I hear a thing like that!

—The holy clergy, said Tom mockingly, didn't open their mouths when O'Connell was goin' round the counthry scatterin' bastards everywhere. Gettin' them be steam, be God!

—I told yous twice before, an' I'm tellin' you for the third an' last time, said the barman furiously, that this double-meaning talk'll have to be heard only outa hearin' of the decent people who come into this decent house for enthertainment; and he again shoved his thick gob over the counter, thrusting it sideways and tilting it upwards at the angry hurler. An', furthermore, he went on, I'm not goin' to have any confusion here over Parnell either; for when all's said an' done, he's gone, an' a good riddance, bringin' disgrace on Ireland's fair name be committin' an immortal sin!

In a mighty rage, the hurler let fly and gave him one in the snot while it was well poked out over the counter, forcing a steady stream of blood to flow down his chin and over the white front of his dickey, and causing him to knock down a serene-looking row of newly-cleansed tumblers with a wave of his arm as he staggered back. He sliddered down to the floor, and sat, glancing now at the crowd outside the counter and then at the broken tumblers lying round him.

—Me nose's slit, he sighed loudly, an' me best glasses gone wallop, an' me only afther cleanin' them, too!

The two constables were afraid of the hurlers, for no one could say, especially a policeman, what a hurler would do when he had a hurley in his hand, so they turned on the other party, very officious, and full of the law.

—Now, said one of them to Tom and Mick, you two members of Her Majesty's Forces betther be gettin' outa this, d'ye hear me? We can't have quarrelsomeness comin' into the quiet of the counthryside. So g'on, now, the pair of yous, before I have to inthervene to prevent any further tendency towards a breach of the peace!

—We'll finish the dhrinks we paid for, before we go, anyway, said Tom surlily.

—The minute they landed in here, said the barman thickly, through a handkerchief held to his nose, they started to row with these decent men here, and he pointed to the hurlers.

—They started no row with us, said the hurlers. What we said an' they said was said in quietness an' calm.

—Here, now, said a constable, touching Mick on the arm, swally up the remainder of what yeh have there, an' be off, like a good man.

—Oh, let the man finish his dhrink in a decent way, said one of the hurlers.

The policeman wheeled round to face the hurler.

—It's a dangerous thing for anyone to thry to obstruct a constable in the discharge of his duty, he said warningly.

—Didya ever hear the song that everyone's singin', now? asked Mick, with a wink at the hurlers.

—No, said Tom; what song is that, now?

—Goes like this, said Mick, and then he chanted, keeping his back turned to the policemen, knowing that this song was the song they hated and dreaded above all others,

> *A Bansha peeler wint wan night,*
> *On duty an' pathrollin' O,*
> *An' met a goat upon the road,*
> *An' took her to be a sthroller O.*
> *Wid bay'net fixed, he sallied forth,*
> *An' caught her by the wizen O,*
> *An' then he swore a mighty oath,*
> *I'll send yeh off to prison O!*

The hurlers tittered and the constables flushed.

—An' what did the oul' goat say? asked Tom.

—God, I've forgotten, said Mick.

—I know, I know, said Johnny eagerly, and he began to sing,

> *Oh, mercy, sir, the goat replied,*
> *Pray let me tell me story O,*
> *I am no rogue, no ribbonman,*
> *No Croppy, Whig, or Tory O,*

I'm guilty not of any crime,
Of petty or high threason O,
I'm badly wanted at this time,
For this is the milkin' season O!

One of the constables glared at Johnny and said viciously, What'r you doin' here in a place like this, me oul'-fashioned, cocky little kidger, with your ears open to catch any language that'll help to knock hell outa all decency in later life?

—I'm with me own two brothers, said Johnny sturdily.

—With your own two brothers, are you, now? Well, it's not in a place like this a lad o' your years ought to be, catchin' a glimpse of things not fit for you to see.

—I'm not goin' to ask your permission to come here, anyway, muttered Johnny defiantly.

—Oh, you're not, aren't you? Lappin' up your lessons well, eh? Guh, yeh cheeky little cur, bulky with impudence! Swinging an arm, the constable, in a rage, brought his hand to Johnny's ear with a box that sent him spinning towards the door, dazed and dumb and bothered.

Dazed with the blow as Johnny was, he saw the lovely sight of Mick sending a short jab to the constable's jaw that tilted up his head with a jerk, and, when the poor man's head was well up, a straight-left beauty to the poor man's chin that sent him in a curled-up heap to the floor. He saw the second constable putting a hand on his baton; he saw Tom taking a hurley from a hurler who gave it up with a wink as good as a nod to a blind horse; and he saw the second constable hesitate when he saw the hurley in Tom's hand and the look of battle in Mick's eyes. So he turned and went to kneel down beside his fallen comrade to give him comfort and bring him peace and make us all be just to him; while the barman hurried and scurried and worried to fetch a glass of brandy for the fallen bowsey, a red dribble dodging down his own nose; and the car-driver hastened to help the barman to help the constable who was helping his comrade; while the hurlers pressed to the door, beckoning Tom and his party to follow them, all hurrying out into the garden, making spacious steps for the gateway, Johnny in the midst of them, with a red ear and it tingling, praying the hand that struck him might be paralysed, that the eyes would have the power to see nothing but the paralysed hand, the ears hear nothing but the people talking about the paralysed hand, and the tongue have but the power to point it out to others.

—Come on, boys, said a hurler, let's scatther, an' get away as far as we can from here.

They heard a long shrill blast from a whistle, and, turning, they saw the dark figure of a constable standing, full-shaped, in the light streaming from the open doorway.

—Jasus, he's blowin' for the rest of them – we'll have to run for it!

—The car, the car, said Tom; let's take the car an' be off!

—We're city men, said a hurler, an' never held reins in our hands in our life.

—Nor have we, either, said Mick.

—I can, I can, said Johnny eagerly; I've often dhrove the milk-man's jennet, an' he's often a hard thing to handle.

They heard an answering whistle from some distance away.

—Up with yous, up with us, said the hurlers.

They sprang up on the car, Mick and two hurlers on one side, Tom and two hurlers on the other, Archie in the rear, with his legs dangling down the back of the car, and Johnny climbed into the dicky-seat, gathered the reins in his hand, gave a sharp gee-up, gee-up, to the nag, and away they all went at a quiet trot down the road. Looking back, they saw a figure run out to the road to rush after the car – it was the car-driver coming after them for all he was worth.

—Eh, there, they heard him cry out, come back, yeh daylight robbers; halt there, with me mare an' car; eh, there, you, come back outa that, holy God, isn't this a good one! Eh, there, come back!

—Gee-up, lass, gee-up, me girl, said Johnny coaxingly, and the mare's trot became quick and brisk.

—Touch her up with the whip, said Archie anxiously.

—Y'ignoramus, replied Johnny sharply, an' you seein' she's cold from standin' so long! Wait till she warms up a bit, an' then we can make her go. Gee-up, gee-up, girl; yep, me lassie!

—Supposin' they search the city for us? ventured Tom anxiously.

—We're safe when we get away, said one of the hurlers. When the constables cool down, they'll find it hard to explain why they were dhrinkin' when they were on duty; the barman'll be anxious for the name of his house; and, whatever the jarvey may be, you'll find he's no informer.

The hedges were now passing them by with speed; away in the far distance they heard a few faint whistles; Johnny caught up the whip and gave the mare a flick or two on the flanks. Away she tore now, the hedges flying by like mad things, for the mare was tearing along at a swift gallop. Holding her with a loose rein, but keeping her well in for fear of a sudden need in front of them, Johnny felt hilarious, saving them all from the horneys.

—That was a gorgeous clip you gave the bastard on the chin, said a hurler, to Mick; it musta given him a new vision of hell open for sinners.

Along past numbers of little cottages, the little lights in their little windows flitting by them like falling golden stars; on over the bridge crossing the Tolka, giving a fleeting glimpse of the white-mantled Blessed Virgin standing alone among a clump of rain and river-soaked cottages; then a swift, winding turn up into Botanic Avenue, catching sight sometimes of the Tolka waters, singing her gentle song as she went slowly by the elders and willows, away on her short and simple journey to the Bay of Dublin O.

Along the Avenue, at a quick lolloping gallop, the tidy-limbed little mare goes on, a-pace, a-pace, a lady goes a-pace, a-pace, a gentleman goes a trit-trot trit-trot, and a horseman goes a-gallop a-gallop a-gallop, couples in each other's arms, lying by the road-side or standing close against the walls, turning to look at the jaunt-ing-car go racing by, with its redcoats and green jerseys arm in arm on the seats, glancing at the nipper driving, bent nicely over the mare, turning her round by the Botanic Gardens, the car swaying, the men holding on, stopping their chatter till the car levelled itself again to go swinging along the Glasnevin Road, several couples wandering slowly along, scurrying aside as close to the hedges as they could get, to let the car go fast past by them, along, along the road, Johnny flushed with pride, thinking he was the American Mail fleeing from the redskins, holding the reins as if he had never done anything but go at a gallop through all the days of his life, slowing down a little now going over Westmoreland Bridge, and pulling her gradually to a stop before the doorway of the Cross Guns.

—Where do we go, now? he asked.

They all leaped down from the car on to the side walk.

—Tie her here to the lamp-post, said Mick, an' let us all scatther before they thrace us here, an' we end our ride with a night in chokey. The jarvey'll find her, never fear, an' not much harm done.

One of the hurlers patted Johnny on the back, saying, Well done, me young bucko; you're the one well able to handle a horse!

—He dhrove like Jehu, said Archie.

The hurlers raised their hands high over their heads and shook their hurleys.

—Parnell for ever! they shouted.

—An' Ireland, too! said Tom.

—An' Ireland, too! shouted the hurlers.

Johnny felt in his heart that he had done a good day's work for Ireland. Then he remembered he had left behind on the counter the lovely branch of crimson and golden berries, plucked for his mother; and his heart got a little sad again.

COMIN' OF AGE

Johnny was getting on in years now, growing old with the world and all who were in it. Lean and lanky he grew, with masses of hair growing low down in front, that his mother laboured to brush back from his forehead, saying he'd look as if he knew nothing if he hadn't a high brow. A few days before his fourteenth birthday, he could manage to read, skipping the biggest words, the stories in *The Boys of London and New York*, and the various coloured-cover penny adventure books, and *Ally Sloper*, a weekly comic, whenever he had the penny to spare for one of them. So, if you ask me, he knew nearly as much as there was to be known, and fit he was to take his place in the world, paddle his own canoe, and fill a job with the best boy going, as soon as he could get one. Every day Archie carefully scanned the 'Situations Vacant' columns of the *Daily Express*, on the lookout for a suitable chance for Johnny.

Early on one fair morning in April, Johnny was wakened by having his shoulder shaken by his mother.

—Get up, she said, get up, like a good boy, for Archie has just come across the very thing for you.

Johnny slowly opened his sleep-dim eyes and murmured, Let him speak, for I can hear as well lyin' down as I can sittin' up.

—Get up, get up, man, said Archie impatiently; and when you've washed your face you'll be betther able to take in what I've got to say to you.

Johnny got up, dressed, and washed his face, wondering how he could be able to understand better when all this had been done. Then he sat down by the fire to listen to what the one and only Archie had to say.

Archie opened out the *Daily Express* and looked earnestly into it. Then, in a stately and dignified voice, he read, A smart, respectable, and honest boy wanted. One just finished school preferred. Apply by letter to Hymdim, Leadem & Co, Henry Street, Dublin. There y'are, he added, the chance of a lifetime.

—Maybe a godsend, said his mother.

—A fine big Firm, said Archie, one o' th' biggest in th' whole city, an' Protestant to the backbone.

—Johnny'll never know what he'll rise to, in a Firm like that, murmured the mother.

—Let him run down, now, to Ella, an' get her to write out a letther for him, applyin' for the job; an' another of her own as a school-misthress, sayin' Johnny was a good boy, an' most attentive to his studies, instructed Archie. Let her just sign it E. Benson, so as to show no sign that it was written by a woman.

—An' I'll ask Mrs Middleton for the loan of her boy's new topcoat, said Mrs Casside, for Johnny to have a betther chance of lookin' the boy the job was meant for; an', if he gets the job, we can get one for himself at a bob a week from oul' Greenberg. Hurry off, now, she said to Johnny, to your sisther, an' get her to write the two letthers; on your way there, buyin' a pennorth o' notepaper an' envelopes, a penny bottle of ink, an' a ha'penny pen, in case Ella 'ud be empty-handed. Then hurry back; I'll have th' coat waitin' for you, an' you can go at once and see if they'll give you th' job.

Johnny girded up his loins and set off at a quick walk to his sister's place in Summerhill, popping into a shop on the way and buying all he needed; quickening the walk to a quicker trot, then to the quickest gallop; sliding down, after a while, to a trot, then to a quick walk for a rest; then breaking into a gallop again, going on like Paul Revere to tell the town the enemy was on the way, till he came panting to his sister, showed her the news his mother had cut from the paper, and telling her what she had to do.

In a hurry, she washed her hands for fear of soiling the letter, and saying that when it was written he'd have to copy what she had written, for they'd know her neat hand was hardly the hand of a schoolboy. So when she had written, Johnny, with his face screwed up, and with much labour and care, wrote in a large lettered hand, the following:

Dear Sirs,

I have observed by an advertisement appearing in the *Daily Express* of this morning's issue, that your Firm is in need of an honest, smart, and respectable boy, and that you prefer to employ one who has just finished school. I venture to say that I have all the qualities required, and, as I have just left school, I beg to offer myself as a candidate for the position.

Very respectfully yours,

JOHN CASSIDE

Messrs Hymdim & Leadem.

Ella then wrote on another sheet of notepaper:

St Mary's National School,
Lr Dominick Street.
The Bearer, JOHN CASSIDE, has been a pupil in the above school, during which period I have always found him a truthful, honest, and obedient boy, and, at all times, most attentive to his studies. I feel sure he will give perfect satisfaction to any employer good enough to use his services.

E. BENSON,
School Teacher

Johnny hurried home with the letters; dressed himself in all his faded finery, putting the almost new blue Melton coat, loaned to his mother by Mrs Middleton, over the lot, and hastened off to join those who were busy battling with the world.

When he came to Sackville Street, he felt hot and a little out of breath. He felt the sweat oozing out between his thighs, making his trousers feel a little damp. He had gone too quick, he thought. His stomach felt as full as if he had just eaten a great meal, but he had had only a cup of tea and a cut of dry bread. Tight it felt as a tightly laced drum. If he could only pop into the job, without having to see anyone about it. Still, he was here, and in he'd have to go, and finish what he had begun. But better wait till he had cooled down a little; never do to show you were in a sweat to get it. Go in, cool and collected, and appear as if you didn't care whether you got it or not: and had just dropped in because you had nothing else to do, and the day was long. He'd sit here for a few seconds, till his heart got down to a quieter beat, and then go on: forward – the Buffs! He sat down on one of the pedestals of one of the General Post Office's great pillars, listening to the tram timekeeper, a brown-bearded man, wearing a half-tall hat,

calling out for the trams to make a start: Sandymount, and away
would go that tram; Palmerston Park, and away would go that
tram too, with a tinkle from the bell the conductor pulled. All
aboard for Palmerston Park, where the gentry lived. Most of
them were moving to where the gentry lived, passing through the
poorer quarters, out to where there were trees, air, and sunshine,
where the gentry lived.

For the tenth time, Johnny took the letters from his pocket and
read them, before he finally sealed them up for ever. Not so bad,
he said, as he licked the flaps and closed them down, for if they
want a genuinely honest, truthful, and willing boy, they needn't
look over my shoulder for one.

He watched for a few moments the soldiers streaming past
him: Hussars, in their gorgeous crimson trousers; Army Service
Corps, with their sober blue-and-white uniforms; Lancers, white-
breasted, red-breasted, or yellow-breasted; Guards, in their
tight little trousers, tight little white pea-jackets, tight little caps;
Highlanders, with their kilts swinging – all on the hunt for girls;
always strolling on the same side of the street, the west side, never
on the other, where all the respectable people walked who didn't
like to make a contact with a common soldier; from the corner of
Great Britain Street, principally, to the Royal Bank of Ireland,
back and forward, stopping when they made a catch, restlessly
moving backwards and forwards, on the hunt for girls.

> *While up the street, each girl they meet,*
> *Will look so shy, then cry, my eye!*
> *Och! Isn't he a darling,*
> *Me bould sodger boy!*

He felt quite cool, now, so he licked three of his fingers, and
smoothed his hair back from his forehead as far as it would go.
He dusted the seat of his trousers, felt that his Eton collar sat still
and safe, pulled the lapels of his blue Melton coat forward, and
sallied up Henry Street, threading his way through the crowds of
people coming out and going into the shops. Right into the big
stores he dived, asking where he could deliver a letter that answered an advertisement wanting a truthful, honest, and willing
boy. The far end of the great shop was pointed out to him, and
he was told that when he passed through a door there, he would
find a Mr Anthony who would deal with the matter contained in
the letter applying for the post. So Johnny went on a long journey

by steep mountains of chandlery, terraces of lamps of every sort, table lamps, tiny lamps, bracket, hanging, hall, and reading lamps; small-wick, wide-wick, single-wick, and double-wick lamps; forests of brushes, hair, fibre, and twig; valleys of curtains, cloth, beads, and bamboo; huge rockeries of ironmongery; while overhead was a great gallery, circling the whole of the ground floor, filled with all kinds of delft and chinaware, beetling over all as if eager to look at all the other wonders piled in the valley below. Through all these he wended his way to a glass-panelled door leading to the packing and dispatch departments. Pushing this open, he came into a long dark store, holding all the future supplies for the shop inside, and divided into heavy benches on which goods were piled, to be parcelled and packed and sent to various parts of the city and suburbs. On one side of this store, near the glass-panelled door, was a boxed-in office, full of windows, so that everything everywhere could be seen by a tiny lift of the head of anyone who might happen to be in it. In this office was a tall lean man, with a head like a fairly thin egg, whose hair began to sprout in the middle of his head, giving him the look of a waning scholar, who glanced up and looked at Johnny with a keen look in a pair of watery eyes that were thinly blue in colour.

Johnny, with his cap held respectfully under his arm, handed the two letters to this man, who was Anthony Dovergull, one of two brothers, owners of this big Firm of Messrs Hymdim, Leadem & Company; the other brother (Johnny found out afterwards) was as jet-black as this one was fair, with a heavy moustache losing itself in a heavy coal-black beard (his brother was clean-shaven), with brilliant black eyes that never knew how to soften. He was as tall as his fair brother, but had thick legs, massive shoulders, like a bull's, that gathered together and bent, when he was angry, like a bull about to charge; and his only smile, seen when the House was doing good business, was like a wintry sunbeam finding a home in an icicle. The dark fellow watched over the front of the Firm, standing on a bridge stretching from one side of the chinaware gallery to the other, stood all the day like a skipper on the bridge of a ship.

Mr Anthony Dovergull took the letters from Johnny, read them silently, and looked Johnny all over. Johnny was glad that he had Middleton's Melton overcoat on him. Then Mr Anthony read the letters again, thought for a moment or two; then looked at Johnny again.

—You are a Protestant, young man, are you not? he asked.

—Oh yes, of course, sir, answered Johnny, feeling that he had a close kinship with the mighty man in the boxed-in office.

—Well, we'll try you, said Mr Anthony. You can start tomorrow morning. Hours, eight till six; wages, three shillings and sixpence a week; rising, of course, annually, if your services are found to be satisfactory. And he dismissed Johnny by turning to resume the work he had been doing when Johnny handed him the letters.

So here he was standing in the street again, a child of fortune, a member of Hymdim, Leadem & Company, and an inheritor of three shillings and sixpence a week. He had made a flying start. He would begin life at eight o'clock the following morning. In the morning his life would break into bud. Aaron's rod all over again; it would bud and blossom. He was a child no longer. He had put childish things far from him. He was a worker. Henceforth he would earn his bread in the sweat of his face. The earth was his, and the fulness thereof. Glory be to God. Out of the darkness had come a saving light.

And Johnny felt that it was good; and the morning and the evening were the fair'st day.

BRING FORTH THE BEST ROBE

JOHNNY WAS up betimes, gay and fussy, in the morning. He took no notice of his mother advising him to get down as much bread as he could, for he'd have a long fast; but hurried over his breakfast, and excited and nervous, got into the new array, brown coat, long trousers, grey cap, and new black boots, got from Mr Greenberg the previous day.

Mr Greenberg was a Jew; not an ordinary Jew, Johnny's mother said, but a most respectable one. He had never carried a pack, but had turned the front room of a little house in a terrace off the Drumcondra Road into a shop. There clients came quietly to be satisfied, after a bargain made in their own houses. He had come to Johnny's house the evening before, and had promised to fit out Johnny from top to toe for five shillings down, and the rest of two pounds ten to be paid at one shilling a week; the instalments to be paid on the first day of every month. Mrs Casside had paid the five shillings deposit, and he had entered it in a little blue-covered pass-book below the articles bought: A brown suit, one pound; a navy-blue topcoat, one pound; pair of boots, ten shillings; and the grey cap, Mr Greenberg said, because of the boy making a start in life, would be thrown in free. Thrown in free, he murmured again, with a sigh. He glanced round the room, saw its scanty furniture, and sighed again. Didn't look like a very promising customer. His eyes roved over the collection of books that remained out of all that Johnny's Da had loved. His eyes took on a look of surprise. He went over to where they were, and took one of them into his hand, a thick, heavy, purple-covered one. It was *The Wars of the Jews*, and he opened it, and began to read.

—One of my poor husband's books, murmured Mrs Casside.

—Ah! said Mr Greenberg, Josephus, Josephus; a great writer; a great man. Our people, our poor people. Have you read it, Mrs Casside?

—No, indeed, I'm sorry to say, she answered. But my poor husband knew it near by heart. Everyone regarded him as a great scholar. Nothing was beyond him.

—Ah! said Mr Greenberg murmuringly, zee gruel, derreeble, veeked Romans! Ven they took Jerusalem and destroyed dee ceety, they crucified us in dousandts, dousandts, and dousandts. Zey could not get enough vood to make zee crosses they needed; dousandts and dousandts.

—What, the Holy Romans? asked Johnny.

Mr Greenberg turned towards Johnny, with a puzzled look on his face.

—He means the Roman Catholics, explained Mrs Casside.

—Not zee Catolics, not zee Roman Catolics, said Mr Greenberg. Zee old Romans, zee ancient vones, years and years ago, hunderts and hunderts of years before you or I vos born. But eet is all ofer now, he added; all ofer now. It ees lif, and – vot you say? he asked of Mrs Casside.

—Live an' let live, she said.

—Live, and let live, he repeated. Ve are – vot you call it? – ceevilized now. He put the book back where he got it, and settled his half-tall hat on his head, and stroked his beard thoughtfully.

—Goodbye, he said, shaking hands with Johnny; you vill find zee goods vot you want: a vonderful bargain. And read zee vars of zee Jews, my boy, ven you haf dime, ven you haf dime. It ees goot to read books; zey dell you zings, and it is goot to know zings; zee more zee better. Goodbye, my boy, and goot luck.

—Rather a nice old boy, for a Jew, said Johnny when he had gone.

—He's all right, replied his mother, but he knows how to charge, all the same. Had I had the ready money, I'd have got all he's given for half the cost, an' less.

Here he was now, dressed in the new garments, at a quarter past seven in the morning, with his mother putting the last touches to them; pulling down his dark-blue topcoat behind him, fixing his cap straight on his carefully brushed hair; going to the door with him, advising him not to be nervous, and bidding him god-speed.

Johnny hurried along the almost empty streets and passed the closed-up shops, opening his topcoat wide so that the few who passed at this early hour could see that he was wearing long trousers. What a swell he looked, and what a man he felt as he trudged gaily and swiftly along. A few trams, with nobody in them, hung around Nelson's Pillar, looking higher and statelier for the want of a crowd. Only the pubs were beginning to open as he went by, grocers' porters slashing buckets of water in front of the brightly-painted fronts to take away the raucous smells and smudges of the night before. Johnny got to the Firm nearly half an hour before the time of opening; and he leaned against the sombre revolving shutters, waiting for whomsoever came to open up the shop for the work of the day. There was nothing but a dog wandering up the street; and even the great General Post Office looked surly and sad. Opposite him loomed up the great drapery firm of Sir John Arnott & Co, another firm, he knew, stocked with good Protestants as tightly as it was stocked with good goods. There wasn't a doubt about it; we were, in some way or other, a goodlier run of people than the poor Roman Catholics.

At five minutes to eight he noticed that men and boys began to gather, and lean against the sombre shutters, just as he was doing, some of them glancing at him, curiously, as they settled their backs into a comfortable position. Eight o'clock struck from the big clock outside Arnott's, and still no one came to open the shop. He edged a little nearer to the waiting crowd so that he might catch a word or two of what was being said.

—Musta slept it out this morning, he heard one man say, when the clock showed it was five minutes past the hour.

—He's given us time for a longer smoke before dinner time,

responded another; but you'll soon see him come gallopin' round the corner. Didn't I tell you, he added, for here he comes fallin' over himself with the dint of hurry.

Johnny saw the long lank figure of him who had given him his job hurrying up the street, black suit, black bowler hat, black gloves, and black umbrella, like a thin black bat fluttering in a hurry along to get in out of the daylight. Anthony came up, and, without as much as a good morning to a soul, opened the black wicket-gate in the centre of the shutters, and hurried in, the crowd of clerks and boy assistants pouring in, one by one, after him. And Johnny, last of all, went in too, and found himself in the lonely darkened shop full of the smell of soda, soap, candles, and beeswax.

They all streamed away to where they left their coats and hats, leaving Johnny standing alone, alone in a darkened world, with the hundreds of lamps hanging overhead looking like stars that had died down, had lost their light, and shone in the firmament no longer.

Presently, he saw a man at the far end of the shop beckoning to him. He went down and stood in front of a man with a pale, handsome, Jewish-like face, who looked him all over, smiled rather sarcastically, and said, Mr Anthony tells me you're the new boy assistant, and you're to come with me so that I can show you what to do, and generally show you the way about the Firm. This man was Mr Prowle, an Orangeman, it was said, who was over the dispatch of all things going away by rail or sea; a silent man, who spoke to no one and no one spoke to him; always looking like a juvenile mariner, waiting on a painted ship upon a painted ocean.

He went before Johnny through the door leading to the dispatch store, and, showing Johnny a huge pile of waste paper, said, Sort that, smooth the sheets out in their different sizes, put holes through them when the heaps are big enough, and string them up for use in parcelling up the goods we send away. When that's done, tie up all those clothes-pegs into dozens, and pile them neatly on the shelf behind you.

While he was working away at the waste paper, Johnny saw two messengers carry a small bench over into a corner of the stores, and cover it with a bright-green cloth, on which they placed a big white vase filled with red and yellow artificial flowers, making it look for all the world like a clumsy-looking altar. Then they carried two big parcels and placed them on the bench covered with a green cloth. Each parcel was backed by a big label, bearing on one the words, For Good Boy, Number One; and on the other, For Good Boy, Number Two. Stuck jauntily into the first parcel was a little paper Union Jack, with a bronze shaft as thick as a knitting needle, and a gilded paper point; on the other parcel, a little Royal Standard of the same kind. In front of each parcel stood a rather faded bowler hat, one lined with white silk and the other with crimson. And everyone who passed by wore a wide fat grin, holding tight to it, and not suffering it to depart when they had gone by. Johnny noticed, too, that Mr Anthony, in his desk above at the top of the store, wore a grin too; a quieter and more subdued one, as if he had just done something good and pleasant and quietly noble.

Johnny was working like a good one, tying the pegs into dozens, when Prowle called him, handed him a slip, and told him to get the things mentioned on it and parcel them up for him.

Johnny stared at the pencilled slip, and couldn't make head or tail of it. Six lb – that was clear enough, but what did *S sp* mean? Or *B w cls*, or *Bwx* mean? He looked and stared and looked again for a long time, till Prowle snatched the slip out of his hand.

—Can't you read? he asked sharply. What school did you go to?

—He went to college, said a packer at the other side of the bench, eager to fall in with Prowle; none o' your common schools for him.

—Six pounds of Sunlight soap, two of British wax candles, and a pound of beeswax – could anything be plainer. You'll have to brighten yourself, me boy, if you want to stay here. We don't want duffers. They're all on the shelves behind you; open your eyes and you'll find them, said Mr Prowle.

Johnny strayed up and down the long avenue of shelves, looking for what was on the slip. Probing the spaces, he came near to the desk where Nearus, the head clerk of the stores, was writing. Nearus was a big fellow, over six foot, and broad-shouldered; good and kind of heart he was, as Johnny soon discovered; but he was rotten at the core, for, on the top of each cheek, he wore the rosy cross of consumption, and a cough told the tale of a tomb.

—What are you looking for, what are you looking for? he asked, in a rough-and-ready way, when Johnny came close to him; but there was a soft note in the bark of his voice. There you are, he added, pointing to some shelves; candles there; soap here; and the beeswax over your little head. He took down the things himself as he spoke, and laid them on the counter for Johnny. If you're in any fix at any time, come to me, and don't fret if I shout the answer at you.

So the long day wore on, with Johnny, under the firmament of heaven, tying up pegs into dozens, sorting out paper, running all sorts of errands, finding out how puzzling little words could be when they were written down on paper, discovering, like an explorer, the new regions of the big Firm, and learning where the multitude of differing stores were packed away in their various places; all the time glancing frequently at the bench covered with the green cloth, and wondering what was in the parcels, and why everyone smiled as they passed the parcels by.

Coming back five minutes before the time at lunch hour, he found Nearus alone, bending over his desk, busy with an army of figures. He glanced up when he saw Johnny signing on in the book that lay, like a warrior taking his rest, beside the big desk of Nearus.

—Eh, kid, he said, is that a new suit of clothes you've on you, or is it only an old one varnished?

—New one, sir, said Johnny; bought only yestherday.

—Well, it won't be worth a wax in a week here, man. No one wears a new suit working. Bring an old coat with you tomorrow, and hide it under the bench to wear when you're working. It's enough to look a toff when you're coming in to start, or going out when you're finished.

—Thank you, said Johnny. I'll tell my Ma when I get home.

—Well, kid, he said, how do you think you'll like your job?

—I'm sure to like it well, said Johnny; all the people here seem so happy and smiling.

He beckoned to Johnny to come a little nearer, and bent over till his mouth was close to Johnny's ear.

—Keep your mouth shut and your ears open, and you won't see much, he said. They're all a gang of superior hangmen here. They're smiling today because they have to, for today is the great day of atonement. Know what atonement means?

—Being at one with someone who has had a row with you, said Johnny.

—If you din't knock it down, you staggered it, said Nearus. Well, we're all, for this one day of the year, at one with Mr Anthony and Mr Hewson, and that's why we're all smiling, my boy.

The master is at one with the man, and the man is at one with the master. He stretched a big and thinning hand towards the bench covered with the green cloth. And that's the altar of friendship, he said.

—An' what's in th' parcels? asked Johnny.

—Goodly threasures for two goodly men, answered Nearus. An old suit that Anthony's tired wearing, and another that Hewson's tired wearing, for Enthrews, the packer here, and O'Reilly, the porter in the front shop.

—They must be two good men, murmured Johnny, for he wist not what to say rightly.

—Too good for God, said Nearus. He leaned over closer to Johnny, and whispered in his ear: Don't ever say anything to either of them; don't let them hear you saying anything to anyone else; don't even let them hear you saying your prayers.

Others began to come back from lunch. Nearus got close to his desk to fight the army of figures again, and Johnny went his way behind the great counter to his tying of pegs, sorting of paper, or any extra thing he might be called upon to do.

The long day wore on, and the quiet evening came, and the work slackened when it was but an half-hour before the time to quit.

And all the house was smiling, all except Nearus; for Johnny thought it would be a good thing to smile too.

Suddenly the big black Hewson came in from the front shop, and, joining the skinny, fair-eyed Anthony, both of them, smiling, sauntered down to where the bench, covered with the green cloth, was standing, looking like a clumsy altar bearing on it outward and visible signs of an inward and spiritual grace. Shortly afterwards O'Reilly came in from the front shop, and stood, smiling, at the north end of the store, while the packer Enthrews stood, smiling, at the other end, gently tapping straw into a case he was packing for the country. The vanmen, messengers, and other packers stood in a grinning group near the big gateway; and the clerks from the various dispatch rooms, and the assistants from the front shop, came hurrying in and stood in a smiling row along the length of the warehouse, their eyes staring at the bench covered with the bright-green cloth. Then, after a fit pause, Mr Hewson beckoned to Enthrews, and Mr Anthony beckoned to O'Reilly; and the two came, each from the other end of the earth, trusting, not in their own righteousness, but in the manifold and great goodness of their two Masters, who were ready to bestow upon them some of the crumbs that would soon fall from the table covered with the green cloth.

And when they drew near, Hewson stretched out his hand and took a parcel, and handed it to Enthrews, at the same time that Anthony stretched out his hand and took a parcel, and handed it to O'Reilly. Then Hewson placed a bowler hat on the head of O'Reilly, and Anthony placed a bowler hat on the head of Enthrews, and lo! both were crowned, and a fine glory shone round about them; and a lowly murmur of praise went up from the clerks, assistants, vanmen, and messengers, as they saw this good thing done, and the murmur testified to the goodwill among men.

And Enthrews opened his mouth, saying unto Anthony, Thanks be unto thee, O sir; your kindness was unexpected, and your goodness endureth for ever.

And O'Reilly opened his mouth, saying unto Hewson, Thanks be unto thee, O sir; your goodness was unexpected, and your kindness endureth for ever.

Then the two men who had been so favoured went into a secret place to take off their old clothes and put on the new garments that had been given them; while Hewson and Anthony, smiling and chatting together in amity and peace, waited leaning against the bench that was covered with the bright-green cloth.

And Johnny, looking on, fancied he heard a voice from heaven saying, Let your light so shine before men that they may see your good works, and glorify your Father which is in heaven.

By and by the two came back rejoicing, clad in their new raiment, walking the one after the other, sellovish pride irrigating both their hearts, lifting their eyes to the hills, passing backwards through a lane-way of smiles; Enthrews with the little Union Jack sticking up from the band on his bowler hat, and O'Reilly with the little Royal Standard sticking up from the band in his.

And all hands were admonished by this display to behave better and to serve honestly the two men who, now and again, deigned to think of common men, and took down from the ownership of might and mercy in the centre of Dublin City, hard by the Protestant church on the one hand and the Catholic church on the other.

A low, lorn murmur of satisfaction rose from the assembled clerks, assistants, vanmen, and messengers; and in the midst of the murmur Mr Anthony and Mr Hewson moved away from the bench that was covered with the bright-green cloth, and walked slowly towards the glass-panelled door leading to the front shop. Then Mr Prowle lifted up his fine voice a little, in a respectable manner, and sang, and all except Nearus, who coughed and leant over his desk with his head bent down, joined in, singing softly, soberly and slyly, for very fear that God might hear them:

> *An' here's a hand, my trusty fiere,*
> > *An' gie's a hand o' thine;*
> *An' we'll tak' a right guid-willie waught,*
> > *For auld lang syne!*
> *For auld lang syne, my dear,*
> > *For auld lang syne,*
> *We'll tak' a cup o' kindness yet,*
> > *For auld lang syne!*

Then it was time to go; and all slunk their several ways home for the night, to eat, to whore, to sleep, perchance to dream. And Johnny went with them. Peace and fellowship were everywhere; but Johnny felt uneasy, and saw that it was not good; and the morning and the evening were the sicken'd day.

WORK MADE MANIFEST

SO HERE he was, a start in life made, ploughing his first furrow in the workaday world of Dublin. Hould on now, an' let Johnny think of what he had to do in a day. It was he that had to do as much as any dry-land sailor. First he had to go to where the vanmen stabled their horses, in a lane off Cavendish Row, to gather the precious money collected by them on bills for goods bought in the shop, checking the amounts appearing in the vanmen's books, and signing for the sums received; throwing the notes and coins into a satchel, amounting to from fifteen to twenty-five quid; hurry back to the Firm to deliver the money over to Mr Anthony, always a little anxious that some day he'd be short of a shilling or two, for the vanmen wanted watching, and a bob would make a big hole in his week's wages. Then, when the money was at rest in the safe, he had to sweep the dirty straw and rubbish from behind the long bench that held the goods going by rail or sea, sweeping the rubbish out to the beginning of the passage

leading to the cobbled lane outside the great wooden gate. As a
Protestant and a member of the staff, he swept no farther, but
handed the heap of rubbish over to a Roman Catholic messenger,
who carried it on to where it would be eventually taken away by
the city scavengers. When loads of new stuff came up in lorries
or in floats, he had to carry in the four- or six-stone boxes, open
them with a steel ripper, and pack the goods, starch, soap,
polish, or blacking in bins or on shelves behind the benches. Or,
he would be sent to another store farther down the lane, bordered
on the other side by slaughterhouses, reeking of fresh and stale
blood, into which cattle or sheep were continually pouring; to
come out as skinned and bloody carcases, carried on the shoulders
of sturdy men, with the purple of battle all over their clothes,
who pitched the gaudy carcases into huge carts, which brought
them to the butchers who cut them up into fancy shapes for the
finer sustenance of man. Here in this further store came crates of
chinaware; and Johnny helped to unpack them, and carry the
chinaware in boxes, hard and heavy and biting into his shoulder,
through the long dispatch store, through the front shop, up seven
flights of stairs – a holy number – to the special rooms where the
chinaware was stored. When there were no more soap, matches,
blacking, or chinaware to be carried in and packed away, Johnny
kept from the deadly sin of sloth by helping to parcel up the
goods that were to go away, putting them in order of delivery on
the benches, in readiness for the vanmen to come and bring them
out to the customers. Or, if he wasn't busy in this way, he'd go
on errands, leaving an order for brushes in Varian's of Talbot
Street; or hump a hip-bath, or a full-length one, over his head
and shoulders to Phillipson's in Stafford Street, to have it scraped
and japanned over again, so that its rusty nakedness might be
hidden from sensitive eyes. It was a long day and a tiring day;
but he had the assurance that for ever, now, he would be certain
of his *Boys of London and New York* every week of his life, for
ever and for evermore, amen.

Every worker in the front shop and every clerk, or the possible
makings of a clerk, in the dispatch department, was a Protestant
of one kind or another. The Catholics drove the vans, took charge
of the crates, muled in the stores, did the packing, and acted as
messengers, pushing huge, deep, wicker three-wheeled prams
filled with goods for customers throughout the day and halfway
through the night for four, five, and six shillings a week. Each
vanman, no matter how late he had arrived back at night – and

none of them ever got home earlier from an ordinary delivery than ten o'clock – had to be at the stables by half-seven in the morning, to water and feed his horse, wash down his van, deliver what money he had to Johnny, harness up, and be at the shop for first delivery by half past eight. On Fridays he was allowed to stretch out his hand for fourteen shillings in a little clean white envelope. All were married men with children, so they hadn't time to mind it. Had they been Protestants, as Johnny was, they'd have known that the daily round and common task furnished all they need to ask; room to deny themselves – a road that daily led them nearer God. Stay quiet, an' you can hear the angels singin'.

Johnny had done all these things, and more; he had mingled with all these people, Protestant goats and Catholic sheep, for one long year; he had done well in his job; he had proved himself to be a trustful, willing, and honest boy; and had been rewarded with a rise, so that he went home, now, every Friday, with four shillings in his pocket instead of a meagre three and sixpence. Yet he wasn't satisfied. There was a sting of discontent in his heart. He had come to hate the shop and hate the men who owned it. Why, he couldn't say, rightly; but though the reasons were dim, the hate was bitter; ay, and he hated all, or almost all, who worked for the two Plymouth Brethren, Anthony and Hewson, who never mentioned God, but silently encouraged a number of desirables to go round and whisper in the others' ears that they would be pleased if any or all came to prayer, meditation, and the reading of the Bible in Merrion Hall on Thursday or Sunday nights at eight o'clock sharp, when Jesus Christ would be present on the platform.

There was one above all the others whom he hated. One there was above all others – oh, how he hated him! His was hate beyond a brother's – oh, how he hated him! This was O'Reilly, the porter, ex-RIC man, opener and shutter-up of the shop, and custodian of the basement where the ironmongery was kept. A sweet boyo! A Catholic that was the hidden eye and ear of the two Plummyth Breadiron. Everyone in the Firm, front and rear, was afraid of O'Reilly, and everyone was sweet to him, with their Good morning, Mr O'Reilly, an' I hope you're well, as this leaves me at present. The four-leaved shamrock, Johnny called him, and left him gaping when he went by without sayin' Good evenin', an' how're you feelin' today, sir, with th' weather soft an' a hard wind blowin' an' winther touchin' our toes, an' all th' green things on th' earth shiverin'; an' you feelin' something must be wrong because you go to Mass, while your bosses go to meetin'-house, thinkin' it hard lines that things can't be done in heaven as they're done on earth so that you could live with them, world without end; an' they thinkin', on their side, that there must be something right with O'Reilly; for didn't the good man defend their faith, their hope, their charity with a baton and a musket in the good young days, an' now, in his oul' age, he was still wary in defending their feat, heap, and charyity by keeping a spy-eye on all those who earned their bread by the skin of their teeth; with his sleek, sliddery sludery sloppery gob going peek-a-boo, I see you idling there, skedulin' the time you took to draw your breath; with Hewson asking him today, an' a far-away smile on his kisser, how were his sons gettin' on at the Intermediate; an' Mr Anthony sayin' to him, tomorrow, how right he was not to let himself or his wife or his children or his children's children resort with the kind o' neighbours circumstances obliged him to live among, addin' that O'Reilly ought to be well aware that O'Reilly wasn't an ordinary Roman Catholic, but really O'Reilly was gifted with the spirit of respectability of the Holy Ghost, given to very few people of really O'Reilly's class; for O'Reilly really breathed the breath of an honest devotion to persons and things most worthy to receive it, which was dispensationable according to the body and soul, life and teaching of their, and, in a minor sense, his, Lord and Saviour, Jesus Christ, amen, cross yourselves, and as you were before you 'listed.

So O'Reilly went on, and prospered, and stuck himself up to his neck in the bog of virtue, an' made holy affiance with the godliness of well-doing, never wearying of letting his bronze bosses know of anyone who swung the lead in the good ship we all toiled in; for everything was on the tongue and in the ear that met the eye that O'Reilly saw with; and a dhry thrio the three of them were, made be God Almighty when He hadn't much moisture to spare, for there wasn't the makin's of a tear among the three of them; an' it musta been a helluva shock to the best of them to have ever read that Jesus wept, feelin' that these tears, idle tears, were the one weakness shown by their Lord and Masstar.

A go-between and helper in the daily din was Sorrasaint, the Manager. Paler than Mr Anthony, with white eyebrows, timidly tinged with yellow, a moustache the colour of straw that had been out in the rain overnight, shallow blue eyes he had, shallow as a

puddle made shallower be a dhryin' wind, an' as tight as a tin
flea he was, ever ready to pounce out and forswear anything in
the way of an ankle undher a white petticoat; an' well Johnny
remembered when he once found, in a crate of china, a lovely
coloured picture of a dancing girl, showing a beaming face and a
lingering leg flowin' about in a foamy sea of lace, Sorrasaint came
up behind, like a thief in the day, snapped the picture out of
Johnny's hand, whipped up a hammer, and smashed the dancing
damsel into smidereens, throwing the hammer, in godly indig-
nation, back into the straw again, an' walkin' away, like a gaudy
Guardsman keen on his sentry-go.

These were the Four Feathers in the bowler hat of the Firm, who
were, as well, deep in the web of God's confidence, an' high in the
highlands of Erin's honour and Erin's pride, getting together all
they could get, an' booking for themselves sunny places on the
bonny banks an' braes of the Christal river, where a union of
angels were busy furnishing Ellessdee-touched villas for them,
ere ever their silver cords were loosened and their golden bowls
were broken.

Johnny had been in the job now for a year and a half, and was
busily waiting for promotion to the position of a clerk, if you
please, over a sectional city delivery. Every day of the year and a
half, bar Sundays, he had eaten his two cuts of bread, that the
shop called lunch, sitting on the step of one of the pedestals of the
General Post Office, looking out towards the bustling street when
the sun gave courage to the spring and dreamy delight to the
summer; looking in towards the portico, with shoulders bunched
up, and the dry bread bitter in his mouth, when the cold winds
blew, or the rain fell heavily; for only the girls of the shop were
allowed to eat on the premises, no matter how the weather raved,
or sputtered her cold venom on those who walked the Dublin
streets, with thin blood in their veins, and thinner clothes to
cuddle their skins from the blast.

But there was always the scarlet and gold, the blue and the
white of the warriors going by him, with their pushers; or a
Lancer officer trotting down the street on a fine bay on a fine day
in a fine way, with his sword and sabretache jingling, and the
plume in his Polish hat behaving well in the breeze; followed, at a
respectable distance, by his faithful servant, maybe a Hussar or a
Dragoon, looking only a little less stuck-up on his horse than
his officer and gentleman master leading the way onward. Maybe,
Johnny would watch the dust of the street, and he eating his daily

bread that God sent him, dancing its cloudy dance along the cobbled way when winds blew swift and sudden; or, better still, the skirts of the young girls blowing up when the wind blew strong, sending a surge through him that he couldn't say was wrong, and didn't know was right; but right or wrong, there it was – a mighty feeling and a strange delight when a black-stockinged leg of a pretty girl came out of a drab skirt, like a sunbeam out of a shadow. Then his thoughts would steal away to Jennie Clitheroe, seeking to put a hand in hers, feeling a little rugged spot on a finger where sewing had chafed her skin. He would dream of a green meadow where they could lie together, deep in the green things growing on the earth, the clover, the sorrel, the strong grass and the trembling, with a cornfield in the distance, golden, and scarlet poppies, sleepy, nodding at their feet.

But he was always too tired, when he came home at night, to go after any of these things. After glimpsing the blue and white, the red and gold of the soldiers; the helms and plumes of passing cavalry; the sudden look of pretty legs sometimes shown by passing ladies; came the labour of bearing piles of chinaware on his aching shoulders down the shit-mottled lane, through the dispatch department, along the front shop, a-glitter no longer, and up the seven flights of holy, hilly, helly stairs, thousands of thimes, hours and hours on end, till the shop closed slowly, and Johnny wended his hot and heavy way home, having helped to keep the great world moving.

And the morning and the evening were the tir'd day.

THE SHAME IS A THIEF AND A ROBBER

JOHNNY, WORKING away, had grown in wisdom, if he hadn't grown in grace. Although there was nothing against him, he knew the heads of the house didn't like him. Many whispers had dribbled into his ear, asking him to come to the meetings in Merrion Hall, but Johnny, saying that he felt it was all very nice and comfortable and godly, didn't ever go; and once, in a fit of recklessness, said to one of the evangelical whisperers that he'd rather open a girl's bodice than open a prayer-book, making the whisperer turn pale and turn tail and hurry away in a hot quick trot. But, still an' all, he had learned a few things. He could make out, without any bother, the differing handwriting of assistants and vanmen; count money quick and correctly; balance three hundredweight on a thruck nicely, and push it safely; lay out orders swiftly, and parcel up goods; pack china-ware with any packer in the shop; stand on a high ladder, and catch, with a cunning hand, packages thrown up to him for packing away on to high shelves; cleverly hand casks of oil; tip over heavy cases towards him, and edge them from where they were to where they ought to be; carry six-stone loads on his back through long distances for hours, without feeling faint at the end of the day; and fight his corner with the best or worst of those who worked around him.

The vanmen and messengers had fought shy of him for a long time, ever suspicious of a member of the staff; but one time, when a messenger happened to be in his way and delayed to get out of it, Johnny had given the fellow a hasty kick in the backside; and had suddenly found himself on his back in the straw from a puck in the snout the angry messenger had given him. He, think-ing he had hit another messenger, got the fright of his life when his rage let him see it had been Johnny, one of the staff, hurrying to help Johnny up, and murmuring, for fear of losing his job, that he hadn't meant it, hadn't known it was Casside, thought it was only another messenger, and begging Johnny, with tears in his eyes, to say nothing about it. Johnny had shaken hands with him, saying, never fear, for a Casside was never known to be an informer; and, after that, Johnny was the heart of the rowl with vanmen and messengers, especially when they found out he could curse with the worst of them.

Johnny was feeling very cocky, and now marched about with a long-handled pen stuck behind his right ear. He had been pro-moted to the bright position of dispatch clerk, over the Sandy-mount Ringsend delivery, at a salary of six shillings a week. Every Friday he handed his mother four and six out of his wages, for he let on he'd only five, which was fair and square, for wasn't it him who earned the money, an' hadn't she only to sthretch out her hand to take it? An' looka all he gave her besides. He had now a free hand in getting goods for the customers his vanman served, so why couldn't he get a few goods for himself? No sooner asked than answered. Johnny in his heart decided that it was neither godly nor wise to muzzle the ox that treadeth out the corn. So, on principle, he never went home without bringing something with him; and, after a while, his mother, with a few

frightened warnings to him to take care, made a few special
pockets in his coat, deep and wide so that things could be spread
out without bulging. So he carried home tiny cargoes of matches,
soap, candles, borax, ink, blacking, ketchup, tins of enamel,
Hudson's extract of soap and Monkey Brand that wouldn't
wash clothes, an odd knife and fork now and again, a spoon
occasionally, combs and hairbrushes, chamois leather, egg cups –
though they were more ornamental than useful – salt-cellars,
night-lights, knife polish, with a picture of Wellington on the tin,
shoe-brushes, clothes-brushes, floor-cloths – particularly prized
by his mother – small scrubbing-brushes, Goddard's Plate
Powder that went to Tom and Mick to clean their buttons and
badges, at tuppence a tin, little white-headed mops for cleaning
lamp chimneys, among other things, with various little toys at
Christmas for Ella's kids, and, any over, for the kids in the
neighbourhood, Johnny getting the blessing of the mothers for
his kind thought of bringing to the poor kids a real ray of
Christmas kinsolation.

It was quite an innocent practice, thought Johnny; not like
the heavy-handed foolishness of poor Botolph, the young clerk
over the Rathmines delivery, who had landed himself in a raw
plight with his picking and stealing; and was turned out of the
Firm for ever one day as soon as he had come back from his
lunch. Through a customer sending back goods paid for to the
vanman at the door, Anthony found that no record existed of the
payment in the vanman's book or in Botolph's ledger; and growing
suspicious, they had watched for a week, and found that the
bould Botolph entered up no bill that had to be paid, nor did any
of them appear in the vanman's book. The vanman, pressed to
explain, stammered that it must be a mistake; threatened with
the police, he blurted out that this thing had been going on for
some weeks; that the money received had been divided, two-
thirds to Botolph and one-third to him; yessir, months, maybe, I
can't well remember when I was led into it; it was Botolph who
had enticed him to thievery, for he was naturally a very honest
man, very, as all the world knew; Botolph had kept on appealing,
persuading, nagging him, till he gave in for the sake of peace;
he often an' often made up his mind to tell Mr Anthony all 'bout
it, but, somehow or other, it went out of his mind; an' wasn't it
a poor thing that a decent, honest, sober, steady, and most
respectable workman an' vanman should have been thrapped into
thievery by a vicious, dangerous, eely gougher.

Botolph standing beside him, pale as the twin brother of death, moistening his cracking lips and biting his hot nails, backing, backing till his back felt the prop of a bench, for he was frightened and getting faint.

And Anthony, stern and stiff and tight-lipped, listened, and said, in a voice loud enough to be heard by the hard o' hearing, while all listened so as not to miss a word of it:

—You have been a vanman here in a Firm that any common man would be proud to work for; you have answered that honour by turning out to be a vagabond, a mean thief, a perverse reprobate, a ragged rogue. Leave my sight, you ruffian!

And the vanman, with tears trickling down his cheeks, departed from the sight of his master, Dyke giving him a vicious kick in the arse, followed by one from Enthrews, and one each from the messengers, while, finally, Johnny got one home on him as he passed out by the gate; but he suffered them all gladly, in return for the sad things he had done, and never putting a single sign of quickness into his steps as he went slowly down the passage.

They had brought down Botolph's sister to be in at the death. In she came between Hewson and Sorrasaint, a plump, reddish-haired youngster with grey eyes and a face full of freckles. Not a one to want to put yoor arms around, thought Johnny, unless your sight was failin'. She had been told of what had happened, and had been given her walking papers, everyone concurring in the impossibility of her staying in a Firm her brother had robbed.

She stood there, dressed in black, with a white frill on her neck, tight white-starched bands round her wrists, a black felt hat with a green bird's wing in the band, and brooch of an ivory deer, running hard, in an oval brass-rimmed case, rising and falling on her bosom.

She stood there, a step away from her brother, two away from Anthony, a little handkerchief sheltering her face, crying softly into it, waiting to hear what Anthony had to say to her brother.

Anthony, when he had seen the stricken vanman fade away round the gateway, slowly turned his head, and gazed on Botolph slinking against the bench behind him, rigid, staring, and seemingly unable even to bend his head away from Anthony's snaky stare.

—Come nearer, sir, come a little nearer, said Anthony.

Botolph shoved himself away from the propping bench, and took a few paltry, shuffling steps nearer to Anthony.

—Were it not that we don't wish to make it known that our

Firm could possibly graft a thief on to its staff, said Anthony, you'd be leaving my presence now tucked into the arms of two policemen. Though the sun may shine on the evil and the good, the sun will not be allowed to shine on the evil here. You have been given the privilege of working for a Firm with a reputation as high as any Firm could hold; you had a fine future in front of you; but you elected to become perverse and dishonest; and have brought shame upon your family and ruin to your sister. Had you not wickedly chosen a froward life, you would today have been receiving your wages instead of your dismissal. Instead of being a trusted servant, you are now but a low-minded rascal and a decently-clad thief. We are all very glad to be rid of you. Get out of my sight, you laundered vagabond!

And Botolph, moistening his stiff lips, trying to keep his twitching legs steady, stumbled away from the face of his master, Dyke giving him a vicious kick as he passed by, followed by one from Enthrews, and one each from the messengers who happened to be within range, Johnny finally getting one home on him as he shuffled out by the gateway into the lane. Botolph bore them all well, sighing for the sad things he had done, and feeling that these things were but a small penalty to suffer for his mischievous behaviour.

—Phew! said Dyke, with his nose in the air, and loud enough for Anthony, Hewson, and Sorrasaint to hear him, thank God that stink is gone! The air already feels a lot fresher without it.

Hewson and Sorrasaint turned and went back to their haunts in the front shop, and Anthony withdrew into his shell of an office, leaving the freckle-faced, red-haired girl, in black, standing against the desk of Nearus, with her face sheltered in her little handkerchief, and the brooch of an ivory deer, running hard, within the oval of the brass circle, rising and falling on her bosom.

After a few minutes of quiet crying, Nearus bent over his desk and touched her on the shoulder.

—Steal away home, girl, he said softly, and lie away as far as you can from everything that has happened to you today.

The touch startled her into movement. She moved away from the desk, keeping the little handkerchief pressed to her face; and the black figure, the felt hat, with the bird's green wing in it, and the ivory deer, running hard, went down the passage, out of the gateway, and passed out of the sight and scene of the shop for ever.

All this had happened yesterday, and Johnny was picturing it in his mind all over again as he walked along Sackville Street,

glancing at the fireman sitting outside his sentry-box, smoking
his pipe under the stars that filled the sky, and ready at a second's
warning to unlock the fire-escape chained through the spokes of
a wheel to a stone post, and hasten, with a crowd of eager civilians,
to push it wherever the fire might be.

Johnny was hurrying on to meet his vanman, Dorin, at
Dooney's pub in Great Britain Street, thinking all the time of the
kicks, Botolph, and the ivory deer, running hard, on the bosom
of a crying red-haired girl. Dorin, a day or two ago, had seen
the heap of cracked delft and ironmongery that Anthony sold
at a bargain price to Biddy, a street hawker who went round with
a donkey and cart reselling the broken ware to the poorest people
cast away into the slums. He had asked Johnny for a cracked
teapot, and Johnny had given him a new one, adding that, if
cautious arrangements could be made, he could give him many
more things. Then had come the exposure of Botolph, and Johnny
had arranged to hold a council meeting between himself and
Dorin in Dooney's pub to arrange the business in a safe way.

Johnny glanced up at a sickle moon hanging in the sky among
a throng of stars. What was it and what were they? He had looked
in the pages of Ball's *Story of the Heavens* and at the pictures, but
it was all too hard for him yet. But he would learn, he would
learn. He wouldn't keep on being the ignoramus Archie had
called him when he ventured to say a word in the argument that
arose in Nagle's pub between Dalton and Archie over the battle
of Aughrim and the Siege of Derry. If his father had made himself into a scholar by boring into books, his son could do the
same. He was studying all words he didn't really know the meaning of, in an old dictionary his father had left behind him. More
than that, he was busy learning something about physical, political, and commercial geography out of his father's old book,
Sullivan's *Geography Generalised*. More than that, he was learning
grammar, too; and history from his father's Merle d'Aubigné's
History of the Reformation, and already knew a lot about Luther,
Melanchthon, Erasmus; gentle Melanchthon, sturdy Luther,
fiery Zwingli, scholarly Erasmus. God's own job they had, to
overthrow the idea of the Pope's supremacy in the hearts of the
people; and harder still to turn the church that had become the
church of Babylon, back into the church of God again. But best
of all the books that Johnny found useful was *The Comprehensive
Summary*, an American book, holding a store of knowledge about
many things, physiology, mineralogy, mythology, with a brief

history of every country and nation that had ever existed, from the Babylonians straight through to the surrenders at Yorktown and Saratoga; winding up with the bugle-blast of the great American Constitution. Johnny got to know a great number of people, Cyrus, Zeus, Semiramis and Ninus, her husband, the builder of Nineveh, mentioned in the Bible; Xerxes, Leonidas, Alexander, who found the world too small to hold him; Hannibal, Caesar, Dathi, Agricola, Aurelius, Hector, Ulysses, Columbus – though he'd often heard of him before – Penn, the Quaker, converted in Cork; Washington, hardly ever heard of here, Franklin, his friend, who in odd moments when he had nothing else to do, fastened a key to a kite and discovered the electric current; and many another who, and a whisper was loud enough to say it in, were big men compared to poor little Hewson and Anthony among their pots and pans and soap and candles. He must remember to lift a few carriage candles tomorrow, for they gave a clearer light, and burned more steady when he was studying than the common ones that flickered and sputtered and hurt his eyes.

—Leon'idas, he murmured, the Leader of the Three Hundred at the Pass of Thermopylae, who knocked the lard outa th' Persians, accented, according to Walker's English Dictionary, on th' antepenultimate, and, once, when an old man came into a crowded theatre and sought a seat, the young Athenians pushed together to keep him out, which, seeing, made the old man hurry away to where th' Lace, Lace, Lace'daemonians were, who in a body rose to let the old one sit down. The Athenians, ashamed at themselves, burst into loud applause when they saw the kind act of th' Lace, Lace'daemonians; and the old man, rising from his seat, said, Th' Athenians know what good manners are, but the Lacedaemonians practise them! All very nice and proper, then, thought Johnny, but a hard thing to do these days.

He crossed over Sackville Street, turned down Great Britain Street, and came to Dooney's pub where Dorin was waiting for him, under the clock, with his eyes on the hands. They went inside, moved to a quiet corner, and Johnny took a small port on Dorin's invitation, while Dorin's eyes beamed over the creamy top of a pint of porter.

—Now, said Johnny, when he had taken half of the port, and Dorin had golloped down half of the beer, to business: After what happened to Botolph, we'll have to keep our weather-eye open.

—It was a lousy thing for him to go and dip his hand into the money, said Dorin; why couldn't he ha' played fair, an' stuck to simple goods, like us?

—An' then, added Johnny, to go scatherin' it around so that everyone knew he was diggin' up buried threasure somewhere.

—Th' white-collared get, said Dorin.

—You've got a boy nearly fourteen years old, have you?

—Ay, have I, said Dorin, an' though it's his father sayin' it, a well-up kidger for any fair dodge goin'.

—Well, said Johnny warningly, when I give you anything, you must never – never, mind you – dhrive up to your own hall door to deliver it. It's soon the tongues of th' neighbours u'd get goin', blow on us, an' I'd begin and you'd end your further days in jail. So I'll never give you anything on any delivery, except your last one, so that you'll never be sure that I won't be dodgin' about the sthreet you live in, an', if I once see your van anywhere near it, you'll never get another thing outa me.

—Be Jasus! swore Dorin, I'd never do a thing like that. I'm not the one to frighten away th' goose layin' th' golden eggs. I'm no gaum. I'll work th' delivery in such a wise way that neither of the boyos'll fall into the suspicion they had lost as much as a burnt-out match.

—What we have to do is this, instructed Johnny. You get your eldest boy to meet you a good way from where you live. Give him whatever you have to give, an' dhrive on, so that he can carry th' things home as if they had been bought in a shop in th' usual way. D'ye understand?

—Entirely, said Dorin; but, Jack, wouldn't th' missus be betther than th' boy?

—Oh, no, no; not th' missus, said Johnny impatiently. On no account, or at any time, let th' missus come to collect th' goods. If a policeman happened to be knocking about, an' saw you givin' it to th' missus, he might be suspicious, an' start askin' questions. No, th' missus won't do. Th' boy'll look more innocent; he'll look as if he were your vanboy, an' a policeman passin' 'll take no notice.

—Be God, I never once thought o' that! ejaculated Dorin, draining a last drop from his tumbler of beer.

—Well, I did. We can't be too careful. He took a slip of paper and a pencil from his pocket. Now, he said, tell us what you're most in need of, for a start?

Dorin tightened his lips, and shut his eyes for a moment, taking a long swig from a new pint he had just ordered, opening his eyes for a second to put the tumbler back on the counter, and then closing them again, so that the darkness might be an aid to deeper thought.

—We need a helluva lot, he murmured, for all we had at th' start's bid us goodbye years ago. Th' missus washes a lot, always thryin' to keep things clean – soap, matches, starch, an' blue, f'rinstance.

—Righto, said Johnny, making some notes. I'll make up a fine parcel o' chandlery for you tomorrow evenin'. Now, anything else – saucepans, brushes, or things like that?

—Aw, Jasus, said Dorin, I wouldn't like t'ask you to get me things like that – we must be fair.

—Fair? queried Johnny.

—Well, I ought to give you something every time you make me a present.

—No, no; that won't do, said Johnny swiftly; none o' that for me. It would make you careless, as if you were payin' for them, an' th' money might make me careless, too. I mightn't watch to make sure you were cautious, an' th' two of us would be landed. No; the minute you don't do what we have arranged for you to do, the bargain ends, an' it will never be begun again.

Dorin seized Johnny's hand and shook it again and again.

—I understand, he said heartily, an' your way's th' way it'll be done. You're a decent lad, a real decent lad, heart o' th' rowl, he said; th' real Annie Daly, he said, one in a thousand, a trusty mate, a lad of a good breed, he said; not like th' rest o' them, nose-rags, toe-rags, flittin' afther Mr Anthony here, an' Mr Hewson there, sucks who would sell their mothers for a smile from a boss, he said; but you're a change from all those, a dear change an' a genuine change; an' standin' out as a sowl man, a solid man, hindherin' th' rich to give help to the poor, sound an' thrue in all your dealin's with your fellow man.

Johnny's face flushed with pride, and he shook hands heartily with Dorin. Then they left the pub, and parted at the corner of Sackville Street.

—Safe home, Jack, said Dorin, again shaking hands with Johnny. Rest assured, he went on, that th' missus'll never fail, come what may, to inthercede for you whenever she goes to Mass, with an occasional blessed candle for company before the shrine o' Saint Anthony quietly beggin' help in our endayvours to knock a little reason outa life.

The sickle moon fair followed Johnny home when he parted from Dorin. He walked faster, and the moon moved quick in the heavens; he walked slow, and the moon mended her pace to keep him company. Slitting the heavens, she seemed like a sly shy face peeping through the curtained stage to see how the house looked. Of all the brightness of heaven, the moon was by far the nearest to him. Where was the sun, now? Somewhere to the east; or, as the old story went, speeding along the bitter waters of the north in Vulcan's golden goblet, on its way to where the sun was to rise again, the first thing in the morning. Strange belief. Ignorance of the early ages. Poor man.

What's this he was to get for Dorin? Dozen of matches, pound o' soap, two packages of Hudson's Extract, one o' candles, some blue an' blacking, a sweeping-brush, and a three-pint saucepan. A fair start, anyway.

The heaven and the earth. Look up, and they don't seem to be so far away from each other. Anyhow, they were made together. In the beginning, God created the heaven and the earth; pretty close, what? Yet, sometimes it seemed that they were a hell of a way asunder.

When he came to the door of his house, he looked up before he went in. The moon was right in front of his face. Reminding him of something. What? Oh, yes: the brassy circle enclosing the ivory deer, running hard, rising and falling on the sobbing breast of a red-headed girl.

Oh, well.

He went in; and the morning and evening were the froward day.

GATHER UP THE FRAGMENTS

JOHNNY WAS standing out in the lane at the back of the stores, looking up and down, and cursing Biddy.

All the breakages that came in the crates, provided they were able to stand on their feet, all the ironware and china and delft, injured in their transport from one place to another in the stores, were gathered together in a heap on a special bench and sold to a big-bodied, big-headed, and big-footed woman who had a face like an Aunt Sally, and was the dead spit of the manager's sister; so much so that this sister, who was the girl's overseer, was known privately to all the staff by the name of Biddy too. Johnny, by Anthony's orders, was waiting for her to come with her donkey and cart to take away the damaged goods, after a price had been arranged between her and Anthony, who battled for all he was worth to get the highest price possible for the desolate ironware and china, to be sold by Biddy afterwards to the poor swarming in the back streets of the city. It was drawing close to closing time, and, if she didn't come soon, by the time the bargain was made, and the things carried out, Johnny would be a long while behind his time of leaving for home; so here he stood in the lane, looking up and down, and cursing Biddy.

It was a happy evening, the sun shining hotly, and the sky overhead a deep, dear blue. The lane, stretching from Cole's Lane at one end, and Moore Street at the other, was half-filled with cattle, lowing in a frightened way; some of them trying to steal or run away from the murky entrances of the slaughterhouses, slipping madly, sometimes, in the slime of their own dung that pooled the cobblestones. There was a heavy reek in the air of filth and decaying blood scattered over the yards, and heaps of offal lay about watched by a restless herd of ragged women and youngsters, taking their chance to dive in and snatch a piece of liver or green-slimed guts to carry home as a feast for the favoured. Johnny was well used to the discordant smell hanging in the air everywhere, for the yards where the cattle were killed were often used by his Firm for the storage of crates that couldn't find room in their own warehouses, an odd shilling being slipped into the hand of the butcher who happened to be making the sacrifices of the day.

Johnny had often slipped in the slime, had often fouled his hands in the filth clinging to the crates, as he pushed them over the blood-soaked cobbles, and he had often washed his guilty-looking hands in the great butt outside, used by the butchers for the same purpose, the greasy water in it always coloured with a bloody tint. The butchers were big bullocky men, greasy with the fat of dying and dead animals; kind under it all, for Johnny often noticed that they gave all they could of the bloody issues into the clutching hands of the tattered poor. They took with a sheepish grin the gracious nod Mr Anthony gave them when he happened to meet any of them, as he sometimes did when he hurried into the outer stores to see that everything was safe and going on well, and no idling was knocking profits out of the Firm; for he had to be gracious to the men who provided him, free of charge, with cow-shit-covered storage space, where Johnny had so often see the dying kicks of cattle, growing weaker, twitching in the last throes; then becoming, all of a sudden, stiffly still; where he had often heard the dying bleat of the throat-punctured sheep, entering their end on the cold cobblestones, dying slowly in their own dung. He had seen the butchers suddenly hold back their knives, and the young and old watchers by the reddened gateway suddenly close their eyes to the bloodied treasures in the yard to bend their tousled heads, cross themselves, and murmur a Hail Mary when the Angelus tolled out its holiness from the bells of Pro-Cathedral.

The great blue sky, like a great blue flower, covered it all, with its golden centre sparkling back from the stones of the cobbled lane, marbled with the green slime and purple pools, some of them smoking faintly, like half-hearted burnt sacrifices to a half-forgotten god.

—This sort of thing, thought Johnny, should be done when the winter's harsh, when there'd be some reason for the poor animals to go out of the world from the stabbing frost and driving rain and the bitter wind. Surely, it is a hard thing to be taken away in a shower of sun, and die under a blue sky's blessing!

Here was Anthony coming out of the back stores, hurrying back to his natural nest to poke his bake into the figures again, figures that had mounted up till they pierced heaven and threw a golden shower over the feet o' God.

Here he came, stooping, suddenly, like a hawk, to pick up a blackened cork that had fallen by the wayside, throwing it, with a true shot, into a box kept for oilcan corks that could be used again.

Here he came, picking his steps to keep his finely-polished boots, shining like his soul, from touching the slimy-shining green puddles, barred with blood; his watch-chain dangling, for his back was beginning to bend; the well-kept head was beginning to shrivel; his frosty eyes were beginning to drip when a breeze blew; sure he stepped, quick and careful, for he was of heaven, heavenly; he knew his Lord, and was known of Him; and followed His voice into the glass-partitioned den for the steady lusty-fisted toll of the takings.

Ah! here was the boul' Biddy, at last, with her donkey and cart; and Johnny hurried in to tell Anthony that she was here, and viewing the desolate delft to decide how much value for the poor lay in the tired and tottering goods.

Along came the bent back; the shrivelled head, the dangling

watch-chain; the frosty eyes, trying hard to send a gracious glance at Biddy; standing in front of her, rocking themselves ever so gently on their toes, and jingling keys and money in their pockets; the frosty eyes watching the seam-patterned face of Biddy staring at the woebegone crockery; the thinned-out mouth waiting for her to fire the first words at the shrivelling head, the bending back, and the dangling watch-chain.

—There's not much here today to make a poor woman's heart lep, she murmured. Sorra much you'll be asking for that pitiful heap of has-beens.

—Now, now, Biddy, be fair; be just. Have another look at it, said the figure, gently rocking on its toes. There's a fine heap of fair goods there, really. And you can have it all for twelve and six – not a farthing less.

—Arra, Mr Anthony, your poor eyes must be seein' double this evenin', the hot sun havin' affected them, or somethin'. Twelve an' six, is it, you said? Is it a silver mine you think I have undher the stable where I keep th' animal? Fine hcap d'ye call it? An' next to nothin' in it that's not more than ready to fall asundher, if you blew a cold breath on them. Won't I have all I can do to hand them over safe to any fool that comes to buy them? No, no, Mr Anthony, fair is fair. Looka th' pots – you'll have to hold your hands undher them the whole time th' thing's cookin'.

—Now, Biddy, Biddy, don't exaggerate. The cracks go barely halfway down the saucepans. With a little care in handling, they'll serve the poor people excellently, excellently. It looks the best, it is the best lot yet you've had before you. Come, now, be reasonable: say ten shillings, then? Look over them while you're carrying them out, and you'll see ten shillings is a reasonable, a most reasonable figure.

—I can see them fairly well from where I'm standin', answered Biddy, never turning her head a hair's breadth, but staring fixedly into the battered heap of goods; see them too well, I do, an' it must be jokin' y'are, sir, an' thryin' to take a rise out of a poor oul' woman. Ten shillin's! Is it deaf I'm gettin', thinkin' I heard someone say he wanted half a sovereign for a bewildered heap of incurable crockery?

—Ten shillings, and worth double, murmured the figure, tenderly rocking on its toes.

—Oh, then, it's not deaf I'm gettin', but only listenin' to a gentleman eager to make his joke to frighten a poor innocent woman. A gentleman who knows th' poor woman 'ud never redeem herself from lifelong poverty if she gave him what he's askin'. Ten shillin's! If th' moon was made o' gold, an' I had it on th' mantelshelf, I might be willin', if I was in a given' mood, to part with th' half-sovereign. For goodness' sake, thry to think of th' job I'll have thrying to mesmerize th' shy buyers into imaginin' th' goods'll hold water, an' won't vanish into glassy dew if they hold them too tight.

Anthony stopped rocking himself tenderly on his toes, and stood stiff, a harder note creeping into the voice that had first been speaking in a velvety way.

—Well, he said, taking his hands from his pockets, and holding them by his sides, the last offer – seven shillings and sixpence.

Biddy turned suddenly to face Anthony, her figure, big and brawny, more supple than his, one hand lightly resting on a hip, her lively beady eyes staring into his so steadily that he bent his head lower than hers, and fingered the dangling watch-chain.

—Make it th' even seven shillin's, she said, an' I'll forget meself an' swing meself into foolishness for th' hundredth an' first time in me life.

—Seven shillings and threepence, then, said the bent head admiring the watch-chain, and say no more about it.

—Sorra a word more, she replied, barrin' a swift sigh over your anxiety not to look a little closer at what you're askin' seven an' thruppence for, for it's seldom I make a murmur against th' judgement of others, seein' that the Man above alone can alther another person's opinion, an', then, only afther an almighty effort, an' I can make bould to say that ever since I was a wee baby in arms, th' curse o' me life has been that I never could sthrive to make me own opinions go further than the margin of me own mind, for fear of imposin' anything in th' way of a notion on another, nosin' afther an aysey an' a righteous livin', an', out of a singular shyness that came natural to me, was never fit to beat down into a genuine bargain any one thing that was waitin' to pass from another's hand to mine, for a consideration, but well knowin' you to be a kind an' reasonable an' thorough gentleman, anchored to the way of fair dealin', it's no way backward I am in askin' you to let the poor lot go for th' first offer of seven shillin's sterlin' down.

—Oh, very well, said Anthony, mixing a sigh with a gracious grin, seven shillings, even money, then.

Biddy gave a mighty hitch to her heavy skirt, and fished out a dirty little linen sack from a hidden hip-pocket in an under petticoat, fished the money out of the little linen sack, counted it carefully, and placed it carefully into the slender, white, long, bony, well-shaped hand of Anthony, while the keys had ceased from rattling, and the money in his pocket was at rest; but the seven shillings were hurried off to the nest at the other end of the store, and placed in a safe, where a record was made of the sale in the accounts book, among the bigger figures, so that another little egg was laid in the nest behind the door.

All the hands had gone home, bar Johnny, who had to stay behind to see Biddy off the premises, and to help her carry the stricken goods out into the harshness of the waiting world. He was cursing Anthony for haggling so long over a blasted thruppence, and keeping him here in this damned den beyond his legal time.

Biddy began to carry out the badly-scarred goods, murmuring a constant stream of thoughts meant for Johnny and the wide wide world, and she handling with cunning every article she carried, watching each of them, as a mother would watch a dim and dying child, saying, Ah, another nearly gone beyond recall, an' too well paid for, God keep the air still, for, if a breeze blows, it's fallin' in coloured dust they'll be, an' th' best part of me half-sovereign buried deep in th' pocket of that grisly-faced perjured poacher – Jasus! that one nearly parted company in me hands – liftin' up his hand for silence when God is thryin' to speak a word for th' poor an' lowly. Ah then, their clawin' hands'll have to be watched an' waved away when they come to buy with their stormy handlin' o' delicate things like these, an' their, oh, badly split, ma'am, this, an' looka th' crack here, ma'am, hardly worth liftin', sure you'd spend the day takin' it from table to shelf or from shelf to table, in desperate fear it 'ud break its back in front of your eyes; then don't take any notice of it, ma'am, for I'm not pressin' you to buy, though, if you said th' thruth, it's particular good sight you'd need to have to see th' crack your thryin' to speak of, an', with a little use, it 'ud maybe close up an' go altogether – heart o' mercy! it was nearly goin' on me altogether, that time – but leave it there, if you don't like it, an' don't be combin' them with your fingers, if you please, for you can't expect newly-minted stuff to suddenly appear for your benefit, an' it's little the people round here 'ud understand th' way to use anything above something that had seen its best days; but th' next time I'm here, Mr Anthony'll find a woman awake to what is due to her, an' can put a flush o' shame on his white sly kisser ever alert for the main chance, ever on th' make, ever head bent over on th' thrack of a lost coin, thryin' to make his Sunday-curtained gob look like a twinklin' star, an' it's oh, wouldn't I like to hammer me fist in it, an' muck it about a bit, an' dim its shinin'; but praise be to the Almighty God, it's little leisure he'll have to jingle his coins an' count his gains snibbed from an oul' innocent creature, when his shrinkin', shudderin' body goes woefully down the icy slope o' death, thin an' tottherin', naked as the day he was born on, with the cowld snow fallin' on th' oul' schemer's head, and the nippin' frost askin' him how's he feelin'.

—There isn't one of them, she said, as she carried out the last few articles, there isn't one o' them any one whit betther than th' best o' th' petty scrawls that creep along to buy them, like to like, an' all chipped an' broken an' all cracked across, fit only for th' ashpit, but consigned to go on makin' themselves useful, an' makin' a holy show o' themselves be doin' everything badly.

She gave a malicious glance at Johnny, leaning against the gate, waiting to close it when she had carried all out, and listening to all the muttering mind of the dealer in dangerous delft.

—All some people's got to do, she said, in a loud voice, is to wait for a chance to pick up another Moses out of th' bulrushes. Blessed be God, it's a grand thing to have th' nice power o' standin' still while th' world works! Ay, an' after, cock an ear, an' then move round sayin' they heard something th' wind whispered into their imagination, steady an' prim to catch any innocent sayin', waftin' round like a thistle-seed plumed, an' turn it into a burnin' bush of a lie! A nice pass things have come to, when a body has to poke her way through a swarm of idlers!

She set the last woebegone article gently down in the straw, took the ass's bridle in her left hand, and gave the sleepy animal a poke with a stick she carried in her right one.

—You can safely shut the gate on me an' me seven shillin's, now, she said to Johnny, an' tell himself he'll not be a hell of a lot the richer for them. An' you, she said sharply, turning on the donkey, giving him another poke with the stick, making him blink into a sleepy stir, yep, now, rememberin' you're carryin' God's gifts to the poor, so go quietly with your clumsy feet, for me heart's in me mouth, in case it's a heap o' chanies I'll have left when we stagger into our destination.

—Farewell, called out Johnny, waving his hand carelessly, as the donkey started, Farewell, sweet Lady o' Shalott!

—Jasus! She jerked her donkey to a sudden standstill, splashed back fiercely through the slimy-puddled lane to where Johnny was about to close the gate, made a slash at him with her stick, that, had it got home, would have broken an ear in two!

—Yeh, yeh genteel, gaunty guttersnipe! she yelled, out of a hoarse scream. I'll flatten your grinny bake, an' knock th' plume outa yer impudence, if you dare again to murmur, let alone to shout afther a decent female th' name of some evil woman of th' long ago!

—Go on, go on, about your business, said Johnny, a little frightened by the glare of fierceness in front of him, as he caught up a hammer from one of the benches to weaken the threat of the stick; go on, home, now, me woman, an' let me shut the gate.

—Oh! she shouted, you'd lift a hammer to a weak oul' wandherin' woman, you would, would you! Murdher you'd do, so you would, you collared an' tied tittherer, without a hem or haw of hesitation, regardless of the cost of reavin' the web o' life from a patient an' scarified Christian! And lifting her stick she made another skelp at Johnny's head; but he parried it with the hammer, and she barked her knuckles against the claw.

—Here, here, what's all this? said the voice of Anthony, who came scurrying down to stand between Johnny and the angry woman, now sucking her knuckle, and hissing with the pain of the wound.

—She made for me with the stick, for nothing at all, said Johnny.

—Oh, d'ye hear that! bawled Biddy. For nothin' at all, says he, an' th' place still hot with th' association of me solid decency with th' name of some unholy throllop of th' distant past!

Anthony clicked his tongue against his teeth, and a frosty look of rage fell on Johnny. Then a long bony finger on a long bony hand was stretched out to warningly tip the shoulder of the angry Biddy.

—Go home, good woman, he said; go home, and rest easy that, from this hour, my hands shall show you civility whenever you have occasion to come here on business.

—Thank you, sir, thank you, she answered with a curtsy. It's a wondher to me that th' makin's of such a fine young bowsey can find a snug niche in the business of a respectable Firm. An' I warn him, she added, turning to go, that if he ever dares to call me outa me name again, the powers that be won't save him from a sudden awakenin' in another world!

Anthony turned his frosty eye to stare at Johnny; silently, he stared at him for a full twenty seconds.

—What did you say to anger the woman? he asked. Come, come, what low-minded gibe did you fling at the woman? he added, as Johnny, holding down his head, hesitated.

—I only said something about the Lady of Shalott, said Johnny surlily.

—Well, we don't want any reference to ladies of this or that place here, he said. Business and only business is to be attended to here. You are to keep yourself in hand, Casside, while you're here; when you're among your corner-boy friends, you can act the jackeen as much as you like. Shut the gate, now, and go home.

—I should be with my corner-boy friends now, said Johnny, in a surly mutter, if you hadn't kept me here an hour afther me right time of knocking off. If I went to Merrion Hall, I'd be well in here as a respectable boy.

A cloudy sneer rippled over the tight thin lips of Anthony, and his bony fingers twisted round each other, like the snakes on the head of Medusa. From a side squint, Johnny saw his pallid face redden, and his frosty eyes glitter with a cold glare. When he had closed the gate, shot the bolts, fixed and turned the keys in the padlocks, he heard the stinging voice, mottled with shivers of anger, speaking to him.

—In Merrion Hall, Casside, there is a welcome only for decent persons, old or young. You would not be permitted to pass the door. The door is ever closed before rough-mouthed young rois-terers. In our place of worship there is no room for an associate of coarse-minded ragamuffins; and, indeed, there ought to be no room for them here either; and, let me tell you, you're near the door, unless you show some sign of realizing that it is a privilege to be employed by such a Firm as ours. Now, off you go home!

Johnny snapped the last key from the last padlock, turned on his heel, and lurched away down the stores, followed by Anthony with the dusky Hewson standing, like a sentry with a rod of steel for a spine, beside Anthony's desk-den, concentrating a cold, resentful, sneering stare at the lurching, rage-tortured Johnny, caught in the act of trying to stammer out a rebuke to his betters.

—It wasn't much of a job, thought Johnny, rapidly, as he lurched along. If he lost it, would he lose the world? Well, if this job was the world, the world was well lost. Was he going to go out from the presence of these two God-conceited bastards

without a word? Without a sign, even, that he didn't care a snap
of fingers for them? An evil spirit took possession of him. He
lurched no longer. He held up his head. He sang out in a voice
that was half a shout,

> *His broad clear brow in sunlight glow'd;*
> *On burnish'd hooves his warhorse trod;*
> *From underneath his helmet-flow'd*
> *His coal-black curls as on he rode,*
> *As he rode down to Camelot.*

Johnny felt that the two jaynusus were standing still, in
wondherment an' fury at what he was doin'. Then he sang louder
than ever,

> *From the bank and from the river*
> *He flashed into the crystal mirror,*
> *'Tirra lirra', by the river*
> *Sang Sir Lancelot.*

With a joyous gesture Johnny tossed the keys on to a bench,
opened the glass-panelled door, passed out, and banged the door
behind him. He heard it being pulled open again, swiftly; heard
Anthony's voice calling loudly after him, Casside, Casside, come
back here; heard Hewson's voice calling louder still, when Anthony's was silent, Casside, Casside, here; come here, sir!

—I'll come back at the usual time tomorrow morning, thought
Johnny, in the usual way, an' with a brave face; an' see what they'll
say; an' if they sack me, well, th' foxes have holes, an' th' birds of
th' air have nests, an' I'll ferret out a place for meself, never fear.

On went Johnny through the darkened shop, swung the wicket
in the shuttered entrance open, passed out, and let it bang back,
turning homewards whistling, a gay march home in the midst of
the glow and murmuring heat of the summer's shining sun.

And the morning and the evening were the fivid day.

ALICE, WHERE ART THOU?

JOHNNY DIDN'T feel comfortable on his way to work the following morning. He was almost sure to get his docket. Well, if he did, aself, he'd stick it out like a man, and tell them they could go to hell for Johnny. That was the only way to meet the situation.

Still he felt uncomfortable and cold, and shivered a little. He hadn't said anything to his mother. Why should he, anyhow? She wouldn't say much, if he was sacked – that was the worst of it; if she'd only burst out an' bark at him, he'd find it easier to fight; but, no; she'd just sigh, an' that was hard to counter. Seven an' six a week wasn't a fortune, but it went a fair way to keep things from fallin' over; so, when it was lost, you couldn't really blame her for sighin' – when you thought of it. Ah, anyhow, another sigh or two won't take much out of a woman who has had a thousand an' two sighs in a lifetime.

An' he had to stick up for poor Dorin forcin' a man to walk, an' his thigh ripped open. Job or no job, he couldn't stand for that. Be God, there she was, walkin' right in front of him – Alice Boyd, the Presbyterian. Yes, a pretty mot, right enough, with her mop o' curly red hair, her glittering green eyes, and her jib as jaunty as the jib o' Jenny.

He hastened till he fell shyly in beside the girl, setting his pace to keep time with the shorter and quicker steps of her little feet, while she carried her head high, for she had dropped into long skirts just a week ago, and felt all the world realized that she was a genuine woman, now.

—Why'r you goin' to work at this early hour o' the morning? he asked her.

—I have to make ready for the comin' of a special consignment of chinaware, she answered.

His tongue felt dry and his voice sounded husky as he said, I wish I was beside you all the time, givin' you a hand; but I'm a clerk, now; an' besides, I'm expectin' to get the push out of the job today.

—Oh! she ejaculated.

—Ay, indeed. I was kept over me time, yesterday, an' I gave oul' Anthony and Hewson what for, so I did. Just you watch, when he comes to open the shop, an' says anything to me; just you watch, an' see what I'll say about him an' his job.

She marched on, and was silent. He looked sideways at her, but his boasting hadn't prompted her to any admiration of him – he could see that; afraid to agree with anyone up against Hewson and Anthony; thinking of her own job. He was in the battle alone.

Passing by Nagle's pub, the porter, who was washing away from the front of the shop the filthy turmoil of the night before, suddenly slashed a bucket of water towards them, sending it streaming under their feet. Alice, with a little scream, caught up her skirt and jumped clear into the street, so as to save her dress from the slush that spread over the side walk. Johnny felt that he should have gone for the unruly porter, but his thoughts were all on the slim leg that Alice was showing in her search for any mark of the water or the slush. Still looking, and tucking her skirt towards the front in an effort to see the back of it, she showed her black-stockinged leg nearly up to the thigh, making Johnny's heart to beat and his face to flush.

—There's no actual damage done, is there? he asked, making over to her.

—I hope not, she answered. Can you see any?

He handled her skirt tenderly and lingeringly, tucking it up still higher, till a rim of white lace appeared, looking white and lovely against the black stocking that disappeared up under it. His hand moved along her stocking, feelingly, shaking a little as it felt the vibrant life running along the leg of the girl.

—You're all right, he said slowly, no damage done; only a tiny splash or two on the stocking. His hand began to sneak up under the rim of white lace, but she suddenly shoved it away and let her skirt fall down to her feet.

—That'll do, she said; I don't like that sort of thing.

They walked on, Johnny keeping as close to her as he could, occasionally giving her arm a saucy pressure with his fingers. About to cross Sackville Street, Alice stopped, looking undecided for a moment.

—You'd better walk one side o' the Pillar, she said, and me the other, to keep the shop from talking; and she stepped from the side walk to cross the street.

—Eh, wait a minute, will you? he said, catching her arm. I'll see you this evenin', comin' home.

—No you won't, for that would be as bad as them seein' us together now.

—After, then, he said huskily, pulling her towards him, and

pressing his knee against her leg; some time, somewhere, tonight?

—I don't know. Maybe I will, maybe I won't, she said.

—Tonight at Binn's Bridge at eight o'clock, certain, sure? We can saunter along the canal, and one arm was going around her, and a hand was trying to lift her skirt.

—Let me go! she cried, goin' on, and everyone looking. She jerked his arm away from her and hurried across the street.

—Don't forget, he called out after her; tonight, Binn's Bridge, eight o'clock – I'll be there!

But she went on, never heeding him. He, on his own side of the street, walked more slowly, passed the fireman guarding the fire-escape, and smoking his pipe at the door of his wooden hut; past the flower-sellers, piling up their old boxes into counters, laying out apples, oranges, and flowers of every hue in rising ranks for the coming day's sale; over into Henry Street, where troops of assistants were on their way to the several stores; and seeing the bony form of Anthony hurrying to open the shop with the speed of a man eager to marry the loveliest girl in the world, or to be at the funeral of his bitterest enemy.

Glancing over, he saw his little Alice hovering near Harrison's, the elegant pastrycooks, where Anthony took his lunch, waiting for the men to go in before her. He felt a tremor of fear when he came to the shop, just as Anthony was opening the little wicket-gate in the revolving shutter. He'd wait till Anthony was well in, before he'd go; but, when the door was open, oul' Anthony stood back and waited for all the rest to go before him, a thing he never done before. So Johnny, making the best of it, had to go up, stoop down, with the cold eyes of Anthony staring down at him, and go in, with the cold eyes watching him behind, and the soft steps following his, follow, follow, I will follow Jesus; anywhere, everywhere, I will follow on; follow, follow, I will follow Jesus, everywhere He leads me, I will follow on, but the followed J. C. this time's Johnny Casside, for when he signed his name in the time-book, the cold eyes were staring down at the moving hand that wrote; and when he was at his desk, gathering together the postal orders that had come in from the customers in his district, there were the cold eyes of Anthony watching him, like a careless cat watching a mouse.

—Get that done quick, said Anthony, for you're wanted for another job this morning.

Setting out the goods required, making them into parcels, labelling them, entering names and addresses on the delivery sheet, were all watched over by Anthony. He was joined by Hewson before the delivery was half ready, and the two of them stood, side by side, watching the work of Johnny. Not a word was said to him of what had happened the evening before; but Johnny knew that they were taking it out of him for the affront he had given them the night previous.

—Want to make me nervous, thought Johnny, and so make a muddle to give a ripe cause for a growl; but Johnny was on his mettle, going about his work methodically, softly lilting Me Lodgins on the Cold, Cold Ground, doing all the parcelling and clerical work with deliberate ease and precision, while the boyos over the other deliveries in the store watched furtively, and wantonly wondhered; glad that a comrade was going through a tough time; all of them putting on an airy look of righteousness, as if to sing slow and soft, behold I am not as Casside is, but truly, ruly, schooly, pewly, fooly, dooly, humble servants, doggedly faithful in all things appertaining to their *simper feedielus*, and they praying all the while that Anthony or Hewson would blaze forth into a hunting reprimand at something that Johnny had done before, or that he was doing now; but, to their discomfort, everything was done fair and well, and Johnny stood beside the delivery, all packed, and waiting for the van to come.

—Now, said Anthony, out you go, and help carry up the new chinaware that the storeman is already unpacking.

So that was the game! Johnny was to be made go back to the menial work of long ago. He was to do what no clerk was, or ever had been, asked to do. He hesitated, whether to go, or fight it out. He saw the smiles on the kissers of the other clerks. They were enjoying the show, slow, slimy, slavish, sluddery buggers, the whole o' them!

—What about seeing the delivery safe off on its journey? questioned Johnny.

—Just do what you're told, said Anthony, with the withered pink line of his mouth thinner than ever.

—Without a murmur, added Hewson, with the vivid red pulpy mouth of him showing over his black beard, like a danger signal.

Johnny slouched out to the lane, ripe with rage, through the line of messengers and packers, all pretending to be busy, but all watching Johnny, first, then eyeing Anthony, following after him, with a smile on his face, a face like a skull with the eyes there still, and a thin film of sallow flesh tightly stretched over the bony frame, a death's head, with the tongue still wagging in it, looking over a high white collar, giving a graceless glance, now and again, at the gold watch-chain dangling in the hollow where a belly ought to be, with Johnny wishing that he was twisting a rope tight round the narrow bony neck.

When they reached the gate, Anthony suddenly turned south, hurrying through a narrow passage of empty oilcans and tapped oil barrels, and shot into a water-closet, waiting for customers behind the cans and oil casks.

—A sudden thought musta sthruck him, that time, thought Johnny. Well, he has to sit down when the call comes, like the rest of us; though how a man of his means can use that horrible horse-trough of a closet, spattered and puddled with filth, I don't know; and Johnny shuddered as his mind's eye saw the terrible human midden, set to serve the whole of the outer stores staff. Prince and peasant, saint and sinner, slaundered lady and slut, each in his own way, and in his own good time, comes to that tremendous exercise. Clay, like th' rest of us, th' oul' sod. Formed out of clay. An' God made man outa th' dust of the earth. The natty suit, the collars an' cuffs, the gold watch an' chain – all dust. Himself is clay in a suit o' clay, hard clay, clay all!

—Eh, Jack, said Cary, the senior messenger, a lad of seventeen, with fiery red hair and a handsome foxy face, what's up? What's he got on yer taw?

—I gave the two o' them a lot o' lip yestherday for keepin' me over me time, said Johnny arrogantly, an' I'll give him a little more if he keeps flutterin' at me heels much longer!

—Me sweet yourself, said Cary encouragingly. Don't let your bone go with the dog. Stick up for yer rights. Th' boyo sourly needs a tellin' off from someone!

He hurried back to his oilcans, for fear Anthony would come out on top of his talking, and Johnny went on down the lane, turning into the stores, filled with crated and boxed goods that came by land, rail, and sea.

—Here y'are, said the head storekeeper jovially, pointing to a heavy box filled with chinaware, put that on your hump, and carry it to th' top room o' th' china warehouse, an', if you fall, don't wait to get up again, for the governor's not in a good mood today, and wants things done in a hurry!

Johnny gave a long look of malice at the face before him, brown-bearded, a narrow nose, with a top on it like a strawberry-coloured acorn; the face of a man who has been a sailor, with a waddle in his walk, and a habit of knuckling his forehead whenever he talked to the honourable Anthony.

Along came Anthony through the great gate to bend over the crate filled with chinaware, moving his white bony hand through the straw, as if he were looking for stray Spanish doubloons.

—How long will it take to empty this crate? he asked of the storeman.

—Not more'n a couple o' hours, sir; or less, the storeman added, with a meaning grin, with a boy waitin' to work with a will, as a young boy should.

Anthony took no notice of the remark or the grin, but stood there till Johnny had shouldered the box and moved off, following him then, and halting only when he reached his desk near the entrance to the front shop, leaving Johnny to sweat along and up the thousand and one stairs to the chinaware top store. Till dinner time Johnny went on carrying his white man's burdens, Anthony's head darting forth, like the head of a bony snake, to watch him every time he passed till the half-hour after twelve sent him out for an hour's rest on a great heap of goods, covered with a tarpaulin, opposite the Custom House, there to munch his two cuts of dry bread and watch the steamship *Argo* unloading her cargo, wishing he was big enough to do that kind of work; lying back on the tarpaulin, sensing its happy red-hot heat from the rays of the sun, so different from where he worked, where there was no sun, and where the dim lights burned the livelong day; watching the ship, and wishing that he could go away with her, a great seaman, in a tall ship ribbed with brass, kissing the girls goodbye, an' ahoy for the seven seas!

But a clock in a pub opposite told him it was time to go back to his job as a landlubber, and crushing into a ball the paper that had carried his lunch, he flung it over the side of the quay to sail away with the ships, away, away, to th' Bay of Biscay O!

Back to the store, bending over the time-book, with Nearus leaning pensively over his desk, watching him, his gentle face pretty pale now, his cheeks hollow, the red spots on the bones of them burning brighter than ever, and a catching cough, every now and again, making him put his wasting hands apologetically over his pallid lips.

—You're in th' boss's black books, eh? he said, after a cough that seemed to shake him up a little.

—Black or white, said Johnny defiantly, it's all th' same to me. Nearus bent over, after sending a swift glance to right and

left, to make sure the coast was clear, and brought his wasting
face close to Johnny's.

—Get outa this job, he murmured, before you're a day older.
You'll never fit in here. They have their knife in you, so clear out
while you're nimble enough to go further an' fare worse. I leave
at the end of the week for Australia to get better air, so that this
little cough of mine may go. Th' Jesus here's a money-changer in
th' Temple. They'll dredge th' life outa you, if you stay long
enough to let them do it.

He sidled safely back to the document on his desk as Dyke
came striding up to sign himself in, pushing Johnny silently
away from the book before he had firmly set down the last letters
of his name.

—Mr Anthony left word that you were to go to the top of the
shop an' help th' girl there to clear a way for the new chinaware –
th' only kind o' work you're fit for, y'ignorant louse!

—Not quite so ignorant as you think, said Johnny quietly;
not even as ignorant as you may be yourself, he added, more
quietly still.

—Scholar, be God, eh! sneered Dyke.

Johnny guessed that Dyke knew little – no more, surely, than
any of his own brothers. He had often heard them talking, and
their talk was always of the things they wore, the things they ate,
the things they owned, a piano here, a tea-set there, the things they
happened to see in the street, or a ride on a jaunting-car to the
sea for an hour's holiday. Just enough to keep going, and to
earn a pound a week. Dyke, he knew, lived with a childless wife
in two rooms, in a three-storey house, in a turning off Dorset
Street, with a flower-box on the window-sill for a demesne. Every
Sunday he marched to church with a jerry hat on his head, a
walking-stick in a gloved hand, and a waxed moustache, keeping
his head in the air, while his lordly wife walked by his side, dressed
in solemn brown, her skirt, helped by a big bustle on her backside,
waving scorn to her neighbours. This sort of people gave up
learning, with a clapping of hands, as soon as they left school.
He was learning because he loved to learn. A burden to them;
a joy to him. They were called; but he had been chosen.

—Scholar or no, said Johnny defiantly, I'll bet you I know
more'n you do! Come, are you game?

—Are you goin' to take the bet, Mr Nearus? laughed Dyke.

—Never mind Mr Nearus, said Johnny; leave him out of it;
I'm challengin' you.

—Go 'way, go 'way, said Dyke – I've forgotten more'n you'll ever learn.

Out of the corner of his eye Johnny saw Alice setting some goods in a bin to be added to an order. He saw that she was listening with all her ears. Here was a chance to show what he was made of. It wouldn't do to let Dyke down him before the girl he fancied. She wouldn't think much of him if he did. O heavy lightness! O serious vanity! Here goes! He turned with a flushed face to Dyke.

—Before knowledge was, where was it thought the sun went to when he set, and how was its diurnal rising explained to the ignorant people who lived on the earth then?

—Tell us, you, for God's sake, said Dyke.

—You don't know, said Johnny. I thought as much. Who was Leonidas, and what country was he king of, and what memorable battle did he fight? Who was Semiramis? Alcibiades? What are copal and indigo, and where do they come from? Jesus, we are told, was a carpenter's son; what was Muhammed? Who was th' headspring of th' Reformation, and on what door of what castle did he pin his ninety-five propositions against th' sale of Indulgences? Go on; answer!

—Oh, let's hear a few more first, said Dyke sarcastically.

—Well, then, said Johnny, warming up, yous have heard o' Shakespeare, I suppose?

—No, then, I haven't, answered Dyke mockingly, but maybe Mr Nearus has. D'ye know anything about th' gentleman, Mr Nearus?

—Oh, we've often heard of that, I think, said Nearus.

—Ay, you've heard of him; but how many of you know anything about him? Settin' aside the Chronicle Plays, name ten of the others. No answer? Yous couldn't. What's th' name o' th' play containin' the quarrel between th' two celebrated families, an' what was the city where they lived called? No answer? Verona, Verona, th' city; Montague an' Capulet, th' families. How does th' play start? Yous don't know even that much! A fight, a grand fight between the servants of the two houses; a fight that sped to th' people of th' city, givin' gashed breasts to some and bloodied heads to others!

—Yeh, get off with you! said Dyke viciously, lifting an arm to push Johnny away with a blow in the chest; but he saw sparks in Johnny's eyes, and his hand fell to his side.

—That's bebber, said Johnny. I let no man bite his thumb at me, sir. I'll carry coals for no one!

Dyke stared at him, and bent his brows, mystified. Johnny felt elated, for he knew that he had astonished Dyke, and that Dyke was bound to scorn his show of knowledge, because of the little he knew himself.

—G'way, little boy, said Dyke, for it's weak your mind's gettin'. Won't carry coals! Do I bite me thumb! Mad, be God!

—You do but show your ignorance, Dyke. I'm not one of your poor dismantled messengers. Fiery Tybalt's ne'er a match for Casside, when Casside's sword's prepared, and Casside stands to face him!

From the corner of an eye, Johnny saw that Alice was going.

—Good God! ejaculated Dyke, staring at Nearus, d'ye hear that? Gone cracked. Right enough – he's mad! And who's Tybalt? he asked Johnny, winking at Nearus.

—Ask me arse! said Johnny shortly.

—Nice kind o' language from a young boy, isn't it? Show's how you were reared. Tinker's talk from a clerk in Himdym & Leadem. Where'd you learn your language from – your mother?

—Leave me mother alone! cried Johnny furiously; leave her out of it, or it'll be th' worse for you!

—There, there, give it up, Casside, said Nearus. How's a man to do his work with this steady sthream of arguin' goin' on under his very nose. Go on to your work, an' don't flame up th' minute you're spoken to.

—That's all very well, Mr Nearus, but I was only tellin' Dyke of what Shakespeare said, an' showin' him a fella with but seven an' sixpence a week may know more than one with a pound.

—Catch! cried Dyke, flinging a parcel, so suddenly, to a messenger, that he failed to catch it, making Dyke hurry over to pick it up and hand it to the messenger in the midst of a volley of abuse, followed by a sharp kick in the backside for his carelessness as he turned away flushed and ashamed, to put the parcel into his barrow. Shakespeare! Dyke went on, with a dry contemptuous laugh, he'll do a lot for you; he'll bring you a rise at th' end o' th' year. Our duty here to our employers is the main thing we should all think about; so take pride in your work, an' leave Shakespeare alone.

Dyke was now bending earnestly over some parcels on the delivery bench, and Nearus was staring at documents on his desk, as if he were gazing, for the first time, at the face of a beautiful girl; for though they had, Johnny hadn't seen Anthony come softly in, and stand near, watching Johnny with a look of querulous complaint on his bony face.

For the moment Johnny existed only for himself, and in himself. They were foolishness; he was wisdom. He had the whip hand over them, for he knew more than they did; he knew that, now. His mind was a light that lighteth every man that cometh into his world. He was well over their heads, mounted on the white horse, the winged horse, called, called – what was it now? The one ridden by Theseus, or was it Perseus? He'd have to look that up again. But he was on the animal, anyhow, and the name didn't matter. Proud as he was of what he knew, nobody could deny that he was willing, eager to share with others. Not Dyke, though. Pearls before a swine; waste, sinful waste. Nearus was different. Ignorant he was, but kind; ay, and manly. Tangled up in a cough, right enough; but a man for all that.

—Shakespeare's not for him, he said to Nearus, indicating Dyke; but for you, Mr Nearus. Shakespeare's there – standing at your elbow. You'll find him worthy of you, I'm telling you.

—Be off, be off, said Nearus, without taking his eyes off the documents he was studying; too busy, too busy now.

—Some fools think he's dull, went on Johnny, heedless of the gentle warning given by Nearus that he should break off the talk, but I'm tellin' you he's not dull; he's all life 'n loveliness; ay, an' even brisk with battle, murder, an' sudden death! There's th' gentleness of the calm lake, if you want it; and there's th' crash o' th' tumblin' waves of a stormy sea if you—

—Look at the clock!

The hard cold voice of oul' Anthony, sounding right over his shoulder! A cold wind blasting the heat of his earnestness.

—Look at the clock, Casside, look at the clock!

Johnny stood where he was, silent. He was trying to think of what he would say, or of what he would do. At last he turned, with an untidy grin on his face, to look at Anthony.

—I was just havin' a little argument with Mr Dyke and Mr Nearus, he murmured.

—What does the clock say, Casside?

—A little argument about th' great Shakespeare, added Johnny.

—What does the clock say? insisted Anthony, the thin mouth disappearing into the contracted jaws of the bony skull.

—It says, said Johnny sulkily, that it is some time past the hour for resumption of work.

—And why are you standing gossiping here, idling your

employer's time? Eh? You don't answer. You weren't so dumb a moment ago, were you? Were you?

—No, said Johnny, with a flash of anger in his voice, not quite so dumb.

—Far from dumb, in fact, sneeringly. Well, neither Mr Nearus nor Mr Dyke, I imagine, wish to carry on an argument with an impudent jackeen – at least, I hope not.

—Hardly likely, murmured Dyke with a tender glance at Anthony, who quietly smiled his approval; but Nearus held his peace.

—And Shakespeare, by all accounts, was an idle fellow, went on Anthony, full of vagabond songs, scarcely a good companion for anyone with a respectable outlook on life.

—A scurvy companion, in fact, said Johnny maliciously.

Dyke touched his forehead with a finger and looked significantly at Anthony.

—Be off to your work, said Anthony to Johnny, and let there be no more foolish talk or idleness, or we'll have just to get someone else more suitable to our needs.

—Out o' th' way! said Dyke, an' let them work who want to work, extending a fist towards Johnny's chest to push him away; but Johnny stepped quickly forward and brought a heavily-booted foot down on his toes, making Dyke give vent to a sharp squeal of pain, hearing it with joy as he turned and walked away to the work awaiting him.

Rage was quivering in him. He'd love to have Dyke an' Anthony be th' throat, squeezing even the terror of life outa them!

A thought came to him, like a full-blown rose: he'd read that somewhere, an' he'd thought it lovely. Where? He forgot. He'd go through the chinaware department, an' maybe see Alice in passin'. He'd fix his eyes on hers with a look that would say betther'n th' best words, ah, aha, me pretty little lady, you heard me talkin' Shakespeare to Dyke, an' know now I'm a fellow worthy of puttin' a hand on your delightful drawers, ay, an' undher them, too; ho-ho, I know me love be her way o' waw-aw-kin, I know me love be her way o' taw-aw-kin, an' when he'd get her out walkin' with him, he'd show her revelations.

Sure as anything, here was Suresaint hurrying down the stairs as if God was afther him! With a polished jerry hat on his head, an' his pallid face lookin' like th' face of a lively corpse. And his gleamin' walking-stick undher his arm. And a white-gloved hand half hidin' his horrible face. Here's his platter-faced sisther,

Biddy, the girls' manageress, her big-arsed, lumpy body lumberin'
up the stairs, never puttin' the slightest pass on him, or him on her,
her face aflame, her eyes starin' right out in front of her as if she
had seen a vision of hell open for sinners. There's th' crook of his
walking-stick caught in the rails of the stairs, jerkin' it out from
under his arm, an' he never stoppin' to pick it up, but rushin'
down th' rest of th' stairs, an' shootin' outa th' shop like one
possessed. And all the while, Hewson, at th' top o' th' stairs,
with icy fire in his eyes, glarin' at th' figure tearin' outa sound an'
sight o' th' shop an' all that therein was.

Suresaint had been caught! Oh, that was it! Th' ripe an' ruly
villain had been caught. His hand had been where his hand
shouldn't ha' been. Up th' leg of her drawers! Miss Vaughan's
most likely. Must be it, else why should his ugly oul' sisther be in
tears, an' he runnin' for his life outa the shop? Th' whole trans-
action was written on the gob of Hewson. What I have written,
I have written. Must a' watched him. Caught him rude-handed!

He passed by Hewson, now reinforced be Anthony, both of
them staring at where Hewson last saw Suresaint; hurried to be
right behind Biddy, noticin' all th' girls nudgin' each other, an'
glancin' joyfully at th' shame of the big-bodied oul' bitch; safe
in th' thought that it was her, an' not them, who were in th' way
o' lamentation.

He climbed up to the very top of the house, stopped before a
door, opened it, and went in to a big attic kind of a room.

Such a sight you never saw, such a sight as he saw, when he
opened the door and went in:

There she was:

Sweet and glowing, fair and sweet; flushed and fair, flushed and
    comely,
like a healthy hawthorn in a smoky street.

There she was, with her little hands moving about in a grimy
bin; sorting out the dusty china, there she was.

> *Rise up, my fair one, and come away, my love,*
> *The time of singing of birds is come;*
> *The praties are dug, an' th' frost is all over!*

There she was, with one little foot on the second highest step of
a ladder, and the other resting on the edge of a bin, her skirt so

crinkled by the stretched-out limb that an ankle and calf of one
fine leg was there for all to see, shining high over the hem of her
white petticoat:

> *There she was, like a lily squandered in a murky pool;*
> *Alice!*

She turned her head, and her eyes lit up when she saw Johnny.
He stood there gaping.

—I was sent up, he said shyly, to give you a hand.

—Well, she said with a pout, you'll have to come a little nearer,
won't you, if you're to be of any use?

He went swiftly over to where she was, and stood there beside
her with a beating heart.

—You heard what happened to Suresaint? she asked.

—I saw him driven forth, an' I guessed the reason.

—Mr Hewson caught him interferin' with Miss Vaughan an'
Miss Grice, she said. They let out on him in a note th' day before
to Mr Hewson; couldn't stand it any longer. His sisther's gone
with him too, thank God!

—Horrible thing for him to do, commented Johnny, No one
with a decent mind 'ud thry to do that sort of thing on a poor
girl.

—Well, he done it, she said. It's not a nice thing to think of,
much less to talk about.

There was silence between them for some time, while she handed
down to him the china that remained in the bin.

—It was grand, she said, th' way you spoke up to that fellow
Dyke, an' to that oul' Anthony!

—Didya hear me? he asked, swelling with pride. It's only th'
beginnin', for Johnny Casside's not to be walked on – not even
be th' lordly queen herself.

—I have to sthretch farther in, now, she remarked, so don't
forget to keep a steady hold o' th' ladder.

He drew closer in to the ladder, his eyes sparkling, his heart
beating, and his hand timidly edging as near as it could get to the
pretty, lace-fringed leg of the girl. She went on arranging the
chinaware in the bin, but, stretching over a little more, the ladder
wobbled a bit, and she let a quiet little squeal out of her.

—Steady, steady, Alice, dear!

—You're not holdin' it right, she said complainingly.

—Let me up there – I'm used to laddhers.

—You wouldn't know how to sort th' china, she answered, giving a graceful toss to her head that shook her wavy hair back from her forehead. No good, just holdin' th' ladder, however tight; hold me, instead, an' I'll feel safer. Oh, that's not any betther either, she said peevishly, when Johnny's right arm had firmly encircled her skirt; you're only making it now so's I can't move at all!

—Well, how'm I goin' to hold you so's you can move about th' way you want to?

—If you can't think of a betther way of holdin' than th' way you're holdin', then don't hold me at all!

He took his arm from around her skirt and again got a grip of the ladder, a tighter one this time.

—What d'ye think, Alice, he said, after a long pause, neither oul' Anthony nor Dyke knew nor wanted to know a single thing about th' plays of Shakespeare. Funny, isn't it?

—I see nothing funny in it, she responded snappily; for Alice Norris doesn't want to know anything about them either!

Johnny was puzzled. It was hard to know what to say to a girl. You never knew when you had them. No use of venturing to put a hand on her knee while she was in this cross mood. He'd chance a remark, anyhow.

—Nice stockings you're wearin', Alice; how far do they go up on your leg?

She glanced down at him with a mischievous light in her eyes, and gave her head a saucy toss.

—That's hardly part of your business, she said.

—I'm goin' to have a look, he threatened.

—You'll make me wriggle if you do, an' knock me off. I'm powerless up here. Help me to keep steady, or we'll never get finished. She smoothed her skirt with rapid, clever strokes of her hand, and pulled it a little higher on her leg. Just rest your hand on my ankle, an' then I'll feel safe.

He placed a hand on her neat little ankle, and slyly slid it up as high as her knee. Then something fierce and lovely shot through Johnny's blood. The rustiness of life fled from him, and a world of blossom circled him round about. The stir of Spring, the flush of Summer, the fruitful burden of Autumn, and the rushing of water in the Winter-time moved, flowed, and jostled together in his being; and God's love and care were here, full measure pressed down, and overflowing were here in the form of a pretty face and a quivering slim leg.

—Your skirt's a lot in th' way, he said, as he tucked it tighter behind her, up, up to the lacy halo of her drawers, halfway up her thigh.

—Fancy now, said Alice, beaming down at him, Anthony an' Dyke knowin' nothin' about Shakespeare! Hardly believable, is it? You'd imagine they'd be ashamed to show their ignorance, wouldn't you?

—Pretended to be proud of it, so they did, said Johnny; but I could easily see a shadow of shame in their eyes. Whoa, careful! he added as Alice seemed to give a little slip, and his hand slid over her garter, over the rim of her long black stocking, to hold and fondle her firm white thigh.

—Nearly down that time, she said laughingly, an' would have been if you hadn't been there to hold me. She took her foot off the rim of the bin, brought her leg back to the ladder beside the other one, and Johnny felt his hand being tightly pressed between her two thighs.

The ladder shook, and she half climbed, half slid down into his arms; he pressed her to him till she was panting for breath, he frantically searching to cover her mouth with his own, while she pantingly twisted her bonny head this way and that to avoid the contact.

—You mustn't, you mustn't, she cried; 'tisn't fair on me!

Suddenly the little head stopped twisting, the red mouth brushed his and rested there, her arms went round his neck, her luminous eyes closed happily, and her slim body answered back every venomous pressure given by Johnny.

He was clawing at her skirt when her eyes opened again, with a start; she tore his hands away, panting and pressing herself out of his grasp, till she stood, breathless and flushed, beside the little dusty window looking down to the distant street. Whimperingly she stood there, trying to smooth down her frightened dress and hanging stocking, patting back into order her rowdy locks of wavy hair, pressing her lips to keep them from quivering, and keeping her eyes well away from Johnny's hungry looks.

—You're a bad boy, she murmured cryingly, a bad boy to take me unawares, like that! To tumble me about as if I wasn't a good girl, such a sudden pounce that I couldn't even get breath to tell you to stop, fixin' on me before I knew where I was, seizin' on me like a savage, windin' me into a fear of a wicked thing impendin', ravellin' every stitch on me into an untidy tangle, plain to anyone careful enough to give a hasty glance at me! There, now, she went on, glancing out of the little window, there's Arnott's gettin' ready to put their shutters up, an' closin' time'll be here on top of us before I'll get anything like a quiet look into th' disturbance that's pictured all over me.

She made for the door with quick steps, keeping her face turned away from Johnny. He grabbed her by the arm as she passed, holding her at arm's length while she struggled to make him let her go.

—Oh, let me go! she said vehemently, let me go, you! I must tidy meself before I'm put to shame be wonderin' glances at the troubled look of my appearance.

—Give's a kiss before you go, Alice!

—Maybe it's a kiss you want, afther th' way you've surprised me with your disregard for a good girl's feelin's. Let me go, she added, whipping her arm from his loosening grip, and never again thry to hurt a young girl when she's helpless.

She turned round when she got to the door, hesitated, and looked a little tearfully at Johnny.

—If you thought a lot of a kiss, you'd take it, and be done with it; an', if you're genuine and want to, you can meet me tonight where you said, an' when we come to some grassy nook, you can tell me more about your Shakespeare; but you mustn't try to pull me asunder when you feel you'd like a little kiss. There, she said, coming back into the room, and looking brightly into his darkened face, I know you didn't mean to be so rough, an' we'll make it all up in th' quietness of th' night when we reach th' lanes o' Whitehall.

When she lifted her sweet face for a kiss, he hesitated, then he bent down and pressed his mouth to hers. She turned away and went swiftly from the room. He waited for some time, then went down the stairs into the shop, now darkened by the shuttered windows, where he saw Hewson and Anthony with their gobs together, and the assistants waiting for the signal to go. When he reached his desk, he took off his old coat and put on his good one, went with the rest out of the shop, and hurried home, thinking of the hour when he'd be close beside his Alice, fondling her, and pressing sturdy kisses on her mouth.

He lilted softly to himself as he went along, never minding a soul:

> *The birds sleeping gently,*
> *Sweet Lyra gleaming bright;*

> *Her rays tinge the forest,*
> *And all seems glad tonight.*
> *The wind sighing by me,*
> *Cooling my fevered brow,*
> *The stream flows as ever,*
> *Yet, Alice, where art thou?*

And the morning and evening were the sixth day.

TO HIM THAT HATH SHALL BE GIVEN

OUL' ANTHONY had got married; had been away for a week
on a honeymoon; had come back with a comical smile cold on
his kisser. He had left father and mother in Booterstown to cleave
to his wife in Harold's Cross, as the Scripture hath commandeth.
While he had been away, the staff had decided to make him a
presentation. Johnny, hard-heartedly, had given a shilling – a
tanner out of what he gave to his mother, and a tanner from
what he kept for himself. Four suitable assistants had spent
suitable nights going about from suitable shop to suitable shop,
seeking a suitable present. At last they got one, and showed it
secretly, by night, to the murmuring staff. It was a clock of black
marble, speckled with grey, shaped like a temple, with two slender
columns, one on each side. Over the top were gilt rays, spreading
out, like the rays of the sun, and out of these rays sprang the
delicate form of an angel, who was pointing to the face of the
clock with one hand and up to the sky with the other. Around the
upper semicircle of the dial were the holy words, *Tempus Fugit*.

They had set off on a jaunting-car, Dyke, Hyland, a Salvation
Army sergeant-major, and head of the cutlery department, Woods,
head of the chandlery – three of the oldest members of the staff –
with Johnny, the youngest, to present the precious gift to Mr
Anthony. Johnny had jibbed at going, for it meant another nine-
pence, a fourth part of the car fare, missing from his treasure-
store; but they had insisted that the most significant and the
least significant of the staff should be there as a testimony of their
loyalty and affection.

Up they drove to Anthony's place, and Johnny was in such a
fluster at being about to enter his employer's house that he had

but time and sense to catch a glimpse of a big house, surrounded by a hedge, with dark solemn cypresses looming out of the dusk, with a smell of lilac everywhere around him, before he found himself in a big, big room that he thought was the parlour, had not Dyke whispered that it was called the drawing-room. For the first time in his life, Johnny found his feet resting uneasily on a carpet. Real Persian, whispered Dyke. For the first time, Johnny found himself lost in a thicket of wonderful things, a huge glistening mahogany thing of doors and drawers, with plates and pitchers of gleaming glass on the top of it. A mighty mahogany sofa here, and stout mahogany chairs there and everywhere. In the centre, oh, a great mahogany table, with a top on it glossy enough for an angel to have a decko at himself and trim his wings by the gleaming of it; a narrow strip of white silk, edged with lace, and embroidered with flowers, ran down it from one end to the other; and in the centre of this, a great epergne of many branches, coloured a light green outside, and a deep pink within, stood, as proud as any seven-branched candlestick on the altar of the Church at Thyatira. Whatnots, sparkling with vases and silver-framed photos, were in every corner. Lovely wallpaper, splashed with deep yellow roses, showed off many pictures on the walls, while a shining piano leaned away by itself in a corner, with the name of Cramer on it in big gold lettering. There was a big fireplace, fenced by a big brass fender, full of big brass weapons, as heavy as those in the hand of Goliath. There were heavy blue curtains on the windows, with lacy ones nearer the glass, foaming with heavy tassels and fringe. A golden chiffonier, with many brackets, having on them knick-knacks of all shapes and sizes, hung over the mantelpiece, and on each side of it were lovely coloured photographs of the married couple, Anthony, to the right, pensive, leaning on a fluted pillar, with a book in his hand; and his missus sitting in a curved stone seat on a terrace, with a big harp beside her.

—A house of glory, thought Johnny, full of good things, lovely to look on and very fair to handle. No books about, thank God, for were they here, the desire to have them would make the envy in me bitther to bear.

He stood stiff and as calm as he could keep, well behind the other three, standing stiff, too, and close together, afraid to stir, facing the door, Dyke holding the clock in both hands before his belly.

The door opened and the two came into the room. Mrs Anthony was dressed in light brown, with darker trimmings, and had ruches of stiffly-starched lace around her neck and wrists. Johnny saw that she was a little less plain than a pikestaff, but not much. The pair of them sat down in heavy chairs, right in front of the group carrying the clock, waiting for someone to say something.

—We've come, sir, and Mrs Dovergull, said Dyke, with a little stammer, his face reddening, after he had been nudged by Woods who was nervously twisting a tiny well-waxed moustache, we've come, c-come to, in o-order to, or rather i-in appreciation of, for the purpose of, we thought it w-would be well to take, er this—

—Opportunity, whispered Johnny, behind him.

—Opportunity, went on Dyke, to show h-how we all felt towards the head of the Firm and his l-lady, an' how proud we all were to be let w-work undher such a fine gentleman.

—Hear, hear, murmured the Salvation Army sergeant-major.

—To you an' your lady, sir, said Woods, suddenly and rapidly, after having been nudged by Dyke, we beg to present this gift of a clock to mark the auspicious occasion of your sacred marriage, an' as a token of the affectionate connexion existing between you, sir, an' all the members of your staff.

—Hear, hear, and amen, murmured the sergeant-major.

Anthony got to his feet, smiling, and Dyke, lifting the clock from his belly, gave the clock into the hands of Anthony, who then carefully placed it in the lap of his wife.

—Oh, dear, said Mrs Dovergull, isn't it a lovely present!

Anthony, looking bonier than ever, passed a hand lightly over his tight lips, looked down at the clock, and turned towards the little group drawn closer than ever together, with Johnny half-hidden behind them.

—Gentlemen, he said, I and Mrs Dovergull thank you all for the lovely and valuable gift you have presented to us. We gladly accept it, gladly, Mrs Dovergull and I; and we thank you all!

He stopped, patted the clock gently, and nearly cracked his face trying to smile. Mrs Dovergull went over to the big mahogany piece, poured out three glasses of dark-red wine, and handed them to the three seniors, taking no notice of Johnny. He watched the three gobs as they drank the wine that had been given to them: Dyke's carelessly, as if wine to him was but mellowed water; Woods', with his eyes half closed in ecstasy, as if his tongue had tasted the wine from God's vineyard, but this was better; and

Hyland's, reverently and cautiously, as if the curious taste surprised him a little, but he didn't like to say so.

—*Tempus Fugit*, murmured Dyke solemnly, noticing that Anthony was looking at the gilded words *Tempus Fugit* – a reminder to us all!

—Time, like an ever-rolling stream, bears all her sons away, murmured the sergeant-major.

—Though Time can seem damned long, occasionally, said Johnny, feeling that he couldn't stand there all the time without saying something. A deep silence fell on the room, and Johnny felt that it would have been better to have kept his mouth shut.

—Tony, dear, said Mrs Dovergull graciously, I think these three gentlemen wish to go now.

Johnny saw Anthony pull a tasselled cord hanging near the fireplace, and heard a bell tinkle in another room. Soon a maid appeared, and stood at the door, while the deputation stirred itself, moving in the maid's direction, guided by a cold grin on Anthony's face and a tight smile on the face of his wife.

—Goodnight Dyke, goodnight Woods, goodnight Hyland; we shall all meet again tomorrow morning, God willing.

Mrs Dovergull's Goodnight, gentlemen, was almost smothered in the chorus of Goodnight, sir, from the three gentlemen, making for the door, which soon closed upon all the glory left behind as they passed out into the silent night, under the star-crowded sky, the majestic timepiece of the universe.

That was the Plough there, towards the north, and to the east, he thought, the Gemini, Castor and Pollux, children of Leda, the mother of Helen, who was the cause of all the uproar in Troy; and there was the Polar Star, the fixed star, the star that shone for Caesar, for he was constant as the Northern Star: poor Caesar, dead and turned to clay, stopping a hole to keep the wind away. Well, it'll be a small hole Anthony'll stop. A little Caesar, faintly present when he stands beneath a star.

They strolled down the residential turning, the three of them together, with Johnny walking close behind, on to the corner where they would get the tram going towards the city.

—He was delighted with the clock, said Dyke.

—Mrs Dovergull's eyes were beaming, said Hyland.

—It'll add a lot to the room, said Woods.

—It would have been all right, if it wasn't for Casside, said Dyke; he shouldn't have been with us. I was against it, from the first. Nice thing to have a jackeen spoiling everything.

—Made a show of us, said Woods; Anthony saw it, an'
Mrs Dovergull, too.

Down at the end of the road, the three of them halted to wait
for a tram, Johnny standing a little away from them. He suddenly
remembered that he'd forgotten he had to get back, and that the
car fare took him only to Anthony's house, so that if they didn't
ask him to join them, or lend him tuppence, he'd have to trudge
the whole way home. He edged nearer to them, trying to get
enough courage to ask them for a loan. A minute or so passed,
and then he heard the jingle of a tram coming along the main road.

—Here she comes! said Hyland.

—One o' yous give us a loan of tuppence to take th' thram back
as far as th' Pillar? he asked shyly.

The tram stopped; the three of them climbed in without saying
a word; the tram tinkled on again, and left Johnny standing alone,
beneath the stars.

Dead tired, he'd been, after that long walk home. Not knowing
the way properly, either, he'd wandered a bit before he'd found
the right way to his own hall door. Well, if this wasn't pay day,
he'd feel too full of the world. He could do with a rest, by God,
he could! Still, today he'd buy the book, rest or no rest; rise or
no rise! He had extracts of it from a book on Elocution, left
behind by his father; and, since the bits of it were so good, what
must the whole of it be like? Splendid as the unspoken word o'
God was splendid! How was this some of it went? Ay, the bit
afther Abdiel had given Satan a bloody coxcomb:

> Now storming furie rose,
> And clamour such as heard in heav'n till now
> Was never. Arms on armour clashing bray'd
> Horrible discord, and the madding wheeles
> Of brazen chariots rag'd; dire was the noise
> Of conflict; overhead the dismal hiss
> Of fiery darts in flaming volleys flew,
> And flying vaulted either host with fire.
> So under fierie cope together rush'd
> Both battels maine, with ruinous assault
> And inextinguishable rage; all heav'n
> Resounded, and hath earth bin then, all earth
> Had to her centre shook.

He had put by thruppence a week till he had one and six towards it, an' today, even if he didn't get the expected rise, he'd

spare the other shillin', come weal or woe, and buy it! And when the day of rest came, he'd spend the whole of it with Johnny Milton.

Anyway, if things happened as they had happened so far, he was sure of a rise of a shilling today. So, then, he'd get the book without the actual loss of a make. For weeks he'd watched the lovely book in its blue and gilt binding in the little bookcase at the back of the open-air bookstall at Hanna's shop; for ever fearing that by the time he got the money, the book would be gone. Every evening, going home from work, he'd gone out of his way to make sure the book was still there. It was there yesterday, and it was bound to be there today. He hadn't done badly so far – he had three of Dickens' and four of Scott's; two of Balzac's and one of Hugo's; Ruskin's *Seven Lamps of Architecture*, *Sesame and Lilies*, *Ethics of the Dust*, *The Crown of Wild Olive*, and *Unto This Last*; Darwin's *Origin of Species* and *Descent of Man*, to be read when he knew more about things in general; two by Fenimore Cooper and three by Dumas; Tacitus' *Germania* and the *Life of Agricola* with Plutarch's *Lives* to keep them company; Reade's *Cloister and the Hearth*; Carlyle's *French Revolution* and Mignet's, too; Bunyan's *Pilgrim's Progress* and Sheridan's *Plays*; Taylor's translation of the *Aeneid* and a *Classical Geography*; Ball's *Story of the Heavens*; and, in poetry, the works of Byron, Shelley, Keats, Goldsmith, Crabbe, Tennyson, Eliza Cook – a terrible waste of sixpence – Gray, and the Golden Treasury, with the glorious Globe Edition of Shakespeare falling to bits; all backed up with Chambers's Dictionary, a stiff purchase, costing three shillings, bought after an old one, left behind by his father, had faded away in fragments. All these, with the old religious controversial works of his father, looked grand, and already made a fine show, above the delft, on the top shelf of the old dresser.

He'd add another fine volume to the stock today, Milton's *Works*, a blind man seeing more than a man with many eyes – that is, if he got the rise he expected. Well, it was next to certain, for everyone was talking about the rises that were due, and someone in the know had said that it was coming today for all who deserved it.

In passing to and fro about his work, Johnny had tried to search for a sign in the fixed look on the gob of Anthony, but there was only there the shuttered look that hid everything behind it.

Everyone was working with a will today. All smiles, too. Manna was expected to fall from heaven. Each looked as if he liked his job and was in love with Anthony. Perhaps they were – for that one day, anyhow. It was an anxious time, waiting, especially for Johnny.

—D'ye know how much you're down for, Jack? asked Carey, a cunning look on his foxy face, and he caught Johnny by the arm as he was passing by.

—Is it th' rise you mean? No; a shillin', I expect.

—One an' six, me boy, said Carey knowingly.

Johnny thrilled, but doubted. Too good to be true. If he got a shillin', he'd be well satisfied. Another sixpence would be too much to look for, afther his row with Anthony too. Still one never knew: no use o' bein' a man of little faith.

—No, no, Carey, he replied, catch Anthony givin' too much. You can't lure me into that fancy. Who told you? Where'd you get that news?

—Ah! said Carey, with a cunning leer, that 'ud be tellin' you. Then as Johnny moved away, he came nearer, and whispered over Johnny's shoulder into his ear: Dyke it was; he knows – don't say I said anything about it.

Passing by Dyke, Johnny got a punch in the chest that staggered him and made him catch his breath. Dyke's face as he saw the pain he caused moved from a keenly pointed smile to a snarling laugh. Johnny, smiling eagerly, put a hand over his breast in mock defence.

—Huh! grumbled Dyke, following up the one blow with a rain of them, why you're picked for a favour, God knows! What Mr Anthony sees in you it would be hard to say. Get away, you lost an' lumberin' looney! and Johnny thought he felt the force of good humour in the blows he ran from.

The rumour was right then – Dyke's manner showed it. He'd say nothing to his mother for a few weeks so that he could add some more books to his store. He had so few, and needed so many. His row with Anthony had left no ill-feeling. Maybe the reverse. You see, a fellow loses nothing by standing up for his rights: to thine own self be true, and it must follow as the night the day, you cannot then be false to any man. Good old Shakespeare – he knew more than most. Of course, he'd let Dyke thump him, without saying a word, but Dyke hadn't really meant to be rough. Just his way o' goin' on. At bottom, he was really a decent fellow. Dyke had told him of the rise in a rough way, but it was decent not to keep the knowledge to himself. Perhaps, even oul'

Anthony wasn't quite so bad as he thought. Anyhow, he'd got to be a little stiff with those who worked for him, or he wouldn't get anything done.

He'd get another book next week. Ay, but what? Dickens? Carlyle? A new Shakespeare? No; th' old one would do grand for a little while longer. He'd not decide; betther prowl round th' stands an' see what was goin'; buyin' a book was a serious thing.

Good God, didn't the time go slow! *Tempus Fugit* me arse! An hour dawdles into an age when you want it to hurry. There's oul' Anthony fillin' th' pay envelopes now, his long bony hands sortin' th' silver, slippin' th' coins into th' tiny envelopes, an' closin' th' flaps with a sly lick o' th' tongue an' a swift pressure of th' slender fingers.

While Johnny was writing a label for a parcel, Hyland halted beside him, his black eyes showing a good-humoured light.

—So Casside's down for a big rise, eh? Nine bob a week now, eh? Let's hope he deserves it. How'r you feelin' about it?

—Oh, all right, said Johnny, wearing an air of indifference; if it hadn't come, I'd have known what to do.

—What? asked Hyland.

—Fling th' job to hell! said Johnny carelessly.

—Really?

—Yea, verily, an' by my own help so I would.

—Talkin' big, jeered Hyland.

—Go to th' devil an' shake yourself! said Johnny.

He saw all the clerks, who had been paid, counting and recounting their gains, sorting the coins out, folding them together, and dropping them back again, gracefully, into their little envelopes, finally placing the envelope, with a kingdom of God look on their faces, into their favourite pockets. He hadn't been called in yet. He hoped he'd be sent for before he had to go to his dinner. He hoped to God he wouldn't have to go up and ask Anthony for what was coming to him. Like th' oul' bugger to make me, thought Johnny.

He heard a tapping on one of the windows of the counting-house, and, looking round, saw that Anthony was beckoning to him.

—There y'are, there's th' signal, Casside, said a number of the clerks.

Johnny, settling his hair on the way and giving a tug to his coat to make it sit straight, hurried to Anthony's little counting-house. The bony hand placed Johnny's little envelope on the ledge of

the desk, without a word. Johnny took it with a Thank you, sir,
and hurried back to his own little desk, his heart beating and his
joy full. He waited till he saw that the clerks were busy bending
over their desks; then he opened the envelope and spilled the
gleaming coins on to his desk that he might have the full feeling
of handling the one and sixpence extra.

Good God, th' oul' fool had made a blunder! There was only
five and six in the envelope – two two-shilling pieces, a shilling,
and a sixpence. How well the blunder was made with his wages!
Now he'd have to go back and argue it with Anthony, a hateful
thing to have to do. He fancied he heard some titters over against
him. With a flushed face and disturbed heartbeat, Johnny hurried
back to the counting-house.

—Excuse me, Mr Anthony, he said, I'm afraid you've made a
little mistake, and he smiled forgivingly; there's only five an'
six in th' envelope, instead of seven an' six, sir.

Anthony looked up from a letter he was slowly typing, and
fixed a cold grave gaze on Johnny's excited face.

—How much did you say? he asked.

—Only five an' six in it, sir.

—That is the correct amount for this week, said Anthony
calmly, and went on with his typing.

—Oh, no, no, sir, said Johnny, seven an' six, sir – what I've
been gettin' for a year.

—If you'd taken the trouble to look at your envelope, Casside,
you'd have seen that we've fined you two shillings, making five
and sixpence the amount due to you.

—Fined, echoed Johnny, fined for what, sir?

—For impudence and disobedience, Casside. Next week we
hope we may be able to give you the seven and six as usual, and
the bony hands went on uncertainly, clumsily, gropingly, at the
typing.

Sick and stunned, Johnny was thinking, and not able to think;
getting back to his desk, blindly; fullness of rage making him feel
tight and breathless, his thoughts broken and confused, mixed up
in a medley of anger that this thing had been done to him so
slyly, so quietly, without a wind of the word reaching him, cool
and calculated villainy – th' bony scoundrel, th' dead-fac'd
whore's melt! Silently and steadily the money had been taken from
him – may th' guts in his narrow belly corrode and swell and rise
and burst out of the slit of his mouth! They all had known of it,
and stayed their work to laugh at him, with Dyke leading them

on, and cheerin' in their throats, in honour of Casside's hardship
– may their ill-got lives be lost in a sludge of woe; may their
hearts be cakes o' rust; and a tangle of rotting fibres burn in every
twist and crook of their bodies, hieing them yelpin' to a bitther
grave!

—How much of a rise did you get? whispered Hyland over
his shoulder.

Without the power of answering, he was so stuffed with anger
and dismay, Johnny crushed his cap on to his head, took his lunch
from under his desk, and walked away out of the shop, down
Henry Street, into Sackville Street, mechanically turning up
Bachelor's Walk, the ringing of the handbells, announcing
second-hand auctions all along the way, sounding as if they were
coming from a far distance. He walked on, deep curses burning
in his heart; walked on till he came to a stop before Hanna's
benches filled with books of all kinds, many of which he would
love to have, and bitter with the one thought that he had lost the
power to buy even the poorest of them. For a while he managed
to keep his eyes off the corner where Milton should be; but his
eyes got there at last; and, sure enough, the book dazzled him,
gleaming like a precious stone from a heap of rubbish, almost
asking him, for God's sake, to come and take it.

Take it? For nix? Steal the damned thing? Good God, no;
too dangerous. The youngster keeping an eye on the books
outside wasn't there; strange, that. Must ha' gone to his
dinner.

He peered through the dusty window: oul' Hanna was at the
far end of the shop. Sorting out a new selection. Johnny's hand
stretched towards the book; his fingers went round the upper end
of the spine, and, gently and cleverly, he pulled the book out,
handling it lovingly.

An old man came up and began rooting among the volumes, an
old man with a hooky nose and a spreading beard, rooting with
piercing eyes among the volumes. Johnny put the book under an
arm and took up another, looking at it with eyes that didn't see,
for there was a trembling mist before them. He dimly saw the
man with the hooky nose, piercing eyes, and spreading beard
take a book to his bosom, turn away from the stand, and enter
the shop to pay for it.

Johnny then put down the book he was looking at, turned, and,
with his heart beating like the heart of a bird caught in a squeezing
hand, and his feet feeling as if they were trying to drag him back

again, he sauntered away with Milton under an arm, expecting
every second to hear a wolfish shout from Hanna calling for a
policeman to come and catch a felon. He went on slowly, wheeling
into Liffey Street, then tore along as fast as a rapid walk could
take him. Excited, panting, and thoughtless, he turned into Upper
Abbey Street, then into Jervis Street, not stopping even to glance
at a casualty case getting taken into the hospital; into Britain
Street, up Sackville Street, into Henry Street again, to bolt into
the Henry Street Stores, flushed, covered with sweat, but with the
sweet book cuddled under his arm.

He had risked a lot to gain a lot, and he had succeeded. He had
a half-crown book in his hand and his week's pay in his pocket.
God was good. No, not his week's pay, for two bob of it was snug
in Anthony's pocket. A Robin Hood outa hell who robbed the
poor to pay the rich. Was he goin' to let himself be robbed?
Afther givin' a hard-earned shillin', too, to help buy him a clock?
An' without a fight, either? He was in the right: no one need
tell him God would put a hand into the pocket of a poor man.
He'd argue it out with Anthony. He'd get what was be right comin'
to him, or go! Hyland, Dyke, an' th' rest weren't goin' to have it
all their own way.

His file was packed with orders, but Johnny put no pass on
them. And wouldn't, till he got what was rightly due to him.
Then, he might; anyway, he'd see. There was Anthony, now, back
from his haughty lunch, pegging away, in his clumsy manner,
with his typewriter. Bony and slender as his hands were, they were
slow and awkward at typing, Johnny could see that. All were back
at their work now, all busy, all but Johnny, who hung over his
desk, trying to think of what to say to Anthony. He couldn't
think, so he'd depend on God to put the right words into his
mouth.

Several times he started for the counting-house, and several
times he found himself back at the desk again, uncertain and
afraid. Once he went as far as the entrance, but his heart failed
him and he came back to his desk. He felt a little sick. He should
have gone when he was roused, when the anger was on him.

Screw your courage to the sticking-place, said Shakespeare.

—Oh, to hell with it! he said, roughly to himself, here goes!

Straightening himself stiffly, he marched to the counting-
house and stood near Anthony, waiting to be noticed. After a long
interval, Anthony raised his head from his typewriter and looked
at Johnny.

—Well, Casside, he said, what's the trouble?

Before he could answer, the dark form and dusky face of Hewson edged its way forward from the background, and Johnny found himself loosely hemmed in between the two God-belauding brothers.

—Well, said Anthony again, what is it, Casside?

—I just came to say a word about the fine, sir.

—All that ought to have been said has already been said, said Anthony shortly.

Johnny conjured up all the new strength that had begun to come into his speech. He had written as many letters as he could to his brothers, trying to put into them all the things he had learned the week before, and choosing the most elegant words he could think of to describe what had happened in the locality. He had done it so well that Tom had praised him for the brightness and skill shown in the letters written to him. So with a little trembling in his mind, he settled himself down here to do what he could in his own defence.

—I don't think so, sir, he said; you, yourself have said but little, and I have said nothing at all.

—Oh! said Anthony in an astonished voice, and what have you to say about it?

Although, now and again, there was a slight quiver in it, Johnny's voice was firm and clear; and he felt that Dyke, Nearus, and the rest of them listened and were wondering.

—Well, sir, said Johnny, I'd like to know, first, what was the impudence and disobedience complained of, where it happened, for which I have been fined what is, to me, a very large sum of money?

—I see we have a lawyer amongst us! said Hewson, with a dark grin.

—It is recent enough for you to remember it well, said Anthony, and I've neither the time nor intention to go over it again with you. You have been fined, and there is nothing more to be said about it.

—That's all very well, sir, but I think I have the right to say something in my own defence. The occasion that brought about what you are pleased to call disobedience and impudence was really my own time; and it was you, sir, who were unjust in keeping me beyond the stipulated hour for leaving work.

Anthony had resumed his typing, pretending not to listen to Johnny, and there was a pause, broken by the jerky rattle of the keys clicking clumsily because of the unsteady movement of Anthony's fingers.

—Besides, sir, went on Johnny, had what you allege against me happened even in the rightful time of the Firm, the amount of the fine, if you weigh it with the weekly wage I get, is altogether too large and unnecessarily severe.

Hewson roughly pushed in past Johnny, anchoring himself beside his brother; and the two of them bent over an invoice of goods, taking as much notice of Johnny as they would of a fly on a distant star.

—I have saved up hard to buy a book I want badly, said Johnny in a louder voice, and the fine had made my well-nourished plan go all agley.

—Book! snorted Hewson; maybe it's a book he wants!

—Casside, said Anthony, with a tinge of a smile on his bony face, attend to your work, and you'll have little need of books.

—I have attended to it well, responded Johnny vigorously, and for the past year not a single complaint has been made against me by a single customer. My need of books is my own need, an' that need's my own business, an' no one else's.

—Casside, said Hewson viciously, it's plain that a fine is the one thing you can understand. Go back to your work or you may have a bigger fine to face this day week!

—I have no fear of a fine next week, for I refuse to be fined now; and what I am refusing today, I will refuse tomorrow.

—Go back to your work, Casside, said Anthony, a little more softly, in an effort to be kind, before you go too far.

—I'll go back when the two shillings taken from me are given to me again.

—Casside, said Anthony solemnly, you will have to submit to the fine imposed upon you, or – and he paused to make what he was about to say more impressive – or leave our employment. You must make your choice.

—I have already made it, said Johnny.

—What is it, then?

—To leave.

After a moment's hesitation, Anthony opened a drawer, rooted in it, took out some silver, and flung two shillings on the desk beside Johnny.

—It is plain, he said, that you are wholly unsuitable to us.

—That's possibly something to be unashamed of, said Johnny bitterly. And let me tell you there's another shilling of mine embedded in the clock you have at home! I could ill afford it. I gave it unwillingly. I thought joining in the gift would make things safer here. I need a book more'n you need a clock; but keep it; it will remind you of me when the clock strikes!

Anthony's face went a flaming red. He bent down over his desk and remained silent. But Johnny stood there, as pale as Anthony was flushed.

—Get out! said Hewson furiously. How dare you mention such a sacred thing? Get out, or get kicked out!

Johnny sensed that the whole staff was disturbed, and he glimpsed a worried look defiling Dyke's foxy face. He had made them sit up. Whenever Anthony looked at the clock, he'd remember what Johnny had said to him.

—No one will kick me out, said Johnny. I'm going. God rest you merry, gentlemen. I'm due a rest, anyway. Farewell, a long farewell to all your greatness.

The fleshy hand of the dusky-faced Hewson sought his shoulder, giving him a push that sent Johnny colliding with the desk of Nearus.

—Get out! he said angrily; this Firm has no room for a vulgar corner-boy!

Dyke snatched the precious book from under Johnny's arm and flung it far down the passage-way into the dirty straw, a messenger meeting it with a kick that sent it away beyond into the dirtier lane.

—Follow your book, said Dyke, to your rightful place in the dirt of the street!

—There he'll find his happiness and his hope, said Hyland.

Nearus looked on and sighed and said nothing.

With his face pale as a lily lying in a dark corner, his mind a smarting hate, and rage rough in him, Johnny gathered himself together straight again, faced the two signalmen of God, saying savagely, in half a chant:

> *I leave th' pair of you with your godliness and go;*
> *And when th' ending day comes, day of wrath, I hope*
> *You two may catch a glimpse of heaven's glory;*
> *Then sink down, sudden, down, deep down to hell,*
> *Amazed and sightless!*

Half blind himself with rage, he left them, picked up his precious book out of the gutter, wiped with a handkerchief the specks of cow-shit from the cover, and wended his way homewards.

And the morning and evening were the seheaventh day.

TOUCHED BY THE THEATRE

ARCHIE WAS now completely gone on the stage, and Johnny was following close behind. Archie lived and fought and died and lived again in the toils of the great persons treading out their glorious lives, gorgeous before the footlights. The theatre housed the quick, the rest of the world encased the dead. Some time before, they had formed the Townshend Dramatic Society, had rented some unused stables in Hill Street for a shilling a week. These they had gutted of all partitions, had whitewashed the walls, putting a deep yellow border round the top of them, with a harp in one corner, a wolf-dog in the second, a round tower in the third, and a huge shamrock in the fourth so as to show decidedly the true nature of the work. From old timber taken from the loft they had made a stage at one end, and benches from what was over. Ould lanterns, bought second-hand, shaded with cardboard, coloured yellow and black, did well as footlights; and a turkey-red twill curtain went up or came down at the ringing of a handbell. The stage was fitted with lovely parlour, hall, and landscape sets, provided from the better parts of old canvas cut away from old cloth thrown away by the Queen's Theatre. Here sketches were given to audiences of forty or fifty, who paid tuppence a head to get in, to see Archie playing the Duke of Gloucester to Johnny's Henry the Sixth; or to see Johnny playing Brutus in the Forum scene, followed by Archie as Mark Antony, friends in the audience shouting the exclamations of the crowd for them; or the scene between Wolsey and the nobles, sorted out to be one, played by Johnny in dark-blue tights, yellow buskins, black trunks, brown velvet coat, and rich green silk cape, lent by Tommie Talton for the bright occasion; while Archie strutted as the Cardinal, in a red gown, topped with a low-crowned, wide-brimmed jerry hat that had been soaked for days in soda to remove the black colour, then dyed in crimson, with red curtain cords laced round the crown, the heavy tassels hanging down over his left shoulder. Johnny had to hurry out after the sly blow at the Cardinal,

> *An' so I'll leave you to your meditations*
> *How to live better. For your stubborn answer*
> *About the giving back the great seal to me,*
> *The king shall know it, and, no doubt, shall thank you.*
> *So fare you well, my little good Lord Cardinal,*

to come back in a long black cloak and wide-brimmed black hat to play the part of Cromwell to give Archie his chance in the Cardinal's great renunciation. As well, they played scenes from *The Octoroon*, especially that between Jacob McClusky and Salem Scudder, Johnny doing McClusky and Archie doing Scudder; and the scene between Corry Kinsella and Harvey Duff in *The Shaughraun*, with lots of others in Dick's little orange-coloured books of *Standard Plays*; though Johnny didn't like the rowdy arguments that went on afterwards, for a lot didn't want to praise Archie, being main jealous of his natural gifts and acting vigour; doing all they could in cold water to disparage everything they'd seen him do, making Archie hot and irritable, threatening to tear down the curtain that his money had paid for, all the time asseverating that without him there wouldn't be much of a Dramatic Society left. Indeed, once during an interval in the performance given by the Anna Liffey Minstrel Troupe, playing in the Coffee Palace, Townshend Street, they had played the quarrel scene between Brutus and Cassius, Johnny doing Cassius, both of them crimson-cloaked, and wearing greaves and breastplates made from stereotype paper, silvered over, that Archie had pinched from the *Daily Express*. But the whole thing was taken silently by the audience, neither hiss nor clap was heard, and Archie got gloomy, and for long after he was content to play one of the corner-men, making a bigger noise with the bones than he did with Shakespeare.

Better times had come. Now Archie was a friend of Tommie Talton's brother-in-law, Charlie Sullivan, who did things of great magnitude when the theatre was the theatre, to an audience who knew what acting was; when he played the great Conn the Shaughraun, the great Shaun the Post, in *Arrah-na-Pogue*, and the greatest Miles-na-Coppaleen the world, or even Ireland, had ever, ever seen; filling the playhouses throughout the civilized world with laughter, softening it with sad and sympathetic tears, and making them thunderous with cheers, the way you'd like to shoulder him high, and carry him through the world's laudation.

But now, with the world's people fading into ignorance and low regards, he had to do the best he could for the drama by playing in the Mechanics' Theatre, in Abbey Street, strutting the stage there before a rough-and-randy crowd who came to while away the time, but who put great pass on the suffering and rollicking that shivered and shone on the stage; with the lights dim when the tears were falling, and the lights high when bravery took the branch, or when fun gambolled its way from the stage into the hearts of the laughing people watching from the darkness. Here Charlie played all the Irish plays, mixing them with *The Octoroon*, *The Corsican Brothers*, or *Saved From the Sea*, Johnny enjoying them on a free pass from a front bench in the pit, his brother Archie having a small part in each of them, training himself for a fuller future.

A kidger had brought a letter to Johnny from Tommie Talton, marked Urgent, asking to come to see him at once, without a minute's delay, on business; and here was Johnny, with his heart athrob, hurrying on to answer it. He turned swift into Temple Street, went past George's Church, dived into The Pocket, and knocked at a genteel door, a little parched for want of paint, with a white plaster horse, for ever on its hind legs, prancing, in the fanlight. This was a token that those who lived there, though a little down in the world, held fast to the fancy of living a select and lofty life among ordinary people. Every fanlight in the place exhibited a plaster horse, standing still, trotting neatly, or dancing sadly on its hind legs, like a tired animal rehearsing for a turn in a circus. These were carried about in baskets, by Italians, mixed with images of St Francis, St Patrick, and Madonnas with their children. Johnny had often watched them being sold; had often wished that his mother had had enough to be able to put one in the fanlight. Sometimes staring at the seller speaking to a housewife at her door, a look in the Italian's eyes motioning him to get away, he'd say, How much do they cost, sir? And the seller would ask, Weech – the holy ones, or the seemple horses? And Johnny, answering, the horses, would be told that the leetle ones were two sheelings, and the beeg ones four; the seller turning to the woman to say, once in zee vanlight, ladie, zay breeng a change, oh, so beeg, that no one knows eet anymore vor zee same house; for zee leetle horse or zee beeg horse een zee vanlight leeft, leeft zee house up, up so high, ladie, zat zee house ees not zee

same no more, oh, no, for eet has been leefted, leefted up, up;
for zee horses geeves zee house, oh, deegneety, much, muchbeeg,
waht you call a lot. Often the ladie would buy, Johnny envying
her the horse, now taken so gently from the basket, though he
knew well it was a sin to covet his neighbour's goods. But he'd
go on coveting while there was anything left to covet.

These houses were let in floors to genteel persons; had oilcloth
on the halls, a stand, where hats and coats were hanged, a big
gilt-framed picture on a sidewall, variegated carpets with brass
rods on the stairs, and an air that seemed to tell you to knock
at the door softly. This was the first fine house he'd entered since
he stood in Dovergull's, when they were presenting the clock;
and though it wasn't as imposing as the other, it was grand
enough to make him nervous; for patched boots and thread-
bare clothes didn't go well with the white horse in the fanlight
or the cream curtains on the windows. He dared say they wanted
him to earn a few pence by placing bills in some of the shops,
telling all that *The Shaughraun* was in full swing at the Mechanics'
Theatre.

He raised his hand to the knocker – a lily growing out of a bunch
of grass – and knocked softly at the genteel door. Hardly had the
sound died away in the nearness, when the door was opened by
a little woman with a shawl over her shoulders whose hair was
grey, who peered out at him through soft, dark eyes, fixed, sorrow-
ful, in a pale troubled face.

—Is that Johnny Casside? she asked. Oh, come in, my son. I've
been listening for your knock this hour or more.

She brought him into a room that was neither big nor small,
with much furniture scattered about. There were big black-and-
blue vases, swelling into wide bowls at the top, standing on the
mantelpiece; from tiny brass hooks embedded in the wide bowls
hung crystal glasses cut to catch the light, and a bright fire,
burning lustily, threw dancing gleams of lovely colours into the
glasses hanging from the vases. Right in the centre stood a large
square mahogany clock, with a coloured pictured panel on it of
two white swans swimming on a blue lake, fringed with dainty
yellow and green palm trees. Over all was a huge coloured picture
of Charlie Sullivan as Conn the Shaughraun, a roguish smile on
his ruddy face, a fiddle strapped to his back, dressed in his
tattered crimson hunting-coat, and the terrier, Tatters, at his
heels. Dispersed round were pictures of him again as Miles na
Coppaleen, with the keg of poteen on his shoulder; as Salem

Scudder, paring a stick with a long yankee knife; and Shaun the
Post, standing well fettered, in a prison cell. Besides, there were
smaller photographs of Tommie Talton as Corry Kinsella, as
Captain Molyneux, and as the military O'Grady in *Arrah-na-
Pogue*. A faded red carpet covered the floor, dotted with tiny
fur rugs to hide the parts that had trembled into threads. In the
middle of the room, a little nearer to the fire, stood a table
covered with a white cloth, and having on it breakfast things for
one.

—Give me your cap, she said, an' sit down be the fire. You'll
have a cup of tea when Tom comes down. Isn't what you're
looking at fine? Charlie himself, taken in his heyday, costing no
end of money, just afther Charlie had shaken hands with kings
an all kinds o' monarchs, elevated be the way he played his parts
before them; an' God be with the old days, an' that's herself, she
went on, pointing to a picture of an angelic-looking young girl
that Johnny hadn't noticed before, me own daughter, me Mary,
in the part o' Moya, who could hold a lily to one cheek an' a
rose to the other without makin' either feel outa place, fitted be
God with a smile that simply made an audience thrance itself
into a feeling of kindliness for the world at large, before she gave
a sigh an' took a soaring lep to heaven outa the throes of thryin'
to bring a new child into the world. I hear Tom's bed movin', the
signal for me to put his egg on, for he's a changed boy, now, that
used to have his breakfast sprawlin' in bed, and the first tint of
the night comin' into the sky; now not lettin' me do a hand's-
turn, dustin' and sweepin' his own room, makin' his own bed to
save his old mother any exertion, lockin' the door, even, for fear
I'd sneak up when he's gone, to lay a hand over things. Here he is,
now, an' here's Johnny Casside waiting for your lordship, dying
for a cup of tea before he harbours a thought of doing the thing
you're going to set before him.

The long lanky figure of Tom came strutting into the room,
dressed in faded black broadcloth trousers and a dazzling white
shirt, spliced in many places, the cuffs frayed sharply, but still
brave and challenging. His pale pitted face was merry with a grin;
his hair a mass of golden curls, parted impudently by a curling-
over quiff, cascading down elegantly over his pock-marked brow.

—Well, Johnny, me lad o' gold, he said intimately, as he slid
into a chair beside the fire, and began on the egg, while Johnny
munched a junk of buttered toast and sipped from a cup of tea,
you know that tonight's Charlie's benefit performance? Well,

Cleggett, who plays Father Dolan, 's gone and got ill; none o' the rest know the part, so we're in the devil of a hole. We want you to fill the part for us, me lad.

—An' well he'll fill it, too, murmured Mrs Talton.

—Aw, no, no; indeed I couldn't, exclaimed Johnny excitedly; but the thrill of a cheering audience went through his beating heart.

—You're goin' to do it, said Tom emphatically. Haven't I seen you doin' the parlour scene to Archie's Conn, an' the one in Ballyragget House to Archie's Kinsella, to the manner born, too? Besides, you know the whole part, don't you?

—Yes, I know it all, said Johnny; the whole play, I know it nearly all.

Tommie jumped up, wiping bits of crumbs from his mouth, his eyes ashine, showing a problem solved.

—Me sowl man, he said heartily; now, Mother, turning to Mrs Talton, measure him so that you can stitch enough tucks in Father Dolan's togs to fit him fair.

The breakfast things were swept from the table. The sombre garments of Father Dolan were spread out, Mrs Talton measuring the length of Johnny's arms and legs and the width of his waist, making chalk lines on the black cloth as she measured, murmuring, Tucks won't be many, long legs, long arms, and fairly wide round the waist; but what about the hat? I can't put e'er a tuck in that.

—He wears it only a couple o' times, commented Tom; so he can carry it in his hand. Now for the theatre, me laddo, to run over the words, and give you the feel of the stage.

Johnny, all of a glow, hurried out with Tom, and they got a tram going to Nelson's Pillar.

—I heard th' oul' one muttering out of her, an' I tidyin' me room, said Tom. What was she blatherin' about? Tellin' you what a white-haired boy I'd become, eh?

—Yes, answered Johnny, how you did everything for yourself, makin' your bed an' all, even lockin' the door so as she wouldn't be able to tire herself doin' things.

—If she only knew, and he laughed loudly, pushing his jerry hat to a rakier angle on his curly head. I was at a low ebb a few weeks ago, and I pawned the blankets off the bed, so I do for myself, an' keep the door locked to prevent her finding out. It was all right then, for the nights were warm; but, Jasus, now I'm perished, an' have to bury myself undher old clothes from the baskets!

They got to the theatre, and found two men setting the first

scene for the play. Part of a house appeared at the left corner,
with steps going up to the door; and Johnny rehearsed the going
and coming down of these steps, till Tom was satisfied that some
of a priest's dignity appeared in his walk. Then they went over
the more important scenes in the play, several times; then every
part of the play where the priest appeared; and Tom's face was a
beam of enthusiasm at the end of it all.

—Bravo! he shouted, running over and clasping Johnny's hand.
Did yous see him, did yous hear him? he added, turning to the
two men who had set the scene.

—Ay, did we, said one of them, an' betther it 'ud be hard to get,
if you et an' slept in Drury Lane, itself, for a month o' Sundays!

—Henry Irving's a great man, there's no denyin', said the
other; but if some I know keeps goin' th' way he's shapin' now,
Irving'll be devulged only as an I roved out kind of an acthor!

Tom plunged a hand into a pocket, took out some coppers,
and tossed four of them to the two men.

—Out for a dhrink! he shouted.

Then there was great haste in hurrying over to a pub, for bread
and cheese and a bottle of stout for Tom, and one of ginger beer
with a ham sandwich for Johnny; then back to Tom's, where he
fitted on Father Dolan's clothes, more tucks being added here
and there, till all was said to be well; then home, with his head
spinning, Tom's advice to lie down and forget it all till the time
came, ringing in his ears; with Johnny's mother, when she heard
it, saying, that even were the stage what it should be, there wasn't
much to be got out of it by any respectable person; everyone
knew what the people there were like, livin' languidly a low life
of gay an' coloured divilment; a lure of envy to them who had
to stay in the straight road; wastin' away a boy's life, sightseein'
the chamberin' of light men with fast women; when you should
remember that neither your father nor mother was ever in a
theatre, except to see the wondhers of Shakespeare's plays, done
be God-fearin' men, full of honest laughter, dimmin' with tears
whenever the occasion called for them; adding, as Johnny was
going out, well, since you've committed yourself, do your best,
and don't, for goodness' sake, make a show of the Cassides by
givin' a bad performance.

Johnny raced all the way to the theatre, finding it dark and
deserted, so that he had to edge away, come back, and edge away
again for upwards of an hour, till he saw one of the men go in.
Him he followed, and was told he'd come too soon, but could go

to Mr Talton's dressing-room and wait there till the time came for him to dress and be made up for his part.

A tiny room it was, made of thin board partitions, with a table scattered over with all kinds of face-paints and powder. The green coat and buckskin breeches of Kinsella were hanging from a hook, next to his own black ones; a little cracked looking-glass was on the table, propped up against a tin box; and on the walls a score or more of photographs and coloured pictures of lovely ladies in lovely dresses; dresses so disarranged by the pose of the girls, or the saucy pull of their dainty hands, that lovely legs were peeping at him from all sides and corners, and swelling white breasts all but out of the fair bodices the charming girls were wearing.

> *My bodice, neat an' modest, oh, is slippin', sir –*
> *Be careful, sir, be careful, please;*
> *The silken thread that holds it up is rippin', sir –*
> *Oh, do be careful!*
> *There now! It's down about me waist,*
> *My pearly goods are all uncased,*
> *I hope they're temper'd to your taste –*
> *St Patrick's Day in the morning!*
>
> *My skirts are up above me knees, I'm dancin', sir –*
> *Be careful, sir, be careful, please;*
> *Your eyes are like twin stars o' fire, advancin', sir –*
> *Oh, do be careful!*
> *Good sir, you gave me quite a scare,*
> *I hope you'll find your huntin' fair –*
> *Yes, yes, you're bound to find it there –*
> *St Patrick's Day in the morning!*

Tommie Talton came bustling in, and Johnny jumped away from the pictures. Tom's hat had a hastier rake on his head than ever; his face was flushed; and some of the smallpox holes in his cheeks seemed to fill up and empty again as he breathed.

—There's every sign of it, Johnny, every sign of it; we've done it, I think, at last.

—Yes? questioned Johnny.

—There's a queue forming already, me son. We're going to have a full house; and no paper, no paper, me laddie. Now sling yourself into your priestly duds, and I'll make you up. We've more'n half an hour, before the curtain rises.

Johnny got into the sober clothes of Father Dolan, and felt a bit astray in them. The tucks, ironed out, were still visible, and the trousers looked a bit wide, though the stiff white paper band, stitched to the coat, made a fine Roman collar. A yellowish-grey paint was thinly smeared over his face to take away the bloom of youth; thin streaks of brown across his forehead and under his eyes added a few wrinkles, and made him look thoughtful and serious. Flour scattered over his brown hair made it grey, and finally, a book, representing, Tom said, a Breviary, was put into his hand, and he was all ready for the fray.

—Don't forget not to take the book from your left hand, said Tom. Always keep the right one free for your gestures. He cocked his head to one side and stared at Johnny. You'll do. Look the part to the life. Perfect.

Tom was dressed for his part of Corry Kinsella, buckskin breeches, top-boots, green cutaway coat, white waistcoat, and grey tall hat. He dabbed some red paint on his cheeks, put short thick lines of black paint, to represent sideboards, before his ears, and a thick streak across his upper lip to represent a moustache. With his hunting-crop in his hand, he stood smiling, waiting the time to go on to the stage.

—We'd better be goin' down, he said, for me bones tell me the time's gettin' short. Remember, he said warningly, to keep your head well up while you're speakin', so that the gallery can hear; never stand in front of anyone an' spoil the picture; and don't forget a priest always walks with dignity on the stage, an' speaks slow an' sure.

They went downstairs, Johnny's heart swelling so that his chest felt tight and his stomach felt queer. Passing through an iron door, splashed with the word SILENCE, they came on to the stage.

What with the lights and the curiously-dressed people standing about, silent and still, and the murmuring that floated up from the audience, the dirty stage and the dusty scenery turned into a golden world.

—Do like you done today, an' you'll do grand, whispered Tom, as he slid softly by to take his place where he was to make his first entrance.

Several people who passed patted Johnny gently on the shoulder; and he knew, if he failed, he'd for ever be undone; but he wouldn't fail, for he'd live the part for the time being.

There on the stage, behind the lights, in front of his eyes, stood the cottage of Arte O'Neill, in Suil-a-beg, with the ruins of

Suil-a-more Castle a few feet away, and the Atlantic Ocean near enough to let the sound of its waves be heard; an' there was Captain Molyneux, of the 49th Foot, come to the place to capture the escaped Fenian, Robert Ffolliott, a convicted felon because he wasn't afraid to speak of Ninety-eight; and the green-coated Squireen Kinsella, striking his top-boots with his elegant whip, striding before the cottage, a villain, doing his friend, Ffolliott, out of his property, coming between the Fenian and his own beloved fiancée, pretending friendship all the time, but conniving with the grey-coated police spy Harvey Duff, to nail Ffolliott again, so's he'd be out of the way; with the black-coated Father Dolan, frantic, knowin' all, but darin' to say nothing conceived in the confessional.

Johnny stepped through the door into the glare, the white light, the dazzling place of play, sensing, though he didn't see, the vast gathering of watchers hidden in the gloom, waiting, wondering, pitching their tents of thought with the players in the pool of light that showed another world of good and bad, gay and glum; knowing and simple people, in silks and friezes, in crimson and green garments, and weather-worn grey, aligned together for good or evil, with God on the alert above to ensure that to the true, out of many tribulations, would come an exceeding weight of glory.

There he stood, now, outside the cottage door, his glance resting on the agitated Kinchella asking himself who was it had sent money to Ffolliott in Australia to keep him from starving; with Johnny's answer sounding loud and clear and strange, I am the man, Mr Kinchella; the play flowing on with Johnny stressing the villainy of the Squireen, answering him when Kinchella pleads for Father Dolan's help in persuading Arte O'Neill to become his wife, I'd rather rade the burial service over her grave, an' hear the sods fallin' on her coffin, than say the holy words that would make her your wife; for now I know, Corry Kin-chella, that it was by your means, and to serve this end, my darling boy – her lover – was denounced and convicted; and Kinchella's snarling denial, 'Tis false! cut be Johnny's 'Tis true; but the truth is locked in my soul, and heaven keeps the key! with the vindictive Kinchella threatening venomously, Then out of this house these girls shall go, homeless, ay, an' beggars, followed be Johnny's declaration with a force in it, like God's hidden thunder, rivin' a villain's last hope, Not homeless while I have a roof to shelter them; not beggars, I thank God who gives

me a crust to share with them! going in slowly, leavin' Kinchella
gnashin' his teeth in the midst of a storm of hand-clapping and
cheers from the audience, incensing him with the feeling that his
playing of the part was safe, while the main characters silently
shook his hand, and the minor ones touched him respectfully on
the shoulder; while the play went on to show the sisther of the
Fenian fallin' madly in love with the English Captain; tellin'
how Conn poached the Felon home out of Australia, and brought
him safe to Father Dolan's house where, in the midst of their
jollity, the redcoats come, informed of Ffolliott's whereabouts
by Harvey Duff; the Fenian runnin' to hide in the kitchen clock,
with Captain Molyneux questionin', an' Father Dolan stutterin'
that he was, was here, but had, had—, an' Conn chimin' in with,
Yissir, he wint away before he came here at all; then the Captain
sayin' solemn, Have I your word as a priest, sir, that Robert
Ffolliott is not under this roof? showin' Father Dolan strug-
glin' with his conscience, saved from a lie be the brave Fenian
rushin' in to shout, No, sir; Robert Ffolliott is here; Conn
consolin' the priest be sayin' that Robert would rather have the
irons on his hand than the sin of a lie upon your soul; endin'
with the grand tableau of the handcuffed prisoner embracin' his
beloved, the poor priest, convulsed with grief, leaning his head
on the table, the Captain pointin' the way out with his naked
sword, an' Conn prevented be the claspin' arms of his Moya
from flingin' a heavy bottle at the Captain's head, with a long,
lone, sad sigh goin' up from the watchin' people. So it flowed on
to the last scene where Kinchella, abductin' Arte and Moya, is
shot be Conn, where Arte throws down the ladder from the cliff,
preventin' any of the villains goin' to the waitin' lugger, on to
Harvey Duff's flight from the furious people, beggin' mercy from
Conn who flings aside the crouchin' Informer, sayin', Ay, as you
spared me, as you spared the men at whose side you knelt before
the althar, as you spared them whose salt you ate but whose blood
you drank. There's death comin' down on you from the cliff
above, there's death waitin' for you on the rocks below – Now,
Informer, take your choice! And Robert, freely pardoned, no
longer needin' to fly to America where Irishmen were held in
honour and threated right, and made welcome, and given power,
and shown favour, where no information was sworn against
them, where no narrow walls were built to hold them tight, where
no ropes were woven to hang them high, where no iron was
forged to mar them manacled; but could stay at home, and

marry his loved one, and Captain Molyneux, too, Englishmen and all, as he was; and Conn, happy at last, with his own Moya, and the priest's blessing at long last given.

And Johnny bowed his head with the rest, standing in the midst of a huge coloured bubble of applause, Johnny watching some of the people mooching out, wading through a drift of orange peel and crumpled programmes, with the curtain coming slowly, slowly down for the last time.

All of them, nearly, hurried away then, patting him on the back as they passed; but Johnny lingered a little, looking at the stage wistfully as the lights began to dim, and the fairy feelin' faded. Behind a wing he heard the voices of two men who played the minor parts of Kinchella's henchmen. He listened, for he had heard his name mentioned.

—Didja ever see the like before? said one voice. Whenever I met the cocky kid strollin' about, like a god who knew nothin', I'd ha' liked to have given him a wholesome paste in the snot!

—Father Dolan, how are you! I've a pain in me arse, lookin' at him. A sad sight I hope I'll never see again. Disasthrous, disasthrous! If you'd done it now – Oh, I'll say nothin'.

—Or you, Jem, but mum, though, not a word. The cocky kid done it; an', oh, Jasus, help the poor theatre!

Johnny hurried up to the dressing-room, where he took off his stage clothes silently, only half listening to Tommie's praise, for a good deal of the glory was gone.

—You were really fine, said Archie, when they were on their way home. Even Sullivan said that only once before had he seen a better Father Dolan – the time he once played it himself. Splendid he said you were.

—I heard him saying everyone was splendid, answered Johnny moodily.

—Ay, in an offhand way; but he didn't harp on anyone as he did on you. I got Harvey Duff over betther than ever before – they hissed like hell!

But the goodness was out of it, and the glory was gone for Johnny. To forget what he had heard the two bastards saying of him, he broke softly into a gay Dublin ditty:

> A sober black shawl hides her body, entirely
> Touch'd be the sun and the salt spray of the sea;
> And safe in the darkness her slim hand, so lovely,
> Carries a rich bunch of red roses for me!

Her petticoat's simple, her feet are but bare,
An' all that she has is but neat and scantie;
But stars in the deeps of her eyes are exclaiming,
She carries a rich bunch of red roses for me!

No arrogant gem sits enthron'd on her forehead,
Or swings from a white ear for all men to see;
But jewell'd desire in her bosom most pearly,
Carries a rich bunch of red roses for me!

—If I was you, said Archie, as they walked along Sherriff Street, I wouldn't go an' get a swelled head.

DEATH ON THE DOORSTEP

TOM HAD finished his time with the colours, and had come home on the reserve with a fine character. His company officer, a Captain Bacon, had done what he could to persuade him to keep with the colours and go in for promotion. Tom had passed examinations in signalling, drill-instruction, map-making, and was skilled in all the then known books of infantry technique of attack and defence; and Bacon had got him the Lance Stripe as quick as he could. But Tom didn't wear it long. Nothing would make Tom put a comrade into the clink, or even report one. What they want, he'd say when the stripe had been ripped from his arm, is not a better soldier but a spying bully. Three different times the stripe went up; and three times it came down quicker still, for it wasn't in him to become a jailer or a judge's lackey. And so, though he loved a soldier's life, he left it, and came back to his own town-land.

On the other hand, Mick hated the life, and was always eager to get far away from the sound of a bugle. His life was a stormy one, and his records were packed with regimental entries. At the moment he was doing twelve calendar months, cells, for up-ending a company sergeant-major who had called him a good-for-nothing Irish bastard.

But Tom arrived home with a grand character from the records in the one hand, and a recommendation for work from Captain Bacon to the Superintendent of the Goods Department of the

Meddleland Railway at the North Wall. He got a job as a goods porter at fifteen bob a week, and some months after, that of a shunter at eighteen shillings a week. So to be near to where he worked, the Cassides folded up their tent and rented two rooms in a four-roomed cottage near the North Wall, the other two rooms upstairs forming the home of a Mr Sheelds, with a wife and eight children; noisy kids, half fed, their clothes things of shreds and patches; for ever quarrelling, rushing up or down the stairs; into the street, out of the street; doing quick and sudden jobs in the hall, fit to break a body's neck, if he happened to step on it, filling the house with the incense of poverty, playing uproariously with chaos till the deeper hours of the night shook them into showy slumber.

One morning, under the grey-blue cloak of an October sky, a morning that had, earlier on, wed itself to a bitter breeze, Johnny and his mother helped to load the few heavy things they had on to a little cart, drawn by a donkey, driven by a young fellow, like Johnny himself, with black tousled hair, and one eye missing; lost in a stand-up fight, he said, with a fella twice me size, who when he found he was gettin' bet, an' had me on the ground, under him, poked a bit o' pointed stick into me eye, and turned it round, so that the doctor had to take it out; but, all the same, when he done it, I nearly did for him for I ruptured him with a friendly kick in the balls. When all the things were piled on the cart, both of them had a good time welting the donkey till they got to the doorway of their new home. Sweating hard, Johnny helped One Eye to carry things in, while his mother went backwards and forwards, carrying the more fragile ware that was too precious to be trusted to the lumbering donkey.

They had been installed in their new home, now, for some time, with a little Protestant church at their back, and a huge Catholic church right in front of their face, the first called St Burnupus, the second St Damaman, Mrs Casside passing the fact by with the remark of, The nearer the church, the farther from God. They hadn't been long in the house when they found it was alive with bugs. Tom and Johnny had been close to sickness several nights when the bugs came out, crawling over their shrinking bodies, spreading a bloody evil-smelling slime over them the times they were squelched savagely between angry groping finger and thumb. With boiling water, half filled with soda, Mrs Casside had scrubbed every bit of wood in the rooms; day and night, for over a month, she fought the bugs, helped by Johnny raking their rotten holes out clean, pouring in poisons, mixed with paraffin, spluttering often, as if she was about to retch, getting some mortar from men working at the end of the street, plugging every hole up, and smoothing them over with a broken-bladed knife; till the time came when she could bring in neighbours to rejoice with her, saying, a silken skin can rest decent now, barring an odd nip or two from a sthray flea which could cause uneasiness to no one.

Things prospered after the bugs had been banished. Johnny was getting an egg nearly every morning, instead of seeing one at Easter only; with meat for dinner often, and an odd pot of jam for tea. The kindly fruits of the earth were coming his way. His mother had a warm petticoat under a warm skirt, and a good pair of boots on her hardy feet. The big box on the lobby was always full of coal, for Tom added quite a lot to his few shillings a week. His wide, clumsy railway uniform of black corduroy was a wonder-sack; and often when he came home, he brought forth, like a conjuror, many a good thing for eating and for wear, such as eggs, butter, cheese, bacon, and tea; boots, caps, shirts, suspenders, and socks. Many of the surplus shirts and boots had been pawned, and with her share of the money Mrs Casside had added a few luxuries to the home, cheap sheets, some cutlery, crockery, cheap blankets, and even a chair, bought from a neighbour whose home had been broken up by a sudden death.

When a crate or case looked promising, Tom, or some comrade, would crash the sharp lip of a heavy truck against it till it burst open; then he'd go to a foreman, reporting a damaged case, leaving it free for discreet and fruitful pillage when the coast was clear. A little from many rather than a lot from one was the motto of the men; and anyone who showed carelessness was left to do his work alone. Mrs Casside for a long time was very nervous going into a pawnshop, expecting a policeman to jump out upon her from a shadowy corner in the shop, though she rarely forgot to offer up a prayer for the safety of Tom and the good name of the household. Johnny was too much afraid to pawn anything, though he ate the eggs, drank the tea, wore the boots, and, when the day was mild enough, opened his coat to show his brand-new shirt to the envious and gaping world.

But this happiness was too good to last long. God didn't want us to get things too easy, murmured his mother. For one day Tom came home to his dinner, cold and shivery, and Johnny noticed his eyes glazy. Dhrink, thought Johnny. He was irritable too, pushing aside his meal of steak and cabbage, grumbling that it was God's killing; and when his mother said it was good and fresh and tasty, he took it up and flung it, plate and all, under the fireplace. Then he sprang up, sending his chair flying, clapped his hat hard on his head and went out of the house, banging the street door after him. That night, late, he came staggering back, telling his mother he felt rotten, with a sharp pain in his chest, like a knife going through it, making him catch his breath badly. His mother handled him like a kid, took off his boots, helped him off with his clothes, smoothed out the bed for him, and covered him up warm. Then she ran out for oatmeal, making a bowl of gruel, forcing the unwilling Tom to swallow it down in hot sips, saying it would be like an inside poultice on his chest, and assuring him he'd be all right again, after a good night's sleep, Johnny sleeping on the floor so that his rest wouldn't be disturbed by anyone in the bed with him.

Throughout most of the night, Johnny heard Tom tossing about, heard his uneven breathing, mixed with the muttering of curses of God on the way these things attack a fellow; coughing, catching his breath; and cursing again; with the old bed he lay on creaking constantly, like a rusty signboard shaking on a windy night. Johnny felt a curious sensation, listening; felt as if something strange, something sinister might bring him pain, and carry confusion into the house, coming out of the hard irregular breathing of his brother Tom.

The next morning Tom was burning, and his breath was coming out of his mouth in coarse, frightened, stiff gasps, and his eyes were glittering in a queer way as he lay there, minding no one, but moving from his back to his side, and from his side to his back again. When she saw him, Mrs Casside sent Johnny off to get a red poor-law ticket, and to deliver it at once to the Dispensary for the attendance of a doctor. The next morning at midday the doctor, Shonelly, came, flat-footed, hard-headed, his cheeks a glossy red, ripening into purple on the tips of his cheek-bones. He had a shining bald head, like a huge island surrounded by a narrow fringy sea of wiry hair; and the backs of his hands were covered with dirty yellowish hairs as if furry gloves were being born to them. He had a thick collar round a bulging neck, so tight that he was hard set to bend his head. In he came, coughing up a lump of phlegm fiercely and spitting it into the fireplace.

—Where is he? he asked impatiently. In here? – Oh, I see –

what's the matter with him? How long's he been like this? Get
outa the way, for God's sake, woman, and let me see him. Huh!
feverish; tongue bad; chest congested. Keep him quiet and warm,
d'ye hear? Or better still, let him go to the Infirmary.

—No, no, said Mrs Casside, not the Infirmary – we're not
paupers.

—It's the best place for him. Come up to the Dispensary and
I'll give you an opening medicine for him; and, putting on his
hat, he made for the door.

—I'm anxious about him, murmured Mrs Casside timidly, and
I'd be glad if you could come tomorrow.

—Ay, and so would many another too, me fine woman, he
said sarcastically; but I've more to do than to stand guard on
your doorstep, ma'am. And off he hurried, telling his coachman
to drive to the next patient, and breaking wind shockingly as he
climbed into his oul' drab brougham.

Days went by, but no doctor came, leavin' poor Christians to
die without movin' a finger to help them, Johnny's mother said, as
she washed Tom all over to keep him cool, essaying to tempt him
into a quieter mood than to be squirming about the bed from
morning till night, and from night till morning.

Up she sat with him, till her face grew haggard and her eyes
grew dim and her firm mouth twitched for want of sleep; while
poor Tom grew worse; grew hotter; his quick breath coming and
going with such a rasping whistle that you could almost hear it
all over the house; his mouth agape, with his mother trying to
trickle spoonfuls of beef tea down his throat, and Tom, near
choking, spewing it out again, all over his bedclothes; his
mother wiping his cracking lips and his sweaty forehead, looking
wonderingly into his wide-open glassy eyes; he coughing till you'd
think his lungs would break, and spitting up phlegm in a gasping
gurgle, tinged with a darkish red colour that his mother wiped off
with a gentle hand, while the other caressed his burning forehead.

One day Johnny, going in to see if there was any message for
him to do, found her half lying on the floor, holding on to the
bed with one hand, and to Tom with the other, and he with one
leg pawing the floor, and she looking at him, a tear slidin' down
a furrow in her face, all the time murmurin', Ah, Tom, Tom, Tom,
I can do no more; I'm done in; I've failed you for once in me life.

Johnny, with fear in his heart, and it thumpin', helped her up,
sat her down on the chair by the side of the bed, and be main

force shoved Tom into the bed again, holding him down there, not rightly knowin' what to do; afraid to stay, and afraid to go for help, for fear of Tom gettin' up an' goin' out to do damage to himself before help could come; all the time keepin' his eyes shut so that he wouldn't see the horrid faces Tom was makin', an' thryin' to close his ears to the strained breathin' that forced itself out of Tom's gapin' mouth.

—I'm afraid for you, my son, his mother kept murmurin'; I'm afraid for you; I failed you this time; but I done me best.

—There's a knock at the other door, said Johnny. I betther go an' see who it is. Here, hold him down till I see.

But she sat on there, her hands fiddling with the quilt; her eyes closing; her breast panting, murmuring away, I failed me son this time, but I done me best.

—Eh, here, said Johnny roughly, shaking her shoulder, there's someone at th' other door – maybe th' docthor. Hold him till I go an' see who it is.

She slowly rose, slid over, falling across Tom's body so as to keep him where he was, an' he babblin' an' babblin' away a lot of mixed-up nonsense.

Johnny, opening the door and going out, saw a clergyman, as big as a big policeman, standing at the other one by the end of the hall, waiting for it to be opened. Johnny was about to turn swift to warn his mother to keep silent, and let the unwelcome visitor go unanswered; but the clergyman, hearing his movement, turned, and came towards him.

—Good day, my lad, he said – and a handsome face he had – can you tell me if Mrs Casside lives here?

—Yessir, said Johnny, before he could think of anything to say to ward him off.

—Oh, she's a Protestant, isn't she? Can I see her? I'm the new minister, Harry Fletcher.

—I'm afraid not, said Johnny surlily; me brother's very ill, an' she's mindin' him.

Just then Mrs Casside's voice sounded shrill and appealing, calling, Johnny, quick, come – he's risin', an' I can't hold him down!

Johnny dashed back into the sick-room, to see Tom half out of bed, his mouth agape, mumbling away, and his mother sliding down to the floor, exhausted, but still with a tight grip on the sick man's arm. The minister stood at the door staring, while Johnny rushed over and tried to push Tom back; but he was too far out of bed, and, push as he might, Johnny wasn't strong enough for the twisting and turning Tom.

Before he knew what was happening, the new minister was beside him, his arms were around the sick man, and Tom was safe in bed again, with the clothes neatly replaced around him, and the strong restraining hand of the minister pushing down on his chest. There he stood, staring down at the mumbling man for fully a minute.

—Mrs Casside, he said, without taking his eyes off the sick man, your boy's in a bad way.

She never answered for some time; then murmured in a steady, dreamy way, Poor Tom! I've failed me poor son this time.

—You're worn out, woman, he said, turning his head to look at her, worn out completely. Why isn't he in hospital?

—There was only th' poorhouse one, she said, an' no son o' mine's goin' there.

—There's the Addlelaid, he murmured; what about the Addlelaid?

—You'd have to have some big nob behind you to push you in there, said Mrs Casside.

He kept silent for a few moments, looking down at the uneasy man, his soft, elegant hand holding Tom safe under the clothes, Johnny at the window looking out at the shades of the Dublin Mountains, pale-blue heads above the houses, Tibbradden, Three Rock, Two Rock, Glendoo, and Kilmashogue, like a semicircle of lovely wonders stretched over the forehead of the city. And the tall clergyman still stood silently there, looking down on the twisting, hoarsely-gurgling figure stretched out beneath him.

—The Infirmary would be better than this, Mrs Casside, he murmured.

—No, it wouldn't, she answered doggedly; they'd just sling him there, and leave him to rave alone. Here, at least, he'll have them who know and love him to touch, till he gets to the end of his journey.

—Run round as fast as your legs can carry you, and tell Georgie Middleton to come here at once, said the tall minister, suddenly, to Johnny.

Johnny, without waiting to put on his cap, ran for his life, sensing that the minister had hit on some idea of how to help them. When he got there, Georgie was reading a Deadwood Dick story; but after a little grumbling, he put his hat on and came back with Johnny.

—Georgie, said the minister, putting his hand on the lad's shoulder, I want you to stay here beside this poor sick man; to watch that he doesn't get out of bed; and to do whatever Mrs Casside may want, till I come back. Will you do this for her and me?

—Yessir, he said at once; nothin' easier.

—Thank you, Georgie. Come along you, he added, gripping Johnny's arm, hurrying him out of the house, up Lower Sherriff Street, till they came to the rank of cabs and cars there.

—Climb up, he said to Johnny, while he got up on the other side; and to the jarvey, Addlelaid Hospital, my man – quick as your horse can go!

Away they went bowling along the roads, Johnny a little ashamed of his shabby get-up, and shy of this well-dressed, smooth, and gracefully-mannered minister. He kept silent, watching vaguely the many patterns of life moving swiftly past, trying to think and adapt himself to all that was happening.

—It's a pity, he heard the clergyman saying, and Johnny turned sideways to listen and show respect, a pity I didn't know of your brother's illness sooner.

That was all he said till they came to the hospital, and Johnny and the minister hurried into the hall. After mentioning his business to the porter, the minister went away with him, coming back after about ten minutes, talking earnestly to a white-robed doctor, who shook hands with the minister, saying, Anytime – the sooner the better. You're lucky to have been given a bed.

They hurried out to the car again, and were off, trotting back to Johnny's home.

—Well, said the clergyman, we've got him in as a patient. God send we haven't been too late.

Johnny murmured a shy amen, feeling that much should be said in return for the minister's kindness.

When they got back, Johnny found Georgie Middleton humming a hymn (which instantly stopped when they entered), like a heathen priest mumbling an incantation; and Johnny could see well that he had been frightened of the sick man, deliriously raving, for a strained look of anxiety vanished clean off his face when they came in, and his hands got busy, pretending to straighten out the creases in the bedclothes. His mother, lying on the old sofa opposite, slumbered heavily, her black hair tossed, her hands twitching a little, and her breast regularly heaving with the happiness of sleep.

When the new minister saw she was asleep, he held up his hand warningly, and whispered, Let her sleep on, now, and take her rest; for the time may come when sleep will be far from her. We'll try to get him off without waking her, and I'll leave a note saying everything's all right. Let me see, now: we'll wrap him like a mummy in the blankets, and bind him with the sheets round the middle and under the knees to hamper his twisting. You, Georgie, help me to roll him in the blankets, and you, he added, turning to Johnny, help hold him when he's in them, while I bind them together with the sheets.

Georgie, with much panting, wrapped the thin blankets round Tom, while the new minister twisted the sheets to make them into long dirty-white scarves.

—Careful, sir, careful, murmured Johnny; don't test them too far; they're very far gone, and they're all we have.

The new minister went to work, binding Tom tightly into the blankets, so that only his arms could move, taking no notice of his ceaseless, raving, disconnected babble.

—Now, said the new minister, when Tom had been firmly trussed, Georgie, you'll have to go with this young man, here, to the hospital to help him on the way. I can't, for I've got to be at a Vestry Meeting in a short time. When I say the word, lift together. We'll leave the poor tired mother sleeping. Are you ready? Now!

They lifted him from the room, through the hall, out into the street, forced him into the cab, and stretched him down as well as he'd go on one of the seats, Johnny holding his head, and Georgie holding on to his legs to keep him from rolling off again.

—I'll pull the windows up, said the new minister, doing it as he spoke, and don't dare open one of them till he's safe in the hospital; and turning to the cabman, said smartly, Addlelaid, my man, quick as you can.

Nothing terribly infectious? growled the driver.

—Nothing. Now off with you at full speed. Georgie has the fare, he added to Johnny.

Johnny tried to keep his eyes off the things that stuck out over the bulky, tossed-about bundle of clothes – a greenish feverish face, glaring eyes aglitter, and a drooling mouth sending out a stream of never-ending words that meant nothing. By and by the heat of the sick body began to fill the closed-up space of the cab with a warmth that distended Johnny's stomach, making him feel as if he were in the tropical glasshouse of a garden, tight shut, the heat mixing with the smell of palms slowly rotting away. So the heat here was tinged with an earthy smell, suffocating, sickening; the heat rising in vapour, covering the cab windows with a thick unhealthy mist, mirroring everything that passed by as vaporous, sinister shadows. Soon the sweat began to run down Johnny's brow and down his belly; and through the sweaty mist he could see that Middleton's face was turning yellow, and that his mouth had tightened, telling Johnny that he, too, was tightening his muscles to keep his belly from heaving. Sometimes Johnny's hand would steal out to open a window; but after what the new minister had said, he was afraid that a draught of air might bring death to Tom; and he prayed that the lack of it wouldn't bring death to him. Would they never reach the damned hospital? He bent over towards Georgie, and whispered, Where 'r' we now? But Georgie's mouth stayed tight, and his hands stayed clenched. Johnny, gasping, could imagine how the slaves felt, packed below-deck in the slave-ship; or how the poor sinner felt on his first arrival in hell; mistily seeing that Middleton had wrenched his shirt collar open, and that his hair was wet and lank and lustreless; while Johnny bent himself as far as he could go to press his belly into a smaller space, and keep himself from puking. But the end came at last when they reached the hospital, the driver jumping down, running over to the big door, and ringing the deep bell.

—Go on, get out, quick, man, and bring them here with a stretcher, cried Georgie frantically, till we loose ourselves from this terrible burden!

Johnny climbed out, shutting the door behind him; but his stomach turned over, and running to the far side of the cab, he had to let himself be sick, scraping it with his foot, like a cat, in a vain effort to hide it a little, feeling a sharp shame, and wiping his slavered mouth in the sleeve of his coat as he hurried in to tell the porter all the details about his brother.

Two men came with a stretcher, pulled Tom from the cab, and carried him into the hospital, away down a long dark corridor; while Johnny sat down on a bench, pale and shaking, fearing every second that he was about to be sick again. After some time, Georgie Middleton came over and stood beside him.

—I have th' blankets an' sheets safe in th' cab, he said; I can do nothin' more here, so I'm goin'. Have you got your tram fare home?

—No, said Johnny, I haven't a make.

—I've only got th' six shillings Mr Fletcher gave me for the fare; and I daren't break in on that; and a solitary wing. Here, he said, after a pause, stretching out a penny towards Johnny, take it – it'll take you halfway home anyway.

—I don't want your wing, said Johnny proudly.

—Oh, aw right, he answered awkwardly. I hope the poor brother'll be awright, soon, Jack, he added; goodbye, old chap; and he left Johnny to his thoughts.

He sat there for a long time trying to think of something out of Milton, or Shakespeare, or Burns, to keep his mind off his uneasy stomach, till a smart young white-coated man with keen eyes came into the hall, looked around, and came over to where Johnny was sitting.

—You're the representative of Thomas Casside? Oh, you are. Why, in the name of God, didn't you bring your brother sooner?

—We thought the hospital couldn't find room for him, answered Johnny.

—Always the same, murmured the doctor testily; couldn't this and couldn't that – always an excuse. Did you try? he asked sharply.

—We thought it would be no use tryin', said Johnny.

—You thought! Oh, of course you did! What have you people got to do with thinking? Do you know your brother's dying?

Curious how they always blame us, thought Johnny resentfully. Had we kept him a little longer to die, there'd have been nothing about it. He would have died silently; would have been buried silently; and, bar a few tears from his mother, he would have been silently forgotten.

—We guessed he was dying, said Johnny out loud.

—Oh, you did, did you? Why did you bring him here, then?

—Our new minister made us.

—He did, did he? And you jumped at the chance to get rid of a nuisance, eh? And you expect us to cure him, eh? Well, you have great expectations! You fetch him here when his lungs are nothing but a crackling bunch of bloodied crêpe, and you expect us to cure him!

—We don't expect anything! cried Johnny hotly. Yous won't even let us die quiet. The new minister rushed in on us, ordered everything, did everything! Give us enough to pay for a cab back, an' I'll bring him home again! And Johnny lepped from the bench, flushed and stormy, to stare angrily at the astonished doctor.

—There, there, boy, said the doctor, drawing in his horns a little. I daresay it can't be helped. You've given us a hard job without the ghost of a chance to do any good. Who minded him?

—His mother.

—Well, she kept his body quite clean, and made him decent to handle, anyway.

—Give us the cab fare, repeated Johnny doggedly, and I'll carry him home again.

—Oh, sit down, sit down, and don't get your rag out. Stay there till you hear the worst; or, if a miracle happens, till you're told you may go home. And he went away humming, I Hear You Calling Me.

Johnny sat down, with head bent, on the bench, trying to think of things that had happened to him long, long ago, seeing them in fleeting and patchy colours, of a red-and-black draughtboard tartan petticoat he had worn at five years of age, making him look like a kid of the Rob Roy Macgregor clan; of when he, Ella, Archie, and Mick were down with the scarlet fever at the one time; and of how their mother had safely nursed them through it all by herself; even making Tom lie with Mick, who had it the worst, so that he might get it too, and so enable her to get the damned thing over once for all; and of the terrible time they had had, when they were well, standing in the street, watching the men disinfect the little house, sealing up doors and windows, and lighting sulphur in the rooms, so that the place stank for months afterwards – but he mustn't be thinking of sickness; and of handling almost the first Lee-Metford rifle the English Army had, brought home for show by his brother-in-law because he was a first-class shot; and of watching him put in the clip of cartridges, and ejecting the bullet from the chamber by drawing the bolt; and seeing him fix the dagger-like bayonet on the muzzle of the new gun.

A middle-aged man, with a merry grin on his bearded face, came out of the corridor into the hall. He nodded pleasantly to Johnny, and kept brushing his jerry hat vigorously with the sleeve of his coat. Presently he came close to Johnny, sent a swift look down the corridors, bent down low to whisper.

—Yeh, phih, he whispered in a whistling way, there's more duffers nor doctors here. He opened his mouth, wide as it could go, in front of Johnny's face, and closed it again. See? A dark spot at the butt o' th' tongue. Want to make out it's cancer. I know different, see? Kep' me in till now to see a specialist. Wastin' me time. I'm afraid it is, says he. Pah! He bent down closer to Johnny's ear and whispered, when I was younger, I was too free with the ladies – that's what it is. But I'm not here to teach them; let them find out for themselves; and he went towards the door. Cancer, me neck! he exploded as he disappeared.

Good God! there was the gong-like clock striking eleven. How long were they going to keep him here?

He half closed his eyes, and again thought back through the years, remembering how often he'd gone along the dusty, weary road to the Pigeon House Fort, passing in through the gateway and through the courtyard, glancing at the old guns sticking their snouts through older portholes, like aged fools thinking themselves for ever young; of picking cockles on the brown strand; of lying on the silvery dunes, in the sun, careful of the speary grass that grew there, sharp as surgeons' knives; or of walking along the breakwater, mighty with well-laid, wide, and deep granite blocks, dark-brown nets spread all over it to dry, velvety emerald-green seaweed tangled in their meshes, like locks from the hair of a mermaid raped off in the bed of the sea; or, when the day danced swift with the wind and the tide came ahead in a hurry, sending shouting waves over the side, their tops breaking out into silver, shaking salty showers over his head, like a sharp, laughing chrism from God.

He shivered; he was getting cold, sitting here so long. He'd think of something warmer than the spray of the sea; or of going to Beggars Bush Barracks to see his brother-in-law at Christmas time, and sitting in a big room, before a roaring fire, on a cold wet night, waiting for the Cloak Call to go so that his brother could leave, wearing his heavy coat; watching the men confined to barracks decorating the room; hanging dark-brown and grey blankets on the walls, fixing squares and ovals of silvered cardboard on them; and, here and there, splashing these squares and ovals of silver with lovely Merry Christmases and Happy New Years in holly berries threaded together, and cunningly fixed to the cardboard with pins. Other soldiers were making paper chains of divers patterns and many colours to cross and re-cross the room just under the ceiling; most of them radiating from a huge golden star in the centre, which was flanked by a smaller silver one at each corner of the room. From the ceiling, too, hung hundreds of thin threads, barely visible, carrying little tufts of the whitest wool, thousands and thousands of them, making it look for all the world as if it was snowing thick and fast; Johnny's brother-in-law standing restlessly at the door, waiting for the bugle-call, while Johnny was eager to stay and tire his eyes out with long and lasting looks at the beautiful things around him.

Then through the babble of the working soldiers came the sudden sound of the bugle-call, Benson's quick, last pull at his coat to make sure the folds were right, his impatient, Come on, me laddo, and the passing away from the glowing fire, the blood-red berries, the rustle of the gaily-coloured chains, the golden star and the silver, out into the wide, cold, bleak square, with the rain falling steadily, passing the sentry, standing stiff, like a drab mummy, in his box, out through the gaping gate, hurrying away to where the tram stopped so as to be in time at the market, before the geese were gone.

Twelve! There's the gong-like clock striking the hour of twelve! The poor oul' wan must be worn out, waiting for news. Well, if Tom hadn't passed out by now, there should be some hope. It was wrong, really, to keep the poor old woman in suspense. They should be able to say, one way or the other. He felt himself falling, and pulled up with a jerk. Jasus! He was falling asleep. He forced his eyes open. The whole place was dim. They'd darkened the hospital for the night. A little dull red glow starred the darkness at the end of each corridor; and a pale dusky jet in the hall barely gave him enough light to make out the walls. He hoped he wasn't going to be kept there till the dawn of day. A new day was here already. Night's candles are burnt out, and jocund day stands tiptoe on the misty mountain-tops. It would hardly be a jocund day for him. What's this the next line was? How the hell did it go? Oh, no use of trying to think out Shakespeare here. Where pain was host, there was no room for poethry.

Strange how the glimmer of little things reminded you of bigger things hid in the heavily-veiled mystery of the past! The tiny pale-blue glimmer dodging the deeper darkness of the hall reminded him of poor little Finnigan's wake, and all that went before it. How a group of them were playing madly on a slope bordering the canal, and Finnigan running down it, couldn't stop, and when he came to the canal's edge, took a frightened lep that landed him with a horrible splash into the middle of it! He could still see the pale bewildered agony of the boy's face, his arms wildly threshing the water, making it foam around; and the ripples circling over it when the little head sank down again, to be threshed into a wild agitation when the head broke through to the surface for the second time. He saw again one frantic boy madly pulling up some bulrushes growing by the side, and throwing them out to the drowning lad, thinking they might be of some use to him, unmindful of his bleeding hands where the fine edges of the bulrushes tore through his flesh. He had shouted to a group of men playing cards in a field nearby, and Mick had come racing along, throwing off his hat and coat, and tearing off a collar and tie as he ran, never pausing, but jumping up from the edge and coming down in a dive with the skill of a kingfisher, right in the centre of the rippling centre where Finnigan had gone down for the last time. He saw the boy again when Mick had ferried him out, standing, bent double, on the bank, water cascading from his wide-open, gasping mouth, his legs shaking, his teeth chattering, his eyes staring, a torrent of sobs tormenting his breast, and he spluttering out that he daren't go home; that they'd morgue him for fallin' in, an' he'd stay where he was till his clothes dhried, so that no one would be th' wiser when he got home.

So all day, there he sat shivering, his friends sitting in a circle round him to hide his nakedness; and when his friends left him in the evening, he still sat on, waiting for a later hour to go home, and slip to bed without anyone knowing what had happened to him; sat there when the stars were out, with a damp shirt on him, and the rest of his clothes hanging from the arm of a lock; sat there shivering, with all the lonely company of night around him.

Some time after, Finnigan fell ill, and was dead in no time; and Johnny went to see him; going into the little room where he lay cosy in his coffin, its deep yellow sides richly polished, the brass handles, wherever the glow from the tall wax candles crept to them, gleaming like genuine gold.

—Come closer, alanna, said Finnigan's mother, an' see how little he's changed. Come closer, for he was fond of you; and it was your own brave brother saved his life.

The smell of the room, a blend of whiskey, tea, the polish on the coffin, and the wax of the virgin candles, filled his nostrils as he came closer to see the face of his young friend changing, slowly changing, to the silent, steady face, the face of his brother, his brother Tom; and as he was stirred with amazement, he thought he heard a sombre voice saying sharply, Get up, who are you, and what are you doing here? This isn't a night shelter for the homeless.

Dimly he saw a young-looking nurse staring down at him, her hand on his shoulder, shaking him.

—What do you do here? she asked. There, the clock is striking two!

—Waiting to hear about my brother, miss. He was brought here as a patient, and I was ordered to wait for fear he'd die.

—Well, she said, you can't wait any longer. They have forgotten all about you. It was stupid of you to wait so long. Here, hurry off, and get to bed.

—He may be dead, nurse, so I'd betther make certain before I go. By waiting so long, I've earned that little privilege.

—What's his name; what's the patient's name? she asked impatiently.

—Casside, Thomas Casside, nurse.

She hastened down the dark corridor, leaving him on his feet, swaying a little, his legs cramped and cold, his eyes heavy with sleep, in the dusky hall of the hospital. After a long, long time she came hurrying back.

—The patient is still the same, she said rapidly. Dangerously ill; but still the same. She drew back a heavy bolt, swung the door open; and he passed out to wander sleepily through the empty streets, with the forlorn message soaking his mind in uneasiness.

When he got home, he found his mother sitting by the fire, humming a tune; the kettle humming another on the hob. He sat down on a chair, and stretched out his cold, damp, stiff hands to the fire.

—They made me wait, he said, to see if he would die. He's holding out yet.

—I know, she said. You shouldn't have waited so long. Hours ago, an easy peace came on me, and I knew he wouldn't die. You take this cup of tea, now, and don't worry.

WORK WHILE IT IS NOT YET DAY

A LETTER from the new minister had got Johnny a job as vanboy in the great wholesale firm of Jason & Son, wholesale newspaper, magazine, stationery, fancy goods, books, and hymnbook merchants, that gave employment to hundreds. This was his first morning at his new work. He was to begin at a quarter to four, an' finish God knew when.

The alarm clock, lying on its face, gave a muffled r-r-ring, as if it was getting a cold, and his mother's voice called out, Johnny, it's three; there, it's ringing for you to get up.

Silently he got up and dressed himself quick by candlelight, for it was very cold. It had snowed heavily all the day before, and it was freezing now. Rapidly he slipped on his trousers, socks, boots, collar and tie, waistcoat and coat, and, finally, a muffler his mother had bought to keep his throat and chest warm. He'd have to get a good topcoat, if the job lasted. He slipped Part One of O'Growney's *Simple Lessons in Irish* into his breast pocket, hoping to get an odd squint at it in some quiet corner while he worked. The tram conductor he had heard singing about Wolfe Tone, the night of the illuminations, had given it to him during a theatrical night in the stable of Hill Street, saying, I couldn't make anything out of it; but you're young, and everyone should know the language of his country; ending be him singing with his head up, lookin' at th' sky, and Johnny's hand clasped in his, all because Johnny was a Protestant,

> *English deceit can rule us no more,*
> *Bigots and knaves are scattered like spray –*
> *Deep was the oath the Orangeman swore,*
> *Orange and Green must carry the day!*
> *Orange, Orange,*
> *Green an' Orange!*
> *Never to falter an' never bethray –*
> *With an amen, we swear it again,*
> *Orange an' Green will carry the day!*

Johnny hunched himself together when he opened the street door, and stepped out into the lonely loveliness of the snowy-shy streets, bitterly gay in the throngs of frosty gems that had blossomed on the bosom of the snow. Each window-pane passed had within its narrow boundaries a silvery city with a host of delicate pinnacles, a wilderness of fragile ferns, or an interlaced forest of fairy trees. The houses looked like stout and steady dames, clad in jet-black velvet, with ample snowy wimples draped on their sturdy heads, and pools of gaslight gave a dusky yellow glow to some, like old gold bows fastened on them to set them off, and show there was a touch of gaiety in them still; while overhead hung a deep and densely purple-black sky shaking out fire from a swarm of glittering stars, as if God were shaking out the golden crumbs from the richly-woven cloth covering His holy table.

A poor boy walking in a silver way, canopied by velvet, purple-black, and dizzily pendent with a weight of jewels that dared the wondering eye.

As he walked along, crushing the frosty gems beneath his feet, he thought of the Irish lessons he was learning: Atá bó in san gurth, there is a cow in the field; agus atá si bán, And she is white. Quite easy, really, when you get goin'. Seán was his name in Irish; his right name, and not John at all. Atá Seán óg agus laidir, agus atá sé fuar. Sean is young and strong, and he is cold – that's thrue, anyway. I wondher what the new minister would say, if he caught him speaking Irish? A Fenian, he'd say, a Fenian! Ignorance, pure ignorance, laughed Johnny; a man speaking Irish can be as loyal to Queen and country as anyone else. A decent minister, though, that had made a great conquest of Johnny. He had won Johnny back to the faith of his baptism; to become once more Christ's faithful soldier and servant. He was sanctifying his kinship with God through the Sacraments, through public worship, through prayer, and through the Scriptures. God would help him, and make this new job he had a stay to the home, now that Tom was idle, having been dismissed because of a strike; and Archie was away on a tour with a *Saved From the Sea* company on one-night stands in the smaller towns of the west and south.

Under the guidance of Harry Fletcher, he had passed through the rite of Confirmation; his head had been touched by the hand of a bishop in the Church of the Twelve Apostles; he had renewed his baptismal vows openly; had helped in the singing of *Veni Creator Spiritus*; and he had received a fuller grace from the Holy Ghost. The day had been a lovely sunny one, in early spring. The hedges and gardens of Clontarf were full of life; the birds were all excitement; the leaves of the trees kept up a whispering chatter with a gentle breeze that ran in and out among them, as Johnny and his companion, Nicholas Stitt, trudged to the church. He passed curly-headed Jenny Clitheroe, quite a young woman now, walking with several companions to the church too. He raised his cap timidly as he passed, and glanced shyly at her; but she closed her eyes, and gave a little disdainful toss to her head. A lady-girl cashier in Sir John Arnott's select drapery house, he was too poor for a nod from her, as she went her way to church, in her green dress, with the walk of a queen.

The church was packed with people, and the organ was singing soft music when they were guided to their seat by the tall, kind, and handsome Harry Fletcher, looking fine in his short white surplice and long, heavy black cassock sweeping gravely round his silken-slippered feet. The girls sat in rows on one side of the nave, becomingly dressed in blue, black, or dark green, with lacy veils on their heads, flowing over their shoulders and down their backs. The boys sat on the other side, trying to look solemn, unconcerned, or confident, all in their best, with tidied hair, white collars, and sternly-polished boots.

From the big east window ahead of him, there were the twelve apostles, baked in brightly-coloured glass, looking down on them, carnivalled in bellalluring robes of blue, yellow, red, green, black, brown, purple, orange, Hebrew umber, Chinese white, and Hindoo crimson, glowing like titian tulips in a Persian garden. The sunlight, now, came strolling through them, their eager faces shone with a thousand tints, their coloured cloaks rippled as if blown by a gentle breeze from heaven, their limbs quivered as if they were about to step forward in a sparkling procession over the heads of the congregation. Rays, like tongues of fire, from their coloured cloaks, flooded and swept away the demure modesty of the lacy girlish caps, joyously changing the sober little ladies into radiant lassies, waiting for the gong to go to dance. But the apostles came not forth, dallying till the sun suddenly slackened; then the sparkling hues faded, and they became again figments of coloured glass, jailed in a leaded window, gorgeous only when the sun was bright with a brotherly interest.

Then they began to go up in pairs, kneeling together at the altar rails to let the bishop lay a hand on each head, and dedicate them anew to God's service. When Johnny knelt there, and felt the soft, white, plump hand of the bishop, peering out from gently-scented lawn that had never smelled from the evil smear of a bed bug, he knew that he had got his first great share in the priesthood and kingship of Christ.

There was the dark form of Nelson looming up before him, now, thrusting his haughty head into the purple sky, looming like a rod of discipline over the people, out of the dark, in Dublin, Ireland's sailor boy, one arm missing and one eye gone; but watching with that one eye the slum kid rolling in the mud; the lady or gentleman rolling round in carriage and pair; the red-slippered bishop in flaunting canonicals on his way to say High Mass in his cathedral; the bobby bringing a drunk safe home to the police station; the bloated, blossom-faced whores waiting for randy men to go with them to the stews to see the sights: high he stands there, while Wolfe Tone's first memorial stone lies deep

buried at the head of Grafton Street. And as Johnny goes by,
he seems to sink as he sank down on the deck of the *Victory*,
saying, Kiss me, Hardy, kiss me quick, me spine is spearsed;
remember Emma, pip, pip, hurrah!

Johnny was soon beside the long outspread pile of Jason's
wholesale department, with its rusty red-brown front, grated
heavily on the side walk to admit the heavy bales of goods; and,
sliding up, he mixed himself with about thirty lads and men,
leaning sleepily against the front of the warehouse, waiting for the
time to come to begin. The stars had gone now; the sky had lost
its tinge of purple, having turned into a heavy sludge of thick
darkness, and broad and wavering flakes of snow were falling fast.

—Who's th' boss here? he asked of a short man with brown
bulgy eyes, now half closed, his head nodding as he leaned against
the wall.

—Show-a-leg, he answered drowsily.

—Show-a-leg? Why's he called that?

—You'll see when you see him, he answered.

Presently, Johnny saw them push themselves away from the
wall, and turn shivery faces towards the wide door. Out of the
soaking darkness came a fat squat figure, hidden in a long thick
coat, side by side with a smaller squat one, both moving in a
rolling waddle to the door. The bigger figure put a big key into
the keyhole, whistling lightly as he did so, swung the double doors
back, and led the troop of sleepy men and boys, coughing the
damp cold out of their lungs, into a vast cavern of inner darkness
that pressed heavily down on Johnny's heart.

—Anyone's got a match, light the lights, said a thin hoarse
voice that came from the dumpy figure, an' th' rest o' you stand
by to take th' papers.

Johnny heard the scrunching of nailed boots on wood, the
striking of matches; then several feebly flaming gas-jets crept out
of the gloom, showing in the dimness a vast room traversed with
many wide coarse benches. In the centre, high over the benches,
ran a glass-panelled roomy corridor, reached by stairs that were
first cousin to a ladder. Here, later in the day, the real boss had his
perch, with his clerks sitting in two rows, back to back, looking
down through the windows on their more hard-working brothers
in the vast and worried room below.

In the shadowy dimness Johnny saw the squat figures, as in a
glass darkly, taking off their topcoats; but when they had waddled
into a timid pool of yellow gaslight, he saw that the bigger one

was short and stout, with a head as big as the globe of the world
in a first-class school, and as beautifully bald, set on a neck that
was no neck at all; he had tiny eyes that glittered like smoky
sparks, and were half hidden by beetling brows, as if over each a
portcullis was about to drop and close both of them up for ever;
but most remarkable of all were the thick legs curving out from
the hips in such a bandy way that, when his two clumsy feet
met below, his legs formed a perfect circle, as good as any correct
compass could draw. When he walked, he seemed to be a huge,
badly-made ball rolling along over uneven ground. These circular
legs leered horribly whenever they wobbled into a pool of light,
for they were enshrined in a pair of highly-polished black leg-
gings reaching to his crooked knees. The smaller figure of his son
showed himself a thinner copy of the fat father, the big head, the
smoky glitter of the eyes, the bitter brows, the splendidly circular
legs, covered in knickerbockers and thin black cotton stockings.
Both of them perpetually wore conceited grins, ever putting a
jaunty air into their waddling, evidently finding a lot wrong with
the straighter legs, normal heads, and natural necks of most other
men.

A van drove up with a cargo of *Irish Times*, followed by others
filled with *Irish Independents* and *Freemans' Journals*, men and
boys hurrying out, and coming back staggering under loads of
papers on their shoulders, and dumping them on the various
benches. Here other men, holding invoices in their hands, called
out rapidly the papers required by country agents; others counted
out the papers with great speed from the heaps on the benches,
throwing them on brown paper wrappings to be snatched up by
others, and parcelled up for the vans to take them to the several
railway stations. It was hurry here and hurry there, carrying,
dumping down, calling out, selecting, wrapping up, tying, pasting
of labels, and flinging the finished parcels of papers into their
different bins; and in the midst of the stress waddled Show-a-leg
and his son, both of them looking like what you'd surely sometimes see prowling about in the dim time of life, among the swishy
reeds, the tangled ferns, and the seamy shade of slimy mosses.

The twisted father and the twisted son put a gayer stir into their
movements than any of the others, working with a sinisterly
merry energy that wasn't merry at all; aimed at showing that
such an early hour should have no terrors for manly men;
seeming to make of the dismal gaslight, full of hiding shadows,
a port of call for sunny places, dancing girls, and the perfume of

many blossoms. Many of the sleepy ones stiffened up straight, slyly borrowing some of Show-a-leg's twisted gaiety, coaxing quickness into their tired bodies; the *miserere meuses* trying to look like kids galloping about for the first time on the golden sands of the seashore; while outside in the darkness the snow fell swiftly in ribbonlike streamers, looking from where they worked like white painted bars stretching across the prison-faced entrance to the warehouse.

Johnny was quietly shoved about so's he'd look ridiculous before the twisted toads. Parcels to be made up were snatched away just as he stretched out a hand to get them; the twine was always in the hands of another when he wanted it; and the paste seemed a mile away when he had to fix a label. Grinning, they all watched Johnny testing his way to be one of them, with the bandy-legged one glowering at him curiously, giving a cue to the rest for a wider grin whenever he nodded his head doubtfully towards Johnny.

—Come along; look alive, boy; take the sleep outa your eyes; leering at Johnny's hesitation to push aside a hand snatching the twine, or a brush from the paste-pot. Pounce on it, pounce, boy, he roared, an' don't stand like a dead three on a lonely road! Is it a special bench you want with a staff to hand you out the work, or what? Here, gripping Johnny's arm, watch how it's done; see? Johnny watching the sagging, puffy cheeks, the tiny glittering eyes, wished for a red-hot iron to make jelly of them. Now, off you go – oh, you've missed that too! Here, you'd break my patience! Go out and carry in the newspapers, for I'm afraid you'll never be quicker nor an oul' aged coolie!

So midst the voices calling out ten *Independents*, twenty *Free-men*, five *Irish Times*, five *Freemen*, twenty *Independents*, ten *Times*, twenty *Times*, five *Independents*, ten *Freemen*; the crackling of brown paper as the papers were wrapped up in them; the swish of the brushes as the labels were pasted on; the scratching of tired feet over the rough boards; the thud of horses' hooves, timid of the frost under them; the inspiring hisss-hissss of Show-a-leg, as if he were currying a horse in a stable – Johnny joined the line of men and boys following each other, bearing burdens of news-papers on their shoulders, like blacks in a jungle so that the whole of distant Ireland might know the newest news.

—Here, said Show-a-leg, suddenly gripping his arm, there's our own vans, at last; load up your van for Kingsbridge, an' look smart. Get a barrow, get a barrow!

Johnny strolled over, struggling to walk with dignity, to a barrow by the side of the warehouse. He stooped down to pick up the pull of the four-wheeler, but a shove on the shoulder sent him to sit on the floor, tempting a loud titter out of the onlookers, and he heard a voice in his ear, saying, Away, wee mon; away to Hull! This is for the Northern – 'way ow'r thot!

Belfast bowsey, trying to please his boss, thought Johnny. He walked about for a bit, looking for another barrow; but they seemed to be all rattling about, some filled with parcels, taking them to the vans; some returning empty for another load. He came back to where the boss was busily loading a barrow.

—All the barrows are engaged, sir, he said.

—It's funny how I could get one, isn't it? Show-a-leg answered. Here, take this one I've filled for you, slow-worm.

He'd take things quietly, if only for the sake of the new minister. After all, they were all children of the same Heavenly Father. Johnny seized the pull-handle of the barrow, and dragged it vehemently out into the falling snow, and on to the frost-bitten pavement. Furiously, he flung parcels into the van till it could hold no more, even with a tarpaulin stretched over to keep them steady and tight.

—Up with you, now, said oul' bandy-legs, an' take your load to the station. Keep your eye on him, he added to the vanman, for God's sake, for he's so innocent he'd deliver the lot to the Mendicity Institution if he wasn't watched!

—I've got more'n enough to do to keep th' horse on his feet, grumbled the vanman, an' he with his legs ready to go every way at once on the icy roads.

They were off, going at a careful canter down the street, round on to the Northern quays, the driver sitting tense, the horse sweating with fear whenever his hooves slipped on the shining road. Several times he was nearly down, but some way or other the driver saved him, digging his teeth into his lower lip as he drove, and cursing the frost deeply when the horse was trotting safely again.

The snow had stopped falling; the black sky had brightened to a purple-bluish hue over their heads, and a silver road slid away under their feet. A darker line below them showed the river Liffey flowing slowly by, here and there a little brighter with dimly-shimmering patches of floating ice. Past the Four Courts, a big black building looking as if it budded out of the purple sky; or was stretching up to get the counsel of Heaven into its ass's ear;

the blinded figure of Justice looking out over the whory hills of
oul' Ireland; over the bridge, its icy covering sparkling in the
lights from the passing van, making it a straight turning into a
fairyland of snowy people living in ice-made houses; out quick
again into the goods yard of the Great Southern, pulling
up, with a loud whoa, before the wide gate of the parcels
office.

—I'll be glad when this cursed frost is over, said the vanman,
pacing about, stamping his feet, clapping his red and swollen
hands against his shoulders, while Johnny piled the parcels on
the counter to be checked; me mitts is frozen; as cold as a kiss
from a dead woman.

—You'd want gloves, murmured Johnny sympathetically.

—Where'd I get gloves on fourteen bob a week? queried the
vanman peevishly. Gloves! Tell me that, will yeh?

—I don't know, said Johnny.

—Yeh don't know, eh? Well, neither do I. D'ye expect a
man of fourteen shillin's a week to be rowled in rugs like Charlie
Jason? Kid ones, maybe, you'd like to see me sportin'. Well, I
haven't gone as low as that yet. Eh, he added, turning to the
checker, didya hear what he's afther saying – that I should be
wearin' gloves!

—Steel gauntlets up to the elbow, he'd like to see us wearin'
maybe, said the checker mockingly.

—Heavy leather, lined with the softest chamois, an' thrimmed
with fur 'ud give us freer movement, said the vanman.

—An' twenty tiny mother-o'-pearl buttons on the wrist, added
the checker.

—An' tassels near the thumbs, laughed the vanman.

—An' sturdy muffs to pack the glovely hands in when the cold
gets colder, said the checker.

—An' furry flounces round our necks as well, said the vanman,
to keep our diddies warm.

—Will the young prophet tell how we wor' to work for our
employers got up in a get-up like that? asked the checker, leaning
over his counter to get a closer look at Johnny. No, he went on,
going back to the sorting of the parcels, when it's cold, it's
cold; and the burden's there to be borne.

—An' th' Man Above is always there to the fore, murmured
the vanman.

—An' th' Man Above is always there to the fore, echoed the
checker.

—Here, up with you again, said the vanman to Johnny, and let's get back. Th' Man Above never meant any of us to be one of the gloved brigade.

Out they were again, trotting with decent haste between the rows of sable buildings, on the sparkling silver road, and under the purple sky. On a night something like this, thought Johnny, the King of All, the Giver of Life, the Prince of Peace was born. Under a slantin' roof He was, sheltered from the snowy ground an' warmed by the heat of the animals who danced all the livelong night with the dancin' stars; the bare trees, shovin' aside the terrifying frost, blossomed, and hung out fruits for one night only, strikin' all frost-hardened thravellers with wonder an' fear; crowds of wild flowers sprang up through the snow, an' bent their coloured faces towards where the little Infant lay; the frozen brooks snapped their icy coverings, brimful of song as they tarried or hurried in their flowing; and many there were who stood still to listen, for they wist not what had happened when they heard a brook breaking into song:

> The Lord of all life from His heaven has come,
> Sing out, sing loud, sing merry, sing long;
> Without note from a fife or a beat from a drum,
> Sing out, sing merry, sing all;
> The Lord of all life in His mercy has come
> To save merry man from his murdherous fall,
> Sing out, sing all!

> Th' winter-worn trees are all sprightly again,
> Sing out, sing loud, sing merry, sing long;
> Ripe apples hang there, with red cherries for men,
> Sing out, sing merry, sing all;
> Only death became lonely, and hurried off when
> Jesus came to save man from his murdherous fall,
> Sing out, sing all!

> The rolling stars reel about, drunken with glee,
> Sing out, sing loud, sing merry, sing long!
> The slow-moving cattle dance jigs on the lea,
> Sing out, sing merry, sing all!
> And panting birds, coming from rooftop and tree,
> Sing of man's rise from his murdherous fall,
> Sing out, sing all!

Kings of great multitudes come from afar,
Sing out, sing loud, sing merry, sing long;
With gifts of three kinds in a fresh golden car,
Sing out, sing merry, sing all;
And rich-scented spice in a diamond-clad jar,
For Him who saves man from his murdherous fall,
Sing out, sing all!

Sprinkle His home with green laurels and yew,
Sing out, sing loud, sing merry, sing long;
With red berries of holly and mistletoe too,
Sing out, sing merry, sing all;
For there's nothing now missing from me or from you,
Since He came to save man from his murdherous fall,
Sing out, sing all!

Play on the dulcimer, harp, and the horn,
Sing out, sing loud, sing merry, sing long;
Th' poor Devil's looking both haggard and lorn,
Sing out, sing merry, sing all;
For Jesus lies happy asleep in the corn,
The Saviour of man from his murdherous fall,
Sing out, sing all!

Bring out the ould fiddle and play Him a tune,
Sing out, sing loud, sing merry, sing long;
Cold December's at one with young hot-headed June,
Sing out, sing merry, sing all;
For th' curse of our birth has been chang'd to a boon,
Since He came to save man from his murdherous fall,
Sing out, sing all!

White linen we'll give to the Virgin so fair,
Sing out, sing loud, sing merry, sing long;
And a bonny bright comb for her radiant hair,
Sing out, sing merry, sing all;
For the Babe a red cross, with a rattle and ball,
To show how we're sav'd from our murdherous fall,
Sing out, sing all!

He brought the Kingdom of Heaven to the heart of man,
thought Johnny, an' —

Suddenly, his thoughts were scattered violently out of his head as he was jerked out of the van, and went sprawling on to the road, thrusting out his hands to save his head so that the palms tore over the frost-covered cobbles, scraping the skin in ragged patches from them, the frost biting into the bleeding flesh, making him feel a little sick as he lay still where he had fallen.

—Eh, get up an' lend us a hand, an' don't lie dhreamin' there! he heard the voice of the vanman shouting.

He dragged himself up from the thorny frost and saw the horse on the ground, entangled in the harness, with a shaft pressing into his belly, plunging about with fright in his eyes; while the vanman was struggling to force the horse down flat, keeping back from the frightened and frantic movements of the horse's head and feet.

—Come over, man, the vanman cried to Johnny, an' help me shove him over, so's I can sit on his head, an' keep him from breakin' a–yeh, yeh bitch's get! he roared at the horse, when the animal's plunging head knocked his shoulder, yeh nearly got me that time!

Johnny ran over, seized the struggling horse's head, daubing it with blood from his lacerated hands, and pushed with the vanman; but the power in the animal's neck was too strong, and he plunged about as wild as ever.

The first tram of the morning came jingling up and stopped beside them. The driver and conductor lepped off and came running over to help their brothers. The four of them pushed together, and the horse's head was slowly forced down flat on the frosty stones.

—Kneel on his head, now, said the vanman to Johnny, till we disjoin th' harness an' shove the van back; but for your life don't stir till I yell at you to jump clear.

Hurriedly and cleverly the three men unbuckled the harness, gently forced the van back till the shaft was clear of the horse's belly, then ran it swiftly to a safe distance. The vanman brought some sacks from the van and spread them out on the ground beside the animal, tucking in some of the edges under his hooves, so that when he tried to rise, his feet might get some kind of a grip on the icy stones. Then standing away, and holding the reins loosely, he shouted to Johnny to stand clear.

When the horse no longer felt Johnny sitting on him, he lifted his head, looked around, then rose, half sitting on his haunches, and with a sprawling, sliding movement, he jumped up, snorting, and stood shivering with fear and the cold, waiting to be put back into the van again. Then Johnny had time to see that the conductor was his old friend of the illuminations and the Irish Lesson Book.

—If y'ass me, said the driver, I'd say if I had Charlie Jason's money, I'd see me horse's hooves were well cocked before I'd let him thravel on an icy road like this.

—A stiff mornin' to be out undher the sky in, the conductor said, coming over, and shaking hands with Johnny. Betther times when we have our own again – Is sinn féin, sinn féin, he said. He bent down his head towards Johnny's ear. Good news about Fashoda, eh? The tricolour in the Soudan, eh? The French are on the say, they'll be here without delay, says the Sean Bhean bhocht – God deliver the good news quick, he added, turning an urgent face up to the dark sky. Goodbye, me son. And away the tram jingled towards the Gateway of the Phoenix Park, the conductor whistling the Marseillaise for all he was worth, and waving a hand to Johnny.

On his way home to breakfast, oul' Show-a-leg gave Johnny the job of pushing a handcart full of parcels to Amiens Street Station, for carriage to Belfast and intermediate places. Johnny swore deeply as he answered, Right y're, sir; but stopped short when he remembered his recent visit to Communion, feeling he'd broken the third commandment. From henceforth he must limit his communications to yea and nay, for more than these cometh of evil.

—Go on, push it, boy, he heard Show-a-leg shouting from the entrance; don't be afraid of it – push it along.

Johnny started it with a straining push through the snow, now lying seven or eight inches deep on path and roadway, going off with a prayer mumbling from his mouth that Show-a-leg might somehow escape from the worm that dieth not and the fire that couldn't be quenched.

It was hard going for him. The damp snow clung to his eyelids, forming a moist veil over them so that he could hardly see; besides, he often had to bend to give greater force to his push, making the soft snow slip so that his feet went from under him, jerking the parcels about in the road. Opposite the police station, in Store Street, he sat down on the shafts for a rest, taking out his little Irish book, bending carefully over it, so that the snow couldn't damage it, and tried to learn a few more words. Atá an sneachta a tuitim síos, he murmured, coining little sentences from what he saw around him. Agus deir Sé leis an tsneachta, bíse ar an dtalamh, is mar sin abhí sé: And he said of the snow, be on the ground, and it was so. When I earn enough in the week, I must join the Gaelic League.

He got up from the shafts, shivering a little, and pushed hard on to where he was going. When he came to the long, steep slope leading to the platform of the Great Northern, he began to pant, and had to bend double to make the handcart move. Slower and slower it went; more and more he panted, till the cart stopped altogether; and he sat down again on the shaft to get back his breath. Weak for want of his breakfast – that's what it was. Since three, and it was now past eight, without a bite wasn't good enough. Six hours of hard goin' and he was still waiting for a cup of tea. His torn hands troubled him, too, sticking to the shafts when he held them too tight. He'd go bail the two Jasons weren't far from a fire. Even in warm weather they'd come in on cars, deep in rugs, mummified in thick topcoats and comforters, looking, all the while, like silent, miserable, bundled-up complaints to God. Acting, too, as if they'd been born in Bethlehem; for he'd read in a paper that one of them had taken the chair at a revival meeting given by the great Gineral Booth, who thought when he was sousing people with words he was sprinkling them with the blood of Christ, Who, in honour of their distant salaam, had decorated them with a nice house, warm clothes to wear, and fair things to eat from a white table-cloth the first thing in the morning. Well, the way of the Salvation Army wasn't his way. He didn't like their rough-and-tumble tribute to God; their turgid rush to Heaven; their way of shouting into the ear of Jesus; their rowdy way of pulling Him about to make Him face their way; their raucous manner of praise, like a drunken man bawling his unsteady way home; their ponderous thought that the more miserable and rotten they were, the more God thought of them.

—Eh, sir, Johnny called to a passer-by, muffled up to the eyes, and carrying an open umbrella to keep off the snowflakes, could you give us a shove up to the top of the slope? A Pharisee, he thought, as the figure carrying an umbrella, and muffled up to the eyes, went on, turning neither to the right nor to the left.

Carriages and cars and cabs packed high with trunks, cases, and rugs passed by, bearing snugly-clad persons to catch the next train to the north.

—Eh, sir, said Johnny to another muffled-up figure slouching along on the snowy footpath, could you give us a hand to shove this up to the top of the slope?

The muffled figure turned towards him, a red nose rose out of the depths of a black muffler, looking like the beak of a bird poking over the edge of its nest, and a cold voice answered, You shouldn't take a job if you aren't fit to do the work the job entails; the nose sunk down again, the muffled figure turned aside and went on its way to the station.

Johnny seized the shafts again, pushing hard, pushing harder, pushing his hardest; but the cart never moved an inch ahead. He sat down again, holding up his hot face so that the cool snowflakes might fall on it and calm his temper. An outside car, now, came trotting down on its way back to the stand to wait for another fare. The driver was so muffled up that his thick scarf seemed to meet the rim of his jerry hat, making him look as if the horse and car were carrying off an empty, tied-up bundle of clothes. It stopped beside Johnny, and he heard a voice from between hat and scarf saying, Can yeh not get up?

—No, said Johnny, an' I don't know what to do. Out since three, and haven't had me breakfast yet.

The jarvey jumped down, swung his horse round to face the station, took some thick cord from under a cushion, and tied one end to the axle and the other to the tailboard of Johnny's cart.

—Keep a tight grip of your shafts, he said, an' we'll be where you're goin' in a second. He sprang on to his seat again, and away went the horse at a quick trot, making Johnny's arms crack with the effort he had to make to keep a firm grip on the shafts of the handcart that went ploughing through the snow. When they were safely under the huge roof of the station, Johnny untied the cord, and put it back under the car cushion.

—Thank you, he said fervently; you were a good Samaritan to me today. Then he saw that the jarvey was the same from whom they had taken the car in the mad drive from the Cat 'n Cage. He saw the jarvey looking at him curiously when he was replacing the cord under the cushion.

—Haven't I seen your gob somewhere before? he asked good-humouredly, rubbing his hands briskly.

—Did you? asked Johnny dubiously. Oh, I don't think so, unless you saw me passing by some day in the street.

—No, not just in the street, said the jarvey musingly; somewhere more important. Doesn't matther, anyway, he added. An' now, one good turn deserves another – a mulled pint 'ud go down well on a day like this.

Had he had anything, Johnny would have given it to him; but he hadn't a red. It was a bitter moment for Johnny. He'd have given a lot to have been able to give a little.

—I'm sorry, he said, but this's my first week afther being idle, I don't know how long; and I haven't had any pay yet.

—Ara, g'on ower that, said the jarvey, grinning, you've got a juice left, surely – deep down in th' oul' pocket, wha'?

—Honest to God – not as much as a make!

The jarvey's face crinkled into a rippling frown as he watched Johnny bending over the cart, pretending to be examining the parcels.

—An' was it for this th' poor oul' animal pulled a caravan o' parcels up a steep an' icy hill? he asked hotly. Is that the kinda reception she gets for doin' you a wide an' weighty kindness? D'ye think just because th' poor animal isn't a Christian, you can make her what return you like for gettin' you out of a hole? C'm on; let's have the juice, an' be done with it!

—I tell you, said Johnny, red and uncomfortable, I haven't got it to give.

—Y'aven't got it to give! echoed the jarvey. I mighta known I was right, for you oul' gob shows well th' kind y'are! He wrapped the rug angrily round his legs and gathered the reins into his hand. Well, he added, giving the mare a vicious cut of the whip that made her jump, if I was that mean, I'd let the world alone, and the mare, the car, and the jarvey tore down the sloping drive at a furious trot.

Johnny packed the parcels into the van of the outgoing train, mad with his mother that he hadn't had enough to silence the jarvey's tongue. The snow still fell; the dawn couldn't stir from behind a dark and broody sky; all the sparkle of the frost had been hidden by the new snow; the purple glow had gone when Johnny, having packed the cart in a corner, went home to get his breakfast.

THE CAP IN THE COUNTING-HOUSE

HE WAS back in the dimly-dead warehouse again. He had been too tired and wet and cold to eat much, so he'd nibbled the bread and swallowed down a cup of tea. While he ate, his mother ran out and came back with a penny box of boracic ointment, anointing his rasped and aching hands with it as he sat by the fire. Every damned joint in his body ached. He had bathed his smarting eyes in hot water, while his mother, kneeling down beside him, tied some sheets of brown paper round his legs so as to keep his wet trousers from touching his skin. Then she took a clean sugar-sack from her bed, made two holes in one end of it, fixed the sack round his shoulders, passed some twine through the holes, tying the ends together so that his back and shoulders should be protected from the falling snow.

—You didn't eat much breakfast, she had said, anxiously.

—I'm too tired to eat, he had answered.

—You look it, she had answered, with a slight sigh. If the job's goin' to hurt you like this, you'd betther give it up – we'll manage somehow.

She looked out of the window, watching the snow coming down softly, so softly, like a week-old mother crooning to her week-old baby; so gently, and yet making work harder than it ought to be. You want a topcoat badly, she had said, turning to Johnny again, when he was about to go; don't try to rush; take everything quietly and with caution; and if, in the end, it proves too much for you, we'll have to look out for something else. Jason's isn't the only place God made.

Here he was back in the dim dead-house again, parcelling papers and magazines; pasting labels; tying string endlessly; in the midst of floating dust, dim light, the passing to and fro of heavy, tired, dragging footsteps, and the murmur of voices saying nothing. The smell of snowy slush, mixed with the smell of damp leather, filled his nostrils, while the steam from human breath formed a heavy haze round the jaded light that the gas gave. Dusky figures, like sagging designs formed by apprentice potters, moved about, topped by motionless faces, moving in the web of gloom, slandering life in silence; while overhead the shadowy clerks crouched in the glassy boxes, like dingy crabs in a dusty aquarium. And all this dead movement and dying murmur went

on in the breathy mist and dusky glimmer, before the fluttering
white curtains of the falling snow, filling the wide entrance with
its lacy flickering strands, dodging here and there, as if in play
with each other, but ever, at last, falling to weave a thicker
covering for the footway and the road.

A musical voice, a dark tenor, is calling out in the mist now,
calling the papers to be placed together to form a parcel for some
country newsagent; it is a gentle voice, but, here and there, a
firmer tone dances into the pattern of the gentle sound. Whose
was it? Johnny, lifting his head to see, moves his glance through
the mist to find the owner of the voice so musically calling out the
sordid names of *Ally Sloper*, *Answers*, *Titbits*, *Pearson's Weekly*,
Sunday Companion, *Scraps*, *Weekly Budget* and *Forget-me-not*.
Nearer now, he sees a tall, slender young man standing beside a
bench, with a wheen of orders in his hand, reading out the names
of the papers written on them. He had a pale face, very gentle,
very handsome, with firm lines round the delicately-formed
mouth. He is gently but strongly built, with the signs of speed
and energy in his taut and upright shoulders and straight back.
He wore a blue suit, and his white neck was encircled by an
unassuming but very neat collar and blue tie. In the lapel of the
coat he wore a button badge, having on it a Celtic cross with the
words The Gaelic League over it, and Country and Tongue
beneath in the Irish language.

—God save you, said Johnny to him in Irish.

A pair of soft luminous eyes looked at him for a moment
wonderingly, then the gently-firm voice responded with God and
Mary save you, my friend.

—I see you go with the Gaelic League, Johnny said, indicating
the button in the other's coat.

—A Gael I am, he answered, without shame to myself or threat
to you.

Johnny hesitated; he saw that the fellow before him had more
Irish than he; he himself knew some, but couldn't put it together
readily; hardly enough for fair and ready speech, yet; but it was
thrilling to be talking in a language others there couldn't understand.

—What's your name? he asked; mine's O'Casside, Sean
O'Casside, a Gael too; born in Dublin, and proud of it.

—Mine's Sean O'Connolly, he answered back; and it matters
not if Belfast, Cork, or Dublin be an Irishman's place of birth.

The darkness outside faded suddenly into sunlight; the snow

fell timidly, and the few flakes dodged from side to side, as if to escape capture and injury from the sunny beams darting down to caress the shivering street flooding the entrance of the warehouse with a golden curtain, the twisting flakes of snow looking like shimmering jewels caught dancing in its golden mesh, giving the warehouse prison a golden door; chasing the cold and dreamy snow into a glittering restlessness like a Quaker virgin, warm with sunny wine, blending a deep meditation with a sprightly dance.

—Do you believe, asked Johnny, that Ireland ought to be free, and that the English are our enemies?

—I believe it, indeed, he answered.

—An' so do I! exclaimed Johnny heatedly. Is sinn féin sinn féin, he went on, echoing the tram conductor. He took Sean O'Connolly's hand, and shook it warmly, I'm one with you, he said; Ireland must be free, and the English Garrison must go!

The slim and firm youth leant over towards him and recited with quiet fierceness,

> *Peannaidh is fiabhras dian i dteas na dteinteadh,*
> *Gan charaid, gan liaigh, gan biadh, gan stad ar íota,*
> *Gan leabaidh, gan rian, gan Dia, gan gean ag daoinibh,*
> *Ar Gallaibh i mbliadhna, o's iad do chreach ar muinntear.'*

Johnny felt a curious and tingling admiration for this handsome young lad who spoke Irish so calmly and well; firmly, too, and with a faint note of defiance in its sounding. Johnny knew that every Gaelic Leaguer was up against the venomous opposition of England's Government, and up against even the scorn of not a few of their own countrymen. Indeed, while they were speaking, titters were heard round about them; and while Connolly remained cool, as if he heard them not, Johnny's face reddened and he yearned to strike away the mocking curves from the mouths of the gigglers.

Happening to glance upwards, he saw the head of Fitzgerald, the boss, sticking out of a little watch-window in the glasshouse. He was craning his neck, and peering downwards to see who were wasting their time talking; Johnny saw, too, in the misty gloom, slow movements of pale faces looking up, while they tried to brighten their dim energy with quicker movements to show the boss that all was well with them.

Then the voice of Fitzgerald spoke from the upper house, and Johnny heard a voice from heaven saying Casside, Casside, no wasting of the Firm's time. Go down to the basement, and get the covers ready for tomorrow morning's dispatch; and Johnny saw that the entranceway was a golden net no longer. The sunlight had crept quick from the cold street; the darkness came down swift from the sky; and the falling snow dropped into a level, steady quietness again.

A young fellow for a Fenian, thought Johnny, wandering from the murky warehouse to go down to the deeper cellars, there to sort out thousands of covers for tomorrow's labour; to paste thousands of labels on these covers, so many to an hour, as he who came before him had done; or get sour looks and hot words from the frock-coated demon in the glasshouse, busy seeing that the lesser divils didn't lose a second getting out the literature of hell: wrappers for the dailies here; wrappers for the weeklies there; and wrappers for the monthlies over yonder; slashing a broad blue mark on each that properly contained the list of papers required and their number, safely pinned to a corner of the wrapper; setting aside in a special place any wrapper in which the list was missing. Ay, a young fellow for a Fenian; young and handsome; young and firm; young and kindly; young, and maybe dangerous, for, like Robespierre, he believes everything he says.

—Fine fellow, that Connolly, he said to a big-footed man tying parcels at a bench, as he was passing to where he was to start his own work. What is he?

—Dispatch clerk, said flatfoot shortly.

—Ardent Gaelic Leaguer, too, went on Johnny; are you one?

—Me? asked flatfoot, with surprise in his voice; is it me you mean?

—Yes, you, confirmed Johnny.

—I have me work to do, was the answer.

Over the paste-pot a lanky-faced lad was dipping a brush, and Johnny, poising his own for a moment, said, Fine young fellow, that Connolly chap – he who speaks the Irish.

—Does he? asked lanky-face; never heard him.

—Ay, does he, said Johnny; and well, too. I have a little myself. I wish I had more. Don't you?

—Move a little away, murmured lanky-face; move away, man; there's always someone watchin'.

—Yes, but wouldn't you? persisted Johnny.

—No, I wouldn't, he snarled. Maybe it's Irish we want! A full pot an' the fire to boil it is what I want.

—But, insisted Johnny, a full pot and a fire to boil it isn't the be-all and end-all of life.

—It is to me with a wife an' three kids, an' fifteen shillin's a week, an' a house in Merrion Square to keep goin'. And he moved away from where Johnny was standing.

When he had been working away for an hour or so, and was bent over the rustling wrappers, Johnny saw a dirty hand slide into the blue-purplish patch of light tingeing the bench from the tiny gas-jet over his head, and a leaflet fluttered down before his face. He read it as it lay there before him:

Come And Be Born Again!
Grand Gospel Meeting in the Christian Union Buildings
Tomorrow Night at Eight.
Adjutant Thrimble of the Belfast Brigade of the Salva-
tion Army will Give the Devil a Knock-Out Blow.
The ex-Boxer will tell what he was when the Devil
had him; and what he is, now that Christ has a Grip
of him.
Come, and receive the Gift of Salvation, without Money
and Without Price!
Silver Collection.
Chairman Jason will ask a Blessing.

Johnny crumpled the little slip in his hand, and tossed it contemptuously on to the cold pavement beneath his feet. A Christian was born again at Baptism. Born of water and of the Spirit. The rest of a Christian's life is a confirmation of that Faith, embraced at the Fount; a sanctification of his nature by the salutary reception of the Sacraments, through which fallen man enters into the very nature and substance of eternally enjoyable Godhead; is confirmed co-heir with Christ Jesus; grows in the grace and wisdom of Sonship, till earth releases him to rise into the unfathomable glory and joy of God, the Father's welcome. God and the Gaelic League; not such a curious crossroad mingling as some Protestants might think; for where in the Protestant prayer-book is there a finer declaration of faith, or a finer spiritual petition, than in Holy Patrick's Cry of the Deer?

He went on pasting the labels on the wrappers. A small hand shot into the little patch of purple-bluish light forming a dim pool on the bench, and a second leaflet fluttered down before his face, saying,

Tomorrow at Eight o'clock.
Gigantic Rally of the Socialist Republican Party of Ireland.
Foster Place.
Come in your Thousands.
Tom Ling and Jim Connolly will speak.
Workers Arise!

Out in the street, snow on the ground, and the wind bitter, to
hold a meeting – Johnny shivered. Socialist – what was that?
Jim Connolly – same name as his friend above; but Johnny had
never heard of him. He crumpled up the leaflet in his hand, and
let it drop so that it got a lodging on the cold, cold ground. He
peered about him, but couldn't make out which of the crouching
figures had dropped the leaflets – one for God, the other for
Man. He had no interest in either. He went on with his work
of sorting out the wrappers. Again a stealthy hand moved into
bluish-grey light, and turning his head, he saw a form slinking
off into the deeper gloom of the cellar. Creeping about like black-
beetles, he murmured; all afraid, bar Sean Connolly. He bent his
head nearer to the handbill lying before him, and read:

Rotunda, Tomorrow Night. Eight o'clock.
98 Great Commemoration Concert.
Address: Shelmalier, Bargy Man, and Kelly of Killan.
Harp; Fiddle; Flute.
Songs and Recitations.
Tickets: 2/6, 2/- & 1/-
Muscáil do Mhisneach, a Bhanba!

Three appeals to him, the humblest Roman of them all: for
God, for Man, and for Country; three so different from each
other, yet all alike in so far that each was made in the dimness,
silently, and in fear. They were beetles here, with different badges
on their backs: some with the cross of Christ; some with the
harp of Ireland; and some with whatever the sign of Socialism
happened to be. The call to freedom from sin, freedom from
employers, freedom from national oppression, had each been
delivered stealthily, in the murky darkness; afraid of the light
because their deeds were good. He didn't like it; didn't like to be
even distantly connected with this fear of being caught in the
pleasuance of an idle moment. He was down among the dead men
here. If he wasn't yet actually lying down, he was sitting up in his

coffin here, with a murky mist for a shroud, and a bluish-grey gas-jet for the light of heaven.

If he stopped much longer here, too, his eyes would suffer from the dim light in the brown darkness. The muscles were stretched already, cockling up in his efforts to pierce through the dimness to see what he was doing. He'd leave. He'd leave with a flag of defiance in his hand, held high. But how?

A soft, slingy touch from a hand came to his shoulder, and a timid voice murmured, You're to go up for your pay. Mr Fitzgerald tole me to tell you.

He climbed up the dismal stairs, passed through the warehouse, into the entrance to the stairs leading to the counting-house, where a number of men and boys, in single file, stretched along the stairs, waiting their turn to go in and draw their money. He saw that as each one entered by the brown and golden door, marked COUNTING-HOUSE, he hurriedly took cap or hat from his head.

Why are they doffing their caps as they pass in? asked Johnny of a wide skull near him in the midst of the cold fog at the foot of the stairs.

—Don't you know your manners? came from the wide skull. Aren't we goin' in where Mr Charles is? An' isn't it a good thing to show suitable respect to those who provide for us? Isn't it a way of showin' Mr Charles what we think of him?

I'll show him what I think of him, thought Johnny; for as he was leaving the job, anyhow, he might as well kindle a flare of defiance before he went for good. He'd doff no cap. Refuse before the others, too. He'd show some of them what he was made of. His body ached; his eyes were red and blurred; and his head was dizzy with the downpour of toil that came on him here. Start from bed at three in the morning; going all the time, nearly, till six or seven in the evening, and getting something like a penny-farthing an hour for the work he did. No time left to read, or to learn by heart all the fine things in the books he had. They gave him Sunday to rest, and to pay his respects to God. Well, he'd take his chance to pay his respects to them, now.

He darted up the stairs, two at a time, and placed himself just outside the golden-lettered door of the counting-house.

—I'll take no cap of mine off, he said, loudly, to be heard by all. I'll wear my cap like a bronze helmet, and pull the beaver down; and he pulled the peak of his cloth cap down over his forehead, far as it would go. The rest gazed at him, moving closer together,

giving him plenty of space so as to show there was no bond between them and him.

—Open the door, and let the gallant boyo in, said the voice
from the wide skull below.

With a rowdy swing Johnny opened the door and went in. A
thick glossy, dark-red linoleum covered the floor; deeply-cush-
ioned chairs were there for the comfort of customers; in front of
him was a long, polished, brass-railed counter panelled with Tuscan glass, making all behind it invisible; in the centre of the glass
panels was a small window with a purple plate of thick glass above
it, having on it the word CASHIER in broad letters of black and
gold. To the left stood a mahogany-partitioned office, its upper
part panelled, too, with Tuscan glass; a narrow door stood in the
centre, and on its pane of glass, purple-bordered, was the word
PRIVATE in big gold letters. Johnny knew that behind the purple,
the gold, and the mahogany Mr Charles Jason sat, not too far
away from a sparkling fire, sweeping his office over with a glow
of heat and comfort. Johnny went over to the cashier's window,
and, peeping through it, saw a perfectly bald, stout-bodied
man bending over a drawer half filled with tiny white envelopes.

—Name, name, sir! snapped out the bald-head as soon as he
heard someone standing by the little window.

—Casside, Casside! snapped back Johnny.

The bald-head stiffened a little at the snappy tone of Johnny;
hesitated; then the ringed hand took an envelope from the drawer
and placed it on the little sill before the little window. Happening to glance up as he did so, the cashier saw that Johnny's cap
covered his head; and the ringed hand snatched the little envelope
back again.

—Take off your cap, he said disapprovingly; but Johnny stood
staring into the face of the bald-head, raising no hand to do so.

—Do you hear me, boy? and the voice of the bald-head was
threatening; take off your cap.

—Give me what's comin' to me an' never mind me cap, said
Johnny, conscious that the door behind him was open and the
crowd was gaping in at them.

—No wages are given to those who know no manners, said the
cashier, angrily and with decision.

The hero-heat that surged through Cuchullain in the core of a
fight surged through Johnny now, and he swelled out with the
dint of fury.

—Hand the money out, he said loudly, a leibide! Hand it out in the zone of a second, you fat, faltherin' caricature of creation, or woe'll find you, quick an' early!

The bald-head stepped back so swiftly that its spectacles hopped off its nose and dangled, from a ribbon, on its belly. The pasty face went purple and its voice panted indignantly, Mr Charles, Mr Charles!

Then, through the little window, Johnny saw the long face, pale eyes, greying golden beard, and bent shoulders of Mr Charles coming into the cashier's office with short mincing steps, on his toes, like a creaking and cracked-up ballet dancer, to stare with wonder at the cashier and Johnny's head thrust through the little window.

—What is it? what's wrong? what's the matter? what has happened? lisped Charles nervously, trying to look fierce, but with a hand on his office door so that he could dart back quick if danger showed a sign.

—This, this blaguard – didn't you hear him, Mr Charles? This, this, cor-corner-boy, here, the cashier stuttered, wouldn't remove his cap.

—That is the custom here, sir, Charles said to Johnny, and it must be honoured.

—Well, said Johnny, it's goin' to be honoured, now, more in th' breach than in the observance.

—He has used, sir, villainous, villainous language – didn't you hear him, Mr Charles? A caricature, he said, and some terrible name I never heard before!

—Where's he come from? Who is he? Who took him into the Firm? asked blond-beard.

—It was a ghastly mistake, whoever did it, sputtered the cashier.

—You go back to where you came from, said Johnny vehemently, thrusting an arm through the little window and pointing a finger at Jason; go back and count your gains behind the back o' Jesus; but before you go, tell this bald-headed boyo to hand over all that's comin' to me, quick!

—Give it to him, hand it to him, let him have it, let him have it, and go! ordered Jason. God bless us, how did such a person ever come to be employed here!

The cashier flung a little envelope on the sill of the little window. Johnny spilled the coins out, counted them, and dropped them carelessly into his pocket. Then he turned, pushed his way through the crowd at the door, hurried down the stairs, out into the darkness and the falling snow. A deep black sky it was, as if God was giving Dublin one of His black looks; unstirred by a star it was; as black as the streets were white, as if the city's face were paling under the black wrath of God.

—Well, thought Johnny, my mother will be glad I left it. Now I can find a little time to read the books I love; for I won't be going to bed, any longer, designed for death with the hard work here.

From a public-house, a little lower down the street, a stream of misty yellow light came from a wide window, forming a dusky golden patch on the side walk outside. In the centre of the yellow glow, like a beetle in a daffodil, stood a dark form, his shoulders gathered up into his neck, a golden trumpet to his mouth, playing tenderly and well, straight to the door, and through the door, to the men and women drinking cosily inside:

> *The light of other days is faded,*
> *And all their glories past,*
> *For grief with heavy wing hath shaded*
> *The hopes too bright to last.*

Johnny jingled the nine shillings in his pocket, pulled up the collar of his coat as high as he could make it go, and turned his steps homewards.

THE SWORD OF LIGHT

JOHNNY WISHED that he had more light; more light to see by; and light in his eye to see with, for the light of the body is the eye. Well, he'd seen a lot more than some with perfect eyes. Strange that God, who had given so much mighty light to the world in sun, moon, and stars, gave so little to some people. The old and new testaments had a lot about light in them; and Christ Himself talked quite a lot about it, even saying that He was the light of the world. Then there was the light that lighteth every man that came into the world – whatever that light could be; Let your light so shine before men that they may see your good works; the light this and the light that, till everyone was dazzled by it. And yet in most places it was as scarce as rubies. Hardly a house that he had been in that wasn't dark in daylight. The sun, they said, shone on

all; yet, really, if you looked round, many saw very little of it. He
knew street after street in which there was no sun. Where was it in
Hymdim & Leadems? Or in Jason's? Was it in oul' Anthony's
smile that had as much heat in it as the singed wing of a moth.
And as for Jason – he kept the sun locked up in the counting-
house. The old sun was doing his best, but many blinds were
pulled down to warn him away; or hide him from those who
needed him most. Like the sunburst of Ireland for ever hidden
behind the King of England's crown. A great shower of jewelled
hands were veiling the sun's face, and hiding his light from many
men.

It was a wintry night. The room was bitterly cold, and dismally
dark, too, save where a yellowish trickle of timorous light crept
through the window from a gas-lamp on the edge of the pavement outside, so long a swing-swong for the children that it now
bent forward over the street, looking like an old man who had
lighted a light in the hope of finding a lost piece of silver. On the
little old table, now the colour of dull ebony, Johnny had been
silently and insistently learning more of grammar, geography, and
of history, by the smoky ray of a tiny oil-lamp, flickering every
other second, making the words dance before his eyes, as if they
were alive and wanted to escape from his boring stare. Whenever
he got tired of these things, he read some bit from the *Deserted
Village*, or from Ruskin's *Crown of Wild Olives* that lay wide
open on the little table before him.

He guessed he must be cold; but his mind was warm, and the
state of the rest of his body mattered little; though he did his best
to keep it from the more biting cold by wearing an old coat over
his good one; two poor pairs of trousers; his muffler tied tightly
round his neck; and his cap crammed down over his forehead. He
had been hard at it since six o'clock in the morning – fifteen solid
hours, and he wasn't tired yet.

Sometimes a sly longing stole over him for a hot cup of tea, a
longing that he banished by a deeper look into the book before
him; there was no fire to heat the water, for the coal had to be
watched, and the little tea they had needed a strict jurisdiction to
make it last out the usual meals for the rest of the week. The
paraffin, too, was nearly out. With his last few coins he had bought
half a gallon; had hidden it in a corner, and had warned his mother
that it wasn't to be touched by a soul, save himself. Now its last
few inches were giving a flickering salute to the glories of Goldsmith, Ruskin, and Marlowe.

He raised the little lamp between his hands, placed it close to his ear, and shook it cautiously. Enough for another night or two, he murmured. Well, so far he had never been shook for what he needed. God had always managed to furnish forth a candle or a drop of oil. Though the barrel of meal had often wasted, the cruse of oil had never failed; and so the light of the past gave a new gleam to the light of the present. He would never be now without the light that lighteth every man coming into the world; for surely this had something to do with that light; was that light which could never be quenched. The light of other days would light the days to come. Shakespeare in his way, Marlowe, Goldsmith, and Ruskin in theirs, were lights showing him where to plant his feet safely; kindly lights guiding him to a fuller light in the future.

He paced slowly and cautiously to and fro, murmuring passages from Shakespeare or Goldsmith, putting sense and feeling into them, quietly; for in the other room his mother slept, and he didn't wish to wake her. She had had a hard day, washing for his sister, Ella, for nothing; and for another woman for sixpence and a glass of porter, which, she said, put new life into her. He paused at the window, and looked out on the naked night. A thin, sour, sharp-faced sickle of a moon tried to peer out of a cloudy wind-tossed sky, looking like a maid peeved with a wind that sullied her neatness. Over beyond the canal towered the ugly bloated spire of the Catholic church, a tapering finger on a fat hand beckoning to the ships that came sailing into the Bay of Dublin. The saint after whom the church was called had gone out alone to meet the clanging Normans when they came trotting on to take Dublin back to their hairy bosoms; the saint asking when his nose got the smell of the steel in the line of their glances, Is it peace, my dear Christian brothers, is it peace? And they had answered sweetly, saying, It's bloody wars unless you and your cross-brained Viking Tooles give way, give wisely, give all. And the saint had bowed, saying, All that we have is thine. Then the iron-skinned warriors stroked their beards, murmuring, It is well. So in the midst of their lances, shields, and battle-axes, the saint rode back in triumph, the people cheering because of his valour in bringing peace and poverty to them.

Nearer than the thick-bellied steeple gleamed the rosy red lights of the railway signals, looking like fiery red buttons on the dark-blue coat of our lady of the night, with the sickle moon a dull gold curb in her night-blown hair.

Every other moment from the shunting yard came the clanging crash of heavy goods wagons striking each other as the shunters harried them from line to line; or, sometimes, a succession of clangs was heard when a running rake of wagons came into sharp collision with another rake so that the two might be made into one.

All round where Johnny was looking, ah, many, many years ago, the Danes and the Irish grappled together in their fierce fight; the last long fight between darkness and light. Here the black-browed Thor went down before the gentle, golden-headed Jesus. Here the white and pearly dove pecked out the eyes and clawed out the guts of the vengeful and vindictive raven. Here the sign of the Hammer shrivelled up in the sign of the Cross; and darkness and fury fled before sweetness and light. Here the skirl of the Christian war-pipe shrilled at the bellowing of the heathen horns, helped by the lapping drone of the sea as his waves came curling in from Dublin Bay. The Danish Dubliners watched from their Woden walls the armies hacking and slashing and slaying and thrusting each other through till the number of heads floating on the waters and lying on the land seemed like a bloody fall of hailstones.

And all the purple laughter of the battle came bouncing out of a game of chess. Brian Boru requested Mailmurra, King of Leinster, to bring to Kincora, Brian's little grey home in the west, three of the longest, loveliest, whitest, most golden masts of timber that could be hewed out from the fair woods of Feegile. Poor Mailmurra couldn't refuse, for he was fief to Brian, whom he hated, seeking slyly to stir up the Danes against the High King. Before this, just for policy's sake, Brian Boru had given him a cloak of bright and precious silk, all edged with gold, with a bright shining silver brooch to keep it company. To ease his annoyance at having to bear the timber for Brian, the King of Leinster got the Chief of Offaly to bear one of the stately masts of golden timber; the Head of the O'Phelans to carry the second; and the Prince of the O'Murries to go with the third. All went well till at the foot of the mountains an argument arose over how to handle horses; the upshot being that O'Phelan called Mailmurra a suckhole, and Mailmurra called O'Phelan a bad dhrop in a good breed, when O'Phelan buttoned up his coat, turned on his heel, an' stalked off, saying, It's snaky-minded a man would want to be to go safe along a road with a Mailmurra; Mailmurra bawling afther him, Bah! back o' me hand to you, bowsey!

So Mailmurra had to set about doin' for himself what the O'Phelan had left lyin' in the road; toilin' so hard with the length of timber that the silver brooch burst away from his cloak, flew off, and disappeared from sight over the hip of the highest mountain. When he got to Kincora, he gave the cloak to his sister, Gormlaith, Brian Boru's wife, who made another brooch for him from a mould of bubbling silver handy on the fire beside her; an' she all the time naggin' him for bein' Brian's servant, dancin' attendance, a thing unseemly for a Mailmurra to do; a thing his father, or his father's father, or his father's father's father, wouldn't do for all the wealth an' valour owned be Greece an' Throy together; the tormented Mailmurra stealing away to look over a game of chess, when she was bent down biting a stitch of thread, hotly played between Brian's son and Kevin of Glendalough, the poor man thinking to do well by his host's son be advisin' him to make a move that lost him the game.

—That was the kind o' counsel that made Dublin's battle of Glen Mawma break on the Danes! snarled Brian Boru's son in the reddenin' face of the poor King of Leinster.

—If I gave counsel then that broke the battle on the Danes, answered Mailmurra, in tortured quietness, I'll give them counsel again that'll make th' battle break on you, yeh pup!

—Let's see you do it then! shouted Brian's son, leppin' up in rage an' scatterin' the chessmen: I dar' you!

With that, on fire with anger, Mailmurra left; and so that he couldn't drink in the great hall that night, went to bed at once, tearin' off at a flyin' gallop before the crack o' dawn, without as much as an I'm off, or So long, or even a kiss me arse, or a ha'p'orth to Brian Boru awake on his canopied bed devisin' out schemes to double-cross the innocent King of Leinster; hearin' of which the white-haired, white-whiskered Brian bounds outa bed with barely a screed on, to send a favourite gillie of the Dal Cash, dressed up to kill, afther the flyin' King to deludher him back again, so's Brian could have a quiet serious chat with him. The gillie goin' all-out caught up with the King on the bank of the Shannon not far from Killaloe, bowin' low to him, and givin' him Brian's message of love an' consternation at him goin' without a word, when the King turned on him suddenly an' let the unsuspectin' man have three such skelps on the skull with a skudgel of yew he had in his hand as cracked the gillie's head in three different places, so that he had to be hurried back home to Kincora on a hurdle, raisin' the ire of the warriors there that a Dal

Cash Munsterman should be cudgelled by a Cal Dash Leinster-man. Seizin' their spears an' mountin' their steeds, they prepared to ride off afther the King, Brian stoppin' the warlike traffic with an uplifted hand, ordherin' them to their beds again, sayin' that Mailmurra would come to no harm on Brian's land; ending with his hand on his heart an' a tear in his oul' eye that they'd demand an answer for what had been done at the King o' Leinster's own doorpost; while the wily Mailmurra, when he got home, sum-moned lesser kings, princes, big chiefs, and little chiefs be bell, book, trumpet, drum, cymbal, flag, beacon, fire, an' candlelight to let them know of the gust of slights an' slanders blown upon him while he sat a guest in the Halls of Kincora, sending messages to the Vikings of Orkney, Shetland, Man, Norway, and Iceland, urging them to come sailing on the first waves that surged into Dublin Bay to join up with the Danes there to force Brian Boru to give battle on the plains of Moy Ealta an' the land stretchin' from the head of Howth to the walls of Dublin on the banks of the river Liffey. So that a game of chess gave rise to the holy slaughter of pagan and Christian the time horrid hairy Brodar, with the great black raven on his chest, runnin' for his life, came upon the tent of poor oul' Brian, an' he on his knees prayin' for all he was worth to the great white Christ, with Brodar shoutin' at him for an oul' crawthumper to get up an' meet his doom, to make Brian lep to his feet an' whip up his sword an' let Brodar have it, slicin' off his legs with a wonderful slanty sweep of hiss sweapon, one from the knee an' t'other from the ankle; though while he was topplin' down, Brodar, aflame in a yell of agony, in the name of Thor, let the good Christian King have the beneficial edge of his biting battle-axe on the white-haired head, splitting it in two to the two lips that were just shouting the holy name of Jesus. And the darkness of hell enveloped the soul of Brodar, and he shot down deep; but the light of God shone round about the soul of Brian, and he went up high; and peace came to Ireland, dancing, and had a most happy weekend.

He must stop his dusky dreaming, and go back to the glow of his work. But he still lingered at the window, looking out at a world of a few dark shapes, the pompous steeple, the red lights of the railway, the yellow pool of light given by the gas-lamp on the edge of the side walk, and the slender, ogling slip of a moon, peering slantwise from the gloomy clouds, like a sly wanton eyeing a timid man from behind a curtain.

A big striding figure flashed darkly into the dusky pool of light and went swiftly by the window. Mr Harry, murmured Johnny, on his way to a Vestry Meeting, or something. The poor man was having a harrying time with the true-blue Protestants because, they said, he was a ritualist, though he asserted he was only determined to carry out the rules of the rubric in decency and order. They had had their eye on him ever since he came to the parish, some of them hissing softly as he came in to lead the church service when they saw the black cassock, which they called a Roman garment, flowing decently from under his white surplice, down to his feet. The Orangemen loudly and defiantly spoke the creed when it was being intoned by the choir, shouting out Popery! when Mr Harry and others turned towards the east as the creed was sung. They shouted at Parish Meetings that the yellow fringe on the communion table turned it into an altar; maintaining that the crimson and golden crosses on the confirmation certificates were busy corrupting the minds of the innocent young Protestant people they were given to, ensnaring them into the woeful superstitions of the Romish church. Stones were flung at the church windows, and a brick once landed on the organ, putting the player out, and causing consternation to the kneeling congregation. It was current all over the parish that the bould Harry would have to give up his sacerdoting practices or go. A good many rallied round him; but they were, like Johnny, the poorer members of the flock, and were, of course, of little use to him. The others closed their purses, making Mr Harry's job a very queer one, slowing down things, and he found it hard to fight against a sullen and resentful Select Vestry. If Johnny had had money or a fair job, he'd have sailed into the fight on Harry's side; but he had neither, so he had to be content to follow afar off. He hadn't had the courage to tell Mr Harry he'd lost his job; he was hoping that he'd be asked about it soon, then he'd tell Mr Harry everything, and Mr Harry would certainly have a lookout for something new for him. Pity he hadn't dropped in as he was passing the house.

A knock came to the door. Harry Fletcher – it must be he. He screwed his face round by the corner of the window, but it was too dark to see who the figure could be. If it was anyone for his mother, he'd send them to hell! He'd let no one wake her. But he was almost certain the knocker was the boul' Harry. He went from the room, opened the street door, and there was his old friend, the tram conductor, with a grin on his face, and his hand stretched out.

—Just slipped down with th' song all written out for you, he said, taking the pipe out of his mouth, and spitting on the pathway; *Speeches from the Dock*, too; an' th' *Life of Wolfe Tone*; an', if you've time to listen, I'll sing the song for you, so's you'll get the air all right.

Johnny brought him into the dark room that was barely aware of the light from the smoky lamp. He was ashamed that he wouldn't be able to offer him a cup of tea. The brightness of Goldsmith and Ruskin faded before the black bitterness of having nothing to give. Not even a bit of a fire for a friend.

—Not nearly as cold as it was, said the conductor, as if he sensed the bitterness of Johnny's thought; not nearly.

—I wasn't feeling a bit cold, said Johnny, so I didn't bother to light a fire.

—Waste o' good coal, murmured his friend; but Johnny noticed with pain that he kept his topcoat on him. There's the *Life*, he went on, laying on the table, in the little pool of light the lamp gave, a paper-covered book. You'll like it – th' way he got round the French Government to send a fleet to Ireland, an' th' bitther curses he let out of him when the great fleet sent to save Ireland had to weigh anchor, hoist sail, an' go back to France. Aw, Jasus, it was cruel! Some day, he said, laying a hand on Johnny's shoulder, you'll come with us to Bodenstown, an' by his grave pray for more men like Wolfe Tone. Here's the speeches givin' what the Irish felons said standin' in th' prison dock, when they faced death or lifelong imprisonment. You've heard *The Felons of Our Land* sung, haven't you?

—No, said Johnny, never.

—No? Well, one verse goes like this.

—Sing soft, whispered Johnny, for Mother's asleep in the next room.

—Righto; I'll sing as soft as a far-away echo. With an arm round Johnny's shoulder, he sang soft and slow and simply:

Let thraitors sneer and tyrants frown, oh, little do we care –
A felon's cap's th' noblest crown an Irish head can wear;
An' what care we, although it be trod by a ruffian band –
God bless th' clay where rest today, th' felons of our land!

Johnny felt the arm round his shoulder quiver, and a strange thrill stole through his own veins, stiffening his body, as he listened to the sad and defiant song.

—You nearly know the air of *Who Fears to Speak of Ninety-*

eight already, the conductor went on in a husky voice after they had stood dead silent for some seconds. I'll sing just two verses soft, an' you can hum the air as I'm singin' to make sure you've got the air right.

> *We dhrink th' memory of th' brave,*
> *Th' faithful an' th' few;*
> *Some lie far off beyond th' wave,*
> *Some sleep in Ireland, too.*

> *All, all are gone, but still lives on*
> *Th' fame of those who died;*
> *An' thrue men, like you men,*
> *Remember them with pride!*

There was a long silence in the darkened room, pricked by the little golden pool of light on the bronze-hued table, broken by the tense breathing of Johnny and his friend.

> *Th' dust of some is Irish earth,*
> *Among their own they rest;*
> *And th' same land that gave them birth*
> *Has caught them to her breast;*
> *And we will pray that from their clay*
> *Full many a race may start,*
> *Of thrue men, like you men,*
> *To act as brave a part!*

—Are the Fenians to the fore yet? whispered Johnny, close to his friend's ear.

—I'm afraid, I'm afraid not, lad, answered the conductor sadly close to Johnny's ear. Then his hand sought Johnny's, and he pressed it. Maybe they are, though. You never can tell. Anyway, we're here, aren't we? What are you readin' now? he asked, to relieve the sense of tension.

—*Crown o' Wild Olives*, said Johnny, by John Ruskin.

—Ruskin? Curious name. Irish, was he?

—A Scotsman who wrote splendidly. Listen to what he says about war: War, the greatest of all games – the play of plays, the great gentleman's game, which ladies like them best to play at – the game of war. It is entrancingly pleasant to the imagination; we dress more finely for it than for any other sport; and we go out to it, not merely in scarlet, as to hunt, but in scarlet and gold, and all manner of fine colours; though, of course, we could fight better in grey, and without feathers. Then the bats and balls are very costly, costing now, I suppose, about fifteen millions of money annually to each nation; all of which you know is paid for by hard labourer's work in the furrow and furnace. A costly game! – not to speak of the consequences. The cost is all paid for, we know, in deadly work somewhere. The jewel-cutter, whose sight fails over the diamonds; the weaver, whose arm fails over the web; the ironworker, whose breath fails before the furnace.

—An' how, may I ask Mr Ruskin, are we goin' to get th' English outa Ireland without it?

—Without what?

—Without war? Ruskin's only another oul' cod, with th' gift o' gab!

—He wrote about other things, said Johnny, a little indignantly, and he wasn't a cod. Listen to this, spoken before a gathering of business men who were about to build an Exchange in the Yorkshire town of Bradford.

—Aw, Sean, Exchange! interrupted the conductor. What have we got to do with an Exchange?

—Listen, listen for a second, man! Here's a word or two of what he said: Your ideal of life is a pleasant and undulating world, with iron and coal everywhere beneath it. On each pleasant bank of this world is to be a beautiful mansion; stable and coach-houses; a park and hothouses; carriage drives and shrubberies; and here are to live the votaries of the Goddess of Getting-on – the English gentleman with his gracious wife and lovely family—

—There, you see, Sean – the *English* gentleman!

—Wait a second: Irish or Englishman – a gentleman's all the same.

—It isn't, I'm tellin' you; it's different.

—Listen, listen a minute more: the gentleman was always able to have the boudoir and the jewels for the wife; beautiful ball dresses for the daughters; and hunters for the sons, and a shooting in the Highlands for himself. At the bottom of the bank is to be the mill, not less than a quarter of a mile long, with a chimney three hundred feet high. In this mill are to be in constant employment a thousand workers, who never drink, never strike, always go to church on Sundays, and always express themselves in respectful language. There, you see – there's something in all that, isn't there?

—An' what's in it but a lot o' blather? Right enough, maybe, for the gloomy English gropin' after little things; for the Saxon sireless squatters an' Clan London's loutish lords, ever rakin' cinder-heaps for specks o' gold; but th' Irish is different – we have th' light.

—The Catholic Faith, you mean? asked Johnny.

—No, no, no, he said impatiently. That's there, too; but I mean th' light o' freedom we're goin' to win from th' English – th' leprosy o' want desthroy them!

The tall figure of Mr Harry Fletcher again flashed past the window, and a second later a knock was heard at the street door.

—It's our new minister coming to see me, said Johnny, with some embarrassment.

—Couldn't I slip out without him seein' me?

—There's only the one way out, said Johnny testily.

—Well, look, said the conductor, pointing behind him, I can half lie behind the sofa there in th' dense of th' darkness, an', unless he's th' eyes of an owl, he'll never notice me. He hurried over and got behind the sofa, sitting down on the floor, so that only the very top of his head could be seen by Johnny who knew he was there. Johnny went out, opened the door, and Mr Fletcher and he came back into the room.

—Hard at work, I see, the minister said, glancing at the books on the table. Good lad; you'll soon know more than the best of us.

—Sit down, said Johnny, hastily shifting the books the conductor had brought him into the darkness; sit down, sir.

—I'm afraid I've disturbed you, the minister said, sitting down on Johnny's chair and putting his bare hands as close as he dared to the blackened chimney of the lamp, trying to get some heat into them; but I shan't keep you away from your glory long. I've just come, John, to bid you and your mother goodbye.

—Goodbye? echoed Johnny, with distress in his voice.

—Yes; I can't stay any longer – there are too many against me.

—Fight them, said Johnny vehemently; fight them, sir!

—I have done so. No, it's goodbye, John; I have to go. My bishop advised that it wasn't a good thing to provoke contention among Christian people.

—Christian people! But you have done nothing but obey the rubric.

—In the spirit, yes; but the deep-set emotions of an ignorant evangelism is still strong, preventing our poor people from seeing the truth in the Scriptures and the Church's tradition.

—Some of them have been at me about you and your ways, said Johnny, trying to turn me against you. They were very bitther about Sanctus, Sanctus, Sanctus, written in gold on the wall above the communion table, turning it, they said, into a High Althar.

Johnny joined in with the musical laugh of Mr Harry. They're saying, too, that you've a crucifix over your bed.

—The symbol of our salvation can hardly be an evil thing, murmured Mr Harry.

—They complain, too, went on Johnny, that you encourage prayers for the dead.

—It has been the custom of the Church for hundreds of years to pray for the dead, said Mr Harry, rubbing his hands, and holding them out towards the little lamp again; and we have lost a lot of comfort and spiritual communion with our departed loved ones by giving it up. Before we go into the presence of God, the best of us need a purifying period in paradise. That was where Christ's soul went when we say He descended into hell; not the hell of the damned, Gehenna; but Hades, the blessed place of the spirits departed in the faith and fear of the Lord. Surely it is good to pray that God may give them eternal rest, and let perpetual light shine upon their suffering souls.

—We say in Irish, said Johnny, of one who is dead, Solus Dé dá anam – Light o' God to his soul!

—Eh? said Mr Harry, puzzled; Irish what?

—Irish, Irish language, you know, murmured Johnny ashamedly.

—Oh yes, yes, quite, murmured Mr Harry so indifferently that Johnny's face was reddened, and he wished he hadn't said it.

—A prayer for the departed, went on Mr Harry, is plainly implied in the prayer for Christ's church militant here on earth, too.

—Quite, murmured Johnny, trying to get back his ease of manner after the thoughtless slip of mentioning the Irish language.

—And you remember that lovely collect, beginning Almighty God with whom do live the spirits of them that depart hence in the faith?—

—We humbly beseech thee, of they gracious goodness, said Johnny, taking the words from Mr Harry, so's to show he knew it, shortly to accomplish the number of thine elect, and to hasten thy kingdom; that we, with all those that are departed in the thrue faith of they holy name, may have our perfect consummation and bliss, both in body and soul – what could be plainer? asked Johnny.

—The Fathers of the Church are even plainer still, John. We must ever strive to keep the fairest expressions of the Faith alive and fresh in our hearts, till such time as the Irish Church may cordially show forth her eternal and beautiful brotherhood with the rest of the family professing the one, holy, and apostolic faith. And now I must go. He rose from his chair, and Johnny saw that he shivered a little with the cold of the room. Is your mother in – can I say goodbye to her?

– I'll waken her up, said Johnny, hesitating to leave the room for fear his friend should be seen crouching down behind the sofa; she's asleep; she's had a hard day, but I'll waken her up to say goodbye.

—No, no; you mustn't do that, said Mr Harry earnestly. Let the poor woman sleep on and take her rest. Give her my love, and say goodbye for me. He pulled at the collar of his coat at the street door, as if he wished to cover his ears. Well, goodbye, goodbye, John – you're a good lad; goodbye, and God bless you. And the next moment Johnny was watching him striding away into the darkness, never to be seen again by him or his mother.

—What was th' pair o' yous thryin' to do? asked the conductor, when Johnny had come back into the little room. Whew! I'm cramped. Was it thryin' to copy our mode o' religion yous were, or what?

—No, no; not at all, said Johnny sharply. What we spoke about was our own religion. We belong to the one, Catholic, and apostolic church.

—There's me for you, now! I always thought yous were Protestants.

—So we are – in a way; but we're Catholics, too.

—An' how in religion can you be two things at the one time?

—They aren't two things; St Patrick founded our church as he founded yours.

—That's the first time I ever heard tell St Patrick was a Protestant. Anyway, yous don't respect the Pope.

—On the contrary, we have a great respect for him.

—Yous have? Well, that's th' first time I've heard Protestants respect the Pope.

—Not all Protestants respect him, of course; the very ignorant ones dislike and deride him.

—Well, that doesn't matther much, so long as they're Irish. How does he stand in, regardin' her?

—He – her – who?

—Ireland; the minister who's just left?

—Oh, he? She never enters his head.

—A gay lot o' foreigners there's in this counthry!

—He isn't a foreigner – he's Irish.

—Irish – an' Ireland never enthers his head!

—There's a lot that way. Some of your Catholics are just as bad.

—Worse! A scowl came on to the conductor's face, and his hands clenched. Sell her, be God, some of them would! Ay, an' did. Leonard McNally, Pether the Packer, an' th' bastards who bethrayed Parnell!

—What d'ye think of the Irish Socialist Republicans? asked Johnny.

—Connolly, Ling, an' that crowd? Not worth considerin'. What we have to do first is to desthroy th' festherin' weeds clingin' to Ireland's feet an' hinderin' her movements.

—And who are they? asked Johnny.

—The Irish Parliamentary Party! and the conductor's scowl got darker, and his hand clenched more tightly. Redmond an' his gang, paddlin' in the flow of England's brutal, bawdy, gaudy grandeur. They are the new English yeomen of the guard, all dhressed in their jackets green; golden English epaulettes are on their shoulders; the English King has given a timely tap to all their shouldhers, an' their knees are bendin'. I'm off now.

Johnny went with him to the door. There was the dull, heavy steeple of the church vaunting its faith even to the sky; there were the bawdy clouds, now hiding, now showing the nakedness of the slip of a moon; and there were the railway lights, staring like red eyes of animals from a jungle of darkness.

—I'm goin' to call you Sean from this out, said the conductor, as he held Johnny's hand at parting; mine's Ayamonn, Ayamonn O'Farrel, from the O'Farrels of Longford. Well, Slán agat, achara. He bent down and whispered tensely into Johnny's ear, Th' Sword of Light is flamin' still!

—What sword of light?

—Th' Fenians! And without another word, he hurried off, leaving Johnny standing by the door.

The Sword of Light! An Claidheamh Solis; the Christian Faith; the sword of the spirit; the freedom of Ireland; the good of the common people; the flaming sword which turned every way, to keep the way of the tree of life – which was it? where would he find it?

He went back into the darkened room, sat down, leaned his elbows on the table and his head in his hands. He glanced at the little smoky lamp and fancied fhat it had changed to a candle – a tall, white, holy candle, its flame taking the shape of a sword; and, in its flaming point, the lovely face of Cathleen, the daughter of Houlihan.

His head bent lower, heavy with thought. There, under his eyes, on the pages of Ruskin's book, lay a glittering silver shilling. Harry Fletcher's gift? Couldn't be; there was no shilling there when he took Harry to the door. It was Ayamonn's gift. Johnny felt his friend knew that, had it been offered, it would in pride have been refused; so he simply left it quietly on the pages of an open book. Johnny took it up and handled it and sighed; then a shudder went through him as he remembered that the minister had gone away for ever, and that he would have to ferret out a job for himself.

I STRIKE A BLOW FOR YOU, DEAR LAND

JOHNNY'S WHOLE world was divided against itself. England was at war with the Boer Republics. His brother Tom, who had had a job of temporary postman at twelve shillings a week and was on the Reserve, had been called up; had been dressed in khaki, helmet and all; had marched, with a contingent of his regiment, the Dublin Fusiliers, through the city, Johnny by his side, carrying his rifle, and had gone long ago to the front, after promising Johnny he'd bring home a bunch of hair from Kruger's whiskers. He had gone up to Natal under General Sir Redvers Buller, and nothing had been heard of him for weeks. Johnny was troubled that he might have perished in the battle of Tugela; for Johnny and Tom had a real affection for each other. Thousands of Irishmen were out there on the veldt, risking all for England; for her honour, and, Johnny thought bitterly, for the gold and diamond mines of Johannesburg. She had been fortified in her attack on the Boers by testimonials from the Basutonians, Zululonians, Matabelians, Bechuanalandians, Bulawayonians, Mashonians, and the Kalomonians, who had all in a great chorus sung hail hallelujah to the great white queen mother, Victoria.

All civilization, save alone the Irish. Ireland had become a place of stormy argument, with Dublin as its centre. Every man, woman, and child fought battles hour by hour, either for the British or the Boers. Transvaal flags were in everyone's house, in everyone's window, or in everyone's hand. At times spontaneous processions formed in the streets, marched through the city, booing every redcoat that passed, and often coming into collision with the irritated police. All fancy-goods shops and newsagents were filled with Boer symbols; streams of ribbons flashing the colours of England's enemies flowed through every street and sparkled in every second window. Every patriot carried in the lapel of his coat a buttoned picture of Kruger, Steyn, Botha, Joubert, or De Wet; and a story went everywhere that De Wet was really Parnell come to life again, and up in arms against the English. Day and night the office of the *Irish Independent* flashed on a screen the latest news, a red light burning for a British victory and a green one for a Boer success, thousands gathering to cheer when the green light shone, and to groan and hiss when the red light was shown. A Transvaal Committee had been formed, with Arthur Griffith and some Irish Members of Parliament, to help the brave Boers to an Irish ambulance. A meeting had been called, but the Castle had proclaimed it; and Dublin tossed her head and clenched her teeth.

Today Johnny and Ayamonn were standing in the crowd watching the lights, when the news was flashed on the screen that the British had lost ten guns, and a great cheer, thundering defiance, made the street tremble in an agony of joy. Ayamonn, hoarse with mad emotion, whipped his hat from his heavily-haired head and waved it round in circles, as he shouted with the crowd.

—We should ha' gone to where th' meetin' was to be, he said, proclaimed or no.

—We're better here, said Johnny; for he didn't relish the chance of a tussle with the police; and here he knew that wasn't likely to happen.

In the crowd, right in front of Johnny, stood a lissome young woman dressed in a gay dark-green dress suit, the skirt barely reaching to her ankles; a black bolero jacket, trimmed with flounced epaulettes which were rimmed with a brighter green than the green of the suit, and flecked with scarlet. She wore high-laced boots that disappeared up under her skirt, which, whenever it was swung by a lively movement of the girl's, showed the fringe of a white lace petticoat. Perched daintily on a curly roll of reddish hair was a dark-green felt hat sporting a black-and-white wing of a bird in its side. Several times Johnny's knee had touched her thigh, timidly at first, then with steadier resolution; and now, with a beating heart, Johnny found that the girl hadn't taken her leg away from his touch.

Ayamonn, full of himself, was gently swaying to and fro, as far as the crowd's pressure would permit, and singing, half to himself and half to the crowd, his eyes filled with a far-away look:

> *My boyish ear still clung to hear*
> *Of Ey–eyrin's pri–ide of yore,*
> *Ere Norman foot did dare pollute*
> *Her in–independent shore;*
> *Of chiefs, long dead, who rose to head*
> *Some gallant patriot few;*
> *Till all my aim on earth became*
> *To strike one blow for you, dear land,*
> *To strike one blow for you,*
> *To stri–ike one blow for you, dear land,*
> *To stri–ike one blo–ow for youooo!*

A woman striding towards middle age, wearing a disorganized straw hat on her tousled head, patched boots, one brown, one black, the brown one darkened with blacking to make it feel more at home with the other. She wore a black-and-white check skirt, the white square making up to the black ones by the grime gathered in street and house, the whole scalloped by wear and tear along the edges. She wore a large brown shawl flowing down to beyond her hips. Suddenly, she darted out from the crowd to a vacant place on the side walk, flung her shawl open with a sweeping flip and tucked it more closely round her body, as if she were clothing herself in armour.

—I don't care who hears me, she shouted, for we're full of life today, an' – puff – we're gone tomorra. To every man an' woman their own opinion, square or round or crooked or cornered, which is only right an' proper, an' a fair division. Sayin' nothin' calculated to hurt a soul, I'll say yous are a lot o' starin' fools, watchin' an' waitin' for somethin' yous'll never be spared to see. I wondher, she went on, raising her voice to a screaming pitch, I

wondher what all of yous, what any of yous 'ud do, if England
went undher!

—Die with joy! a man's voice shouted from the crowd, and a
great cheer added an amen to the declaration.

The protesting woman flapped her shawl like a bird flapping its
wings, gave a clumsy little lep from the pathway into the air,
flapping open her shawl again, and closing it tighter as she did
a nervous defiant dance on the pathway.

—There's ne'er an element of surety in your shoutin', she
yelled, or the pourin' out of your poor white ignorance an'
coloured venom. It 'ud be fitther for yous to work to help yourselves than to set yourselves dhreamin' of help for the Boers; for
listen to me – in about as much time as it 'ud take a clever hand an'
a sharp knife to peel an apple, England'll put the sign o' death on
Kruger an' his gang!

The lissome young lassie standing in front of Johnny, with her
leg touching his knee, moved angrily, and turned her pretty head
to stare at the yelling woman; and Johnny cursed the oul' one
for an ignorant, meddling bitch. Then with a handsome wriggle of
her young body, the girl slid from the crowd and stood, red-faced
and defiant, before the ill-dressed, blustering woman yelling out
for England.

—Will you go home, for God's sake, woman, she said fiercely,
an' clap yourself in bed, since you can't help yourself to a suitable
understanding! We're serious people here, in no way wishin' to
confuse our decency with the dirty tournament of England's
attack on inoffensive peoples.

—General Roberts, General French, an' General Kitchener,
three Irishmen – remember that! shouted the blustering woman.
They'll soon put the lonesome sign of death on Kruger an' his
gang!

—Will they now? asked the young woman. You know all about
it, don't you? Well, if I read the news right, Gatacre didn't do it at
Colesberg, or your great Lord Methuen at Magersfontein, where
he led thousands of th' poor bewildered Scots o' th' Highland
Brigade to leave an everlastin' farewell to their wives, sisthers, an'
sweethearts. And your Butler hasn't done it at Colenso, has he?

A policeman, big and brave, for he knew there were hundreds of
his brothers less than half a street away, came up, and eyed the
pretty lass with an evil look, his mouth, thought Johnny, wathering
for an excuse to haul her to the station, so that he might handle
her hidden loveliness while he was doing his duty.

—Eh, you, he said to the lissome lassie, draw it mild an' let the woman have her say. The law allows free expression of opinion to all.

—Come on back here, sweet lass, whispered Johnny, going over slyly, and timidly touching the girl's arm, and never mind that ignorant and insignificant woman; but she brushed his enticing hand away, and he went back to the crowd abashed.

—Irishmen all! yelled the older woman, flapping her shawl, doing her little lep up from the pavement after every sentence, Kitchener, Roberts, Kelly-Kenny, French, Mahon, fightin' for England. Five o' th' best, an' Irishmen all – remember that, now!

—Maybe you've forgotten how th' English went clattherin' down Nicholson's Nek, so's you couldn't see their heels for dust, went on the young lassie, an' thousands now of their best are floatin' fast dead an' down th' Tugela river, headin' out for the sea!

—Irishmen all – you can't get over that, now! screamed the oul' one. Whenever oul' England's in a quandary, up comes th' Irishman, tearin' up he comes, an' turbulent to pull her out of it – ah! me faithful, darlin' Dublin Fusiliers!

A surge of many people cheering came from some distance away, like the first rolling billows of a tidal wave. Ayamonn sniffed, tossed up his head, and listened.

—Something's goin' on below, he said; come on, me boy!

—We're all right here, said Johnny, pulling back, and it's safer to stay where we are.

—We don't want to be safe, cried Ayamonn, making off for the wider vista of Dame Street, followed by the pretty red-haired girl; and the crowd, turning from the lights, swept down, carrying Johnny with them close to the girl, knocking over the boisterous oul' one just as she was doing her little lep from the pathway, and flattening the burly constable against the wall of a building. When they streamed into Dame Street, they mingled with a tremendous crowd, cheering fiercely, and waving hundreds of Boer, Irish, French, and American flags. Some way after the head of the crowd was a brake, a long car, benched on both sides, drawn by two frightened hearse horses. A stout, short, stocky man, whose face was hidden by a wide-awake hat, was driving them. Several other men, pale-faced and tight-lipped, sat on the seats, facing each other; and with them was a young woman with long lovely yellow hair, smiling happily, like a child out on her first excursion.

—Look, Sean, me boy, look! shouted Ayamonn, didn't I tell

you we wouldn't take things lying down much longer! That's James Connolly dhrivin', and that little man with the square jaw's Arthur Griffith; an' th' lovely lady's Maud Gonne – help us, Jasus! an we'll win our freedom yet! Come on!

The horses were moving along at a steady trot, the crowd were keeping up a trot in unison, and after the brake a large mass of heavy-coated, helmeted policemen trotted sullenly, and as nimbly as their bulky bodies would allow. That part of the crowd nearest to the police were laughing animatedly and jeering into their red and sweaty faces, goading them with cries of Shake a leg, there, bring your knees up; take id aysey, me poor men; hay foot, straw foot; keep your chests in an' your bellies well out; it's a damned shame to have th' poor men runnin' their guts out – cruelty t' animals, so 'tis; at th' double, min – quick march; eh, keep back there, an' give th' min breathin' room.

—Keep as close to th' brake as you can, said Ayamonn, pulling at Johnny's arm, while Johnny kept fast hold of the girl's hand, who twined her dainty fingers round his. Pushing hard, they were soon but a few steps behind to one side of the brake, near the great persons who were sitting, tense and tight-lipped, there. In high good-humour they all were, with the police helpless, jammed in the crowd, looking ridiculous as they lumbered along stiffly in an unsteady trot.

Now brakes filled with police forced their way through part of the crowd and followed those trotting along on foot. Passing by the gates of the Castle, there, snug in that deep gash of the city's body, were drawn up all the squadrons of the Horse Police. There they sat their horses, darkly seen for a few moments by those marching by, in the shine of silver on helmet and tunic; gloomily they sat there, a frozen frieze on the façade of the Castle, motionless; not a jingle from stirrup, bridle, or bit, not a hair of a helmet-plume stirring. As they passed and saw, the murmuring, chattering people grew silent, and nothing was heard but the trotting fall of the feet of the crowd; nothing seen but the dark forms, silent, behind the shine of the silver. And Johnny remembered when he last saw such a sight he was safe on the top of a tram, warm and confident, close to his mighty mother's side.

The procession swung into Parliament Street, everyone tense, silent, expectant, waiting. Johnny heard the sound of a sharp order, saw the dark figures coming to life; heard another sharp order, and saw many flashes of light as swords were drawn; saw the plumes stirring as the horsemen moved; heard another shouted order, and the squadrons came galloping down on the crowd. Johnny tried to push a way towards a side street, holding on to the hand of the girl, but they were wedged fast in the crowd, and they were swept beyond it. He saw the people in the brake stand up to watch the charging police, and the driver checked the horses to half turn round and look back over the heads of the swaying crowd. The flashes of steel light were rising high and falling on the heads of the people. The air was deafened with shouts and screams and curses. Those nearest the edges began to seek safety in the side streets; the manly jog-trot of the procession was now but a medley of scuffling feet; the clack of iron hooves on the stone setts, mingled with the cries of those who hadn't yet felt the fall of a sword, and the sombre silence of the Horse Police, trotting here, trotting there, prancing their horses against the tumbling breasts of the people, lifting their heavy sabres as if drilling to the musical notes of a murderous tune, to let them fall on frantic heads trying swiftly to wag aside from each glittering blow.

The people were resisting now. Poles, sticks, bars of iron, and bare fists were contesting the fight with the police.

The horsemen had made a mistake by coming down on them too quickly, giving them no time to scatter, so that wedged together, cut off from a way of escape, the sabre-stormed people were forced to fight back. The Dubliners were angry, and, caught like this, they became a troublesome mass of fighters. Stones snapped asunder some of the chin-chains, and police were riding about bareheaded, with blood trickling down their faces. Some of them had been pulled from their horses, and were struggling on the ground beneath a mass of pummelling fists. Their batons were being used by men in the crowd, and a few had swords which they gripped tensely, but didn't like to use.

—We're caught in a thrap! said Ayamonn hoarsely, grinding his teeth, caught in a thrap!

Johnny put his arms across his chest, pushing out as strong as he could, to keep his ribs from cracking, the sweat rolling down his face and his breath coming out in bitter panting gasps. The girl, flattened beside him, had closed her eyes, and her little red mouth was gaping open. Many dark figures were writhing curiously on the road, dotted here and there with a helmeted body, crouching down on hands and knees, blood dripping on to the setts from some hidden wound. A horseman, well in advance of his comrades, was forcing a way towards Johnny and his two friends, kneeing his horse through the crowd, hacking away with a sabre gleaming sourly in the grey air. Johnny saw a gleam fall on the face of an elderly man, saw a bloody cheek suddenly separate itself from the face and fall away from it, to be frantically clapped back to its place, with a yell, by the stricken man, who suddenly sat down on the road, moaning, pressing his two twitching hands to the horribly gashed face with all his power. Still Johnny stood staring at the slashing horseman, coming closer; still Ayamonn crouched, his arms held high, sheltering head and face; still the pretty girl stood with her eyes closed and her little red mouth gaping. Back, inch by inch, came the crowd, melting before Johnny as the horseman advanced to where but a few yards separated them from the slash of his sabre. A man in front of them, carrying a gaudy Boer flag, screamed when he saw the gleam circle over him, and then sank down without a murmur when the flash fell, letting the flag go from his grip, and as it toppled backwards, the staff came to rest on Johnny's shoulder. Now the horseman curveted round to where they stood, and Johnny saw a pair of eyes, like flaming carbuncles, fixed on him from under the helmet's peak; saw the thick mouth of the half-mad man opening and shutting nervously, the heavy yellow teeth clashing together as he roughly swung his horse round to where they stood. In the madness of fear, Johnny gripped the pole of the flag with both hands and blindly thrust it forward at the rider with all his might as the horse came prancing round on his hind legs. The hard, sharp, wooden spearhead of the flagpole caught the rider on the side of the neck under an ear, and Johnny caught a glimpse of an angry red tear where the spear had struck, as he tumbled off his horse with a sliding crash on to the hard ground, letting a smothered grunt out of him before he lay stunned and still there. Johnny felt a horse's hoof grazing his leg, splitting a trouser-leg from knee to ankle; he saw Ayamonn running furiously over to the fallen rider; saw him stamp his heavy boot on the horseman's face, and though the hard rim of the helmet saved the face from being caved in, Johnny plainly saw that the iron heel had left a horrible bloody blob on the rider's chin; he felt Ayamonn pulling him madly by the arm, and shouting at him, This way; up this street, for Jasus' sake, or we're for it when the others come!

Then they ran; the three of them ran up a side street, ran through the streets before them till they had utterly lost the sound of the tumult in the place they'd left behind them.

Diving into a pub, Ayamonn called for three halves of malt, hot, to get them sober, he said, and to take away the chill that follows the brazen heat of a battle. Johnny smiled, tried to look indifferent, then hurried out to lean against a lamp-post and be sick on the road, Ayamonn watching him anxiously from the doorway.

—All right? he questioned. It's the terrible pressure of the crowd that's upset your stomach. Come in an' get th' ball o' malt down you, an' you'll be right as rain.

—Yes, said Johnny, the pressure of the crowd – that was it; but in his heart he knew that it was fright and the things he had seen. He was no soldier. Never would be – he felt it. There was no use trying; but he'd say nothing before the girl. He went back into the pub.

—That was a glorious prod you gave th' helmeted bowsey, said Ayamonn – right undher th' lug! Save us, you did. He'd ha' sliced us as you'd slice a salmon. God, I did laugh when I seen him hurtlin' off his horse! Well, we stood up to them today. Our dhreams are comin' thrue. Eh, he said suddenly to the barman who had put three whole balls of malt on the counter, I said halves; and Johnny knew that he hadn't enough to pay for the whole ones.

—That's all right, whispered the barman, leaning over the counter, th' dhrinks are on me, see? I guess what you've been doin' – standin' be th' Poor Oul' Woman, wha'?

They all shook hands with the barman, murmured good health, and lowered the steaming amber whiskey. Johnny felt the cold leaden pain in his belly change into a delightful glow of comfort, and his face flushed with a new contentment. He saw the colour creeping back into the girl's face, the sparkle leaping into her dulled eyes, and he saw, with a thrill, her two pointed breasts falling and rising deliciously behind the sweet shelter of her bodice. He caught her arm in his hand and squeezed it, pressing it tighter when she smiled happily back at him.

—Look at his leg, she said, indicating to the barman Johnny's torn trousers; a prancin' horse done it. A wondher he wasn't desthroyed! And the scared face of the falling horseman again came before Johnny's eyes.

—Now, we'd betther scatter, said Ayamonn, when they'd come out of the pub: I this way, yous that. Slan libh till we meet again; and off he went, while Johnny and the girl, in a roundabout way, walked to Ballybough, she with her arm in his, and he pressing it close to his side. He felt lovely thoughts singing her beauty straying through his head, but his heart beat so fast, and his chest felt so tight, that he could hardly say a word.

—You're limping a little, she said, when they were passing over the Tolka.

—The leg's hurting a little, he said.

—Here we are, she said, stopping before a cottage in a little avenue. You'll have to come in for a second an' let's have a look at it. I can put a stitch in your trousers at the same time.

—No, no; I couldn't, he said shyly; thanks all the same, though he longed to go in and seek out a chance to fondle her; I'd better leave you now, really.

—You're a shy fellow, she said, laughing. There'll only be th' two of us, so you needn't worry, and she opened the door with a latchkey. She gave him a pull towards her, saying sharply, Ah, go in, man, or you'll give the neighbours another chance for a fancy-born story.

They went into a little room to the right off a narrow hall, furnished with a table on which was a white cloth and the stuff for a meal, some ham, bread, and an egg in a cup waiting to be boiled, while a shining tin saucepan sat itself within the fender before a brightly-burning fire. Along the wall, under the window, ran a sofa with two big crimson and dark-green covered cushions on it; two rather stiff upright chairs, leather-bound; against the wall opposite, a mahogany cupboard, having on it a gilded vase and many photos of the girl in various positions, with a parasol on the seashore, sitting on a carved stone bench, with a book in her hand, leaning against a fat and fluted pillar; and one, that made Johnny's eyes linger there, of her in low bodice and tights, and a saucy smile on her wide and neatly-curved little mouth. A warm brown carpet, sprinkled with large blue blossoms, covered the floor, and yellow curtains prettily draped the window. The wall-paper was cream-coloured, with trellises of yellow and pink rose-buds everywhere your eye went. Pictures from the Christmas number of *Holy Leaves* covered some of them, and a few were hidden safely by a green-coated Robert Emmett waving a plumed hat over the mantelpiece. Johnny's eyes gave a swift glance at all those bright things, but came back to linger on the photo of her little ladyship wearing the low-cut bodice and the charming tights.

—That's a good one, she remarked, noticing where his eyes had strayed. I'm a good dancer, and whenever there's a panto or anything on with a chorus, I get a job in th' front rank. An uncle of mine lets me have a couple of quid a week, so I don't do too badly. An' how d'ye like me, she added roguishly, in a fie-for-shame costume?

—You look lovely, he said earnestly; you look lovely as you are; and you would blossom forth fair in anything.

—I see, she said, her face flushing pleasantly, you can put a silvery sound into your words when you want to deludher a poor girl. But sit down there till I see to your leg, an' we can talk afterwards.

She put a kettle on the fire, and fetched a basin and a towel from another room. When the water was hot, she poured some into the basin and gently bathed his leg with an old clean linen rag.

—There's a bruise there, she said, an' it has bled a little. When the wound was clean, she smeared some vaseline on a white handkerchief and tied it firmly round his leg.

—There, that should feel easier now, she said. When we've had some tea, I'll do your trousers. Me name's Daisy, she added, Daisy Battles. She went on chatting while she made tea and boiled two eggs. She cut some ham, and placed an egg before him. Eat, she said; you must be nearly starving.

He felt too full and excited and expectant to eat, but he swallowed the egg and drank a cup of tea, watching her making a tidy meal of it.

—Me skirt an' petticoat an' what I wouldn't like to mention are all creased an' twisted with the crush of the crowd. I'll have a job to get them into a proper shape again. Well, it's all for oul' Ireland anyway.

When they'd finished eating, she pulled the table back with a swift movement to the far end of the room, and placed the sofa lengthwise in front of the fire.

—That's much nicer, she said. Sit you down here, an' take off your trousers while I get a needle and thread. Go on, she added, laughing, seeing him hesitate, don't be so shy – I won't look at you, I promise; and she hurried out of the room. Flushed and agitated, he took them off, sat down on the sofa, took off his jacket and draped it over his bare legs. When she came back, he saw she had a dark-green shawl swung from her shoulders down to her hips, fastened over her bosom by a large oval brooch framed in dull gold, having on it a naked girl in ivory standing daringly out from a black velvet background. She sat down beside him, took up his trousers, and began to mend the rent in the leg. He guessed now that there was nothing beneath the dark-green shawl but a thin chemise or something. Frightened, he turned his gaze to the fire, and saw there a glance of agony on a twisted face, a blazing red mark under an ear, and a chin smashed into a bloody blob. He turned his face to watch her stitching.

—God, she said, looking down at his feet sticking out from under his jacket, what tiny feet you've got! An' hands, too! patting one of them; lady's hands an' lady's feet. But you've lost your tongue. Haven't you ever talked to a girl before?

—Of course I have – in Irish, too.

—In Irish, eh? You know Irish then?

—Of course I do.

—What's tabhair dham póg, then?

—Give me a kiss, of course.

—Well, give me one, can't you? Well, you take care not to hurt yourself when you're kind to a girl, she said, after he had bent shyly over and kissed her lightly on the cheek. What body would believe you bowled a policeman from his horse? There now, that looks a little better, and she held up the trousers with the long rent neatly sewed together. No one'll know you were in a fight, an' you goin' home; and she flung them over the back of a chair behind the sofa.

—That's a nice brooch you're wearing, he said, pressing closer to her now.

—Isn't it? A present from the oul' uncle, taking it out of the shawl, and handing it to him. Supposed to be Vaynus. Naughty girl in the altogether. She shook her shoulders, and the shawl fell from her, leaving her in chemise and stockings. You'll scorch your jacket, and she whipped it off his legs, and flung it on the chair behind. My goodness, I can hear your heart thumping from here!

—Isn't yours thumping too? he asked. Let me feel; and he pulled loose the bow-ends of the ribbons, opening her chemise halfway down so that her taut white breasts with their rosy nipples appeared bare before him; and he pressed his hot hands over them. Then he tugged at her chemise to raise it higher on her legs, and she half rose from the sofa to let him do it properly, before she stretched down on it to wait for his coming.

Some hours afterwards she was lying on the sofa, the shawl around her, the brooch, with its dull gold rim framing the naked lady, fastening it together over her bosom; but the naked lady was naked no longer, nor did his hands ache to tear away the dark-green shawl hiding again her many buoyant beauties.

—You're in a great hurry, she said, looking at him through half-closed eyes. Can't you stay a little longer?

—I can't he said. I have a lot of work to do.

—Work! she echoed. Work on a day like this? What kinda work?

—I have a lot of things to learn, Daisy.

—Well, she said, giggling, you've learned a lot with me today, haven't you? You'll be a knowin' fellow from this out. Won't you come to see me soon again?

—Yes, of course I will. Goodbye for the present – I must be going.

—Well go, she said, sharply; no one's keepin' you. You're a good boy, she said in a softer tone, holding out her hand. There, as he pressed it hard, don't break it. You have me half dead, she added roguishly, an' poor me thinkin' you too shy to do anything dangerous! Shut the door softly afther you; and closing her eyes, she lay back on the sofa with a happy long-drawn sigh as he left her.

ALL HEAVEN AND HARMSWORTH TOO

JOHNNY'S BROTHER, Archie, had thrown up the stage as a bad and mad job. After serving as a property master in Dublin's Theatre Royal, he had gone on a crazy fit-up tour in the west with a company playing *Saved From the Sea*. One of the nights he had been put to take the money at the door; had found that when no more came, he had taken just enough to pay a third-class fare to Dublin on the midnight train. Leaving the rest of the company to do their best to keep the people happy, he hurried to the station, flung himself into a carriage corner, and arrived home, covered with white Connemara dust, wearing an old narrow-caped long coat, used for the part of Myles na Coppaleen, with three-ha'pence in one pocket and a hen egg in the other. One day, some time after, walking a country road, he had seen a big, long, well-dressed gentleman in trouble with a punctured bicycle. He came over to help, and being skilful with his hands, he soon sent the gentleman home on his way rejoicing. While mending the bicycle, the big gentleman had chatted to Archie, and mentioned that his firm, the Harmsworth Irish Agency, was in need of a clerk; and the bould Archie had ventured to offer himself for the job. One good turn deserving another, Archie got a month's trial, and proving satisfactory, the big, long man, Herbert Knox McKay, of His Majesty's Militia, and Dargaville Carr, the senior partner, had agreed to make Archie's job permanent at a pound a week. So here Archie was now, for over a year, confidential clerk of Messrs Harmsworth's Agency, trading in the Irish distribution of *Answers, Forget-me-not, Home Circle, Golden Stories, Home Chat, Sunday Companion, Comic Cuts* and *Chips*, the pioneer ha'penny boys' papers, the *Marvel, Union Jack*, and *Pluck*, the *Wonder, Boy's Friend*, and the pioneer sixpenny monthly, the *Harmsworth Magazine*. Johnny had now got a sort of a temporary job there, too, of five hours' work on five days of the week for five shillings a week, which paid the rent, provided two dinners in the week of threepence-worth of liver, or of scraps of meat for a stew, and tuppence-worth of spuds, still leaving tuppence in hand for a possible emergency.

Archie, flying high, had married the daughter of a clergyman's son's son, but neither Johnny nor his mother had seen the lady; for Johnny's broken-down appearance didn't look nice, and their home was no fit place to bring the daughter of a clergyman's son's son. The poor man, so it was said, had been fond of the bottle; and his family, after his death, and before it, were left in the rough and rocky lap of poverty. But Josephine Fairbeeley still remained a lady. On a visit to the office to see Archie, she had passed Johnny by one day – a little stumpy, plain, perky-faced lass, with an air that said to all she thought beneath her, I'm a lady born, a lady bred, an' when I die I'll be a lady dead. The one other assistant, a fellow named Drolly, gathered, it was said, cheaply out of a Foundling Hospital, in a muted whisper told Johnny that that was Archie's missus. She passed out again, with a disdainful nod to the foundling and a trivial glance at Johnny, unembarrassed, for she wist not who he was; but passed out with the pointed chin stuck out, a proud tilt to the snub nose, and a veiled glow of self-esteem shining from the dull grey eyes set deep in her perky, pawky, pucklike face. A sting of resentment shot through Johnny's emotions at being set aside for fear the knowledge of kinship should bring the wilt of shame into her walk and the frown of distant association on to her pawky face. But it lasted only for a brief while; for Johnny was building a house of his own in which there was no room for his brother or his brother's wife. And scornful thoughts of things outside of it

were hardening his heart. He knew now that he was far and away
his brother's superior, who never ventured to dispute an opinion
of his, knowing, if the argument went far, he'd but show an ignorance he was eager to hide. At the moment, Johnny was trying
his hand at German, but his funds allowed him to purchase only
a second-hand tattered German grammar for threepence, that
led him nowhere; and he was fain to wait a better time to bring a
chance to get some better books to help him. Anyway, he was
learning his own tongue gaily; and his already fine grasp of
English gave him always a readiness, and sometimes put a sparkle
into what he said to many who had been blessed with an everyday
chance from the time they were born. Poor Archie was but small
beer to him now.

He wasn't long in the job till he found that the foundling was a
sneak, encouraging the enthusiastic Johnny to try to convince him
of the rights denied to their country; listening attentively to his
warm and eloquent arguments, and then running off hot-foot to
pour all, and more, of what Johnny had said into the wide-open
ear of Militia McKay. And ever after in life Johnny found that all
charity boys were dangerous; and here began a feeling of hatred
to the Christian kindness that half-filled bellies with food, and
stuffed the mind with fear and meanness. This bright specimen
was a bouncing brave of the Young Men's Christian Association,
and didn't stop there; oh no, he must make himself a member of a
clean Christian clique whose dirty duty it was to prowl round –
after having had first a cold bath to keep their privates from rising
in alarm – and give a godfly reprimand to any man seen speaking
to a whore; or to go through the country lanes where courting
couples lay close, threatening to inform the police of an act against
public decency if a skirt went higher than a knee, or a manly finger
dared to touch a trouser button. Johnny thought that if this discordant hound of heaven ever strayed towards him, and he with a
girl, he'd make a daub of his ugly face; muck and mash and
mangle about his ugly face, and make a daring daring daub of it;
hoe the image of God out of it; and leave it lying lost and lorn in
vacancy!

One day while Archie was at the bank, and Johnny was waiting
for Drolly to fill in parcel dockets before taking the packages to
the transport agents, the boul' Herbert Knox McKay walked in,
gigantic in the full-dress uniform of an officer in the King's Royal
Rifles – sword, sabretache, an' all. He lingered in the delivery and
packing room to show himself off to Johnny and the foundling.

He was well over six foot, big-chested and broad-shouldered, but one of his knees was made of clay. A mile of a walk would send the leg sagging, in spite of it being bound up with all sorts of surgical tapes. Whenever he was in uniform, he took a car as often as possible so as to save the poor game-leg. When he had popped in, Johnny had been reading a book which he shoved into his pocket, but not before the warrior had noticed it. There he stood, facing Johnny, a gloomy figure in the foggy room, looking, in his uniform, like a smoky manual trickling from the nearest crack to hell.

—Reading, eh? What have you been reading? he asked.

—*The Life of Theobald Wolfe Tone*, sir.

—Good God! he nearly shouted, and stalked into his office. In a few moments he was at the door again, the yellow face, stuck into the sombrely-plumed busby, staring at Johnny. That sort of thing isn't read here; not here; not in a Harmsworth Office. I'm surprised you haven't the decency to think of your respectable brother. The uniform I'm wearing is the sign of what all connected with Harmsworth's believes and honours, and represents what is to go on here.

—You mean belief in monarchy, sir, do you?

—In monarchy, yes; and in everything sacred to every decent man!

—Well, sir, insisted the foolish Johnny, if you can spare me some of your time, I shall be happy to argue the why and where-fore of Republicanism.

—Republicanism? With me? Argue with me! Goood God! And the uniformed figure disappeared behind a banged door.

A fear-God-and-honour-the-king fellow, thought Johnny, who neither honours his king nor fears his God; for if he honoured the king, he would honour all men, since the king is but an exalted symbol of the subject; and if he feared God, he would readily argue with his fellow man, for is it not written, Come, let us reason together, saith the Lord of Hosts. Well, what I have said, I have said; but from the cold glint he saw in the Militia Captain's eye, he knew things would never be the same again here, and that the money for the rent, the liver, and the spuds was in danger.

He remembered, as he waited, how when McKay and McKay's wife had taken a new house and had shifted the furniture in, though not quite ready to live there that day, he had got Johnny to watch for two nights running in case of burglars. Johnny had gone to the tall, wide house, with its lovely bay windows and laurelled garden; had lighted a fire in the kitchen to keep him company; had sought for food and found none; had hurried back home for some tea and bread from his mother's small store; had watched faithfully the two long nights, a poker handy in case of invasion. On the third morning, and it pouring with rain, the boyo and the wife had come bustling in to take possession. She at once ran over, seized the tongs, and hastily began to take from the fire those lumps of coal that, though blazing, hadn't yet become red, piling them safely and prudently on the hob for future use. McKay went from room to room, followed by Johnny, to see that everything was there. He craned his neck from one of the windows, and said, Oh, he's there all right. Johnny saw that it was the gardener he meant; for, looking in the same direction, he saw the man digging, an old sack round his shoulders.

—I suppose he shouldn't be out in that rain, murmured McKay; with a bad cough, too; but he seems to like it.

—He's afraid, said Johnny; afraid to give up. Shall I run out and tell him?

—No, no, said McKay; don't disturb him. He probably wouldn't feel comfortable if he thought he wasn't earning his money fairly. You can go now, he added to Johnny; everything seems all right.

Johnny hesitated, expecting a fee, but none was offered; so he shrugged his shoulders resignedly, remembering he had told his mother the vigil would mean a few more bob for them, and that she'd scarcely credit the story that nothing had been given; yet he shrugged his shoulders, took his billy-can from the hob, saying to Mrs McKay, There, you've more room now to store the coal; turning on his heel, he left them salvaging as much of the coal as they could. Prudence, he thought, is one of the cardinal virtues.

Fairly common minds that consorted with the faith of the common newspapers, thought Johnny, watching the advance of the world through the mind of the baronet; Harmsworth, the Immanuhell of journalistic vulgarism, arraying the legitimate gets of King-Kong in the robes of glory once worn by the saints, sages, prophets, and poets of England.

The senior partner, Dargaville Carr, was an opposite to Mr McKay. He was slender, handsome, with a boyish face, ever tinted with an indifferent smile. He was good-humoured, careless, with the charming manner of an Irishman who cared not how the world wagged so long as he had satisfaction waiting on his desires. Rarely he came to the office, and when he did, he came dressed fit to kill, with a fine geranium or a dainty rose fast in his buttonhole. He came with a quick good morning to everyone, a quicker run to the inner office, an opening of the big rolltop desk, a shutting of it again, and away he was with another hearty smiling good morning to everyone. Johnny liked Dargaville Carr. Johnny had seen the original agreement between Carr on the one hand, and Harmsworth on the other: wherein was laid down in set terms, in fair handwriting, that for several hundreds of pounds, duly paid over by the said Carr to the said Harmsworth, the said Harmsworth, Journalist, would contribute his brain to the founding of a weekly journal to be called *Answers to Correspondents*, which, when founded, and in circulation, the aforesaid Dargaville Carr, Gentleman, would contribute a further sum in sterling, in return for which he would receive, without fail, the benefit of the profits flowing from the sale of the said paper in Ireland; and any Irish profits that might come from each and every and all subsequent and subsidiary publications that might spring off the foundation of the original weekly journal.

So it was that a Harmsworth, called forth by destiny and the needs of the English people, heard the English calling Come over and help us, as St Patrick had heard the voice of the Irish calling centuries before; so he said to his lord, Carr, Lord, here am I; send me, that we may deliver the goods, sanctify the English, and lead them backward to the knowledge belonging to their pees and queues; that I having been desirous, above all other things, of pupularity, may, at the end, drink dupe of the peerian spring that flows sweet Afton beyond the common ken of man's a man for a' that, and brings hellarity to all who drink its waters. And his lord gave him a bag holding two hundred shekels of gold: Go in pride, my sin, make England thy wish-pot and cast thy shoe over shedom; for it is written: in Dublin shall one be born before whom all hads shall bow, and infonts and succkerlings shall give thee willcome, and the great ones there shall be akneeled and anulled for ever. And it shall come to pass that thou hast pitched thy tint in England, then shall I send thee a bag of shekels as big as the one thou now hast, forasmuch as thou wilt do as much and more, unto me when the shekels multiply their numbers. And he answered all that I have is mine.

It was Johnny's job to bring all the packages of papers, with which the firm dealt, to the stations, or newsagents who preferred to deal with them direct, rather than with Jason's; to hunt the goods out of the boat's hold at the North Wall whenever they were late; to help in the sorting and parcelling of the papers; and to pack away the unsold copies for transport as waste paper. He pushed the packages to their various places in a handcart that had long since seen its best days. One of its rests was broken, and swung about like the broken leg of a horse; two spokes were missing from one wheel; one of the iron tyres was loose, and Johnny had to carry a hammer with him wherever he went to give it an odd knock back into its right place; and both linchpins were broken, so that they had to be carefully tied in with twine to keep the wheels from falling off – a constant source of worry to Johnny, who had always to keep an eye fixed, now on this wheel, now on that, to make sure each was all right, and watch his way through the traffic at the same time. This old car, bought second-hand, was part of the firm's economy, as was the saving of old paper, old rope, and old twine.

Cursing and sweating, he pushed the haggard car along, on a lovely evening in the late spring. Packed high it was with the latest number of the *Harmsworth Magazine*. Rotten Dublin; lousy Dublin, what had it for anyone? What had it for him? Poverty and pain and penance. They were its three castles. The gates of Dublin: poverty, pain, and penance. And the *Harmsworth Magazine*, giving, with the aid of its kind, to Dublin the glory that was Greece and the grandeur that was Rome. Now he was a barrennut. Thank God, the Gaelic League was doing all it could to turn the Irish people from a descent into a vulgar and idiotic Tophet; but, so far, with little success. The Orange cover of *Answers* covered the whole country. The priest had it in the inner pocket of his soutane; the teacher had it on his desk; the student had it under his arm; the labourer had it round his lunch; the soldier had it in his sentry-box; the postman in his bag; and the policeman had it on his beat; for *Answers* stooped to conquer. Tomorrow would be the day for that joy journal; and he'd be carrying a heavy cargo again, for there was a new competition on, offering as first prize a thousand pounds down, or two pounds a week for life. An' everybody would be stretching out a hand for it. Lousy, rotten, tiring Dublin, an ignorant perjury of life.

He pushed on through Parliament Street, up Cork Hill, through Lord Edward Street, into Cornmarket, delivering here, delivering there, till he reached James Street where he emptied the ould handcart of its last parcel. Then he sailed down Watling Street to go homewards by the quays, for he loved to see the river Liffey when the sun was setting, passing by many shops and houses looking like poor bewildered whores bullied with too long a life.

Harmsworth and his henchmen! He pictured them assembling round their master to hear the orders for the year: Bullcalf, Feeble, Snout, Mouldy, Shallow, Wart, Fang, and Snare. He heard him say unto them: Attention! We're here to follow, not to teach. Look out for likely whims, and cater to them. Who are we to look down on ignorance? No, look up to it, for it has great power. Get down to it; you won't have to go far. The less you know the better. What do you know? What can you know? What do you want to know? Nothing. Repeat that after me. Don't forget these essential points: One, the English girl has ne'er an equal. Two, marriage is a mainstay, with the baby, and, of course, Mother. Three, the prickle of a sprig of holly in everything you say about Christmas. Four, England will always weather the worst; and don't let either God or a good story be far from your elbows. Better learn all that off be heart. Salem. It's your life. We are the eyes of the world, the ears of the world, the voice of the world. We bring the second ark. Shiloh. Learn that off be heart too.

The twilight was getting close to the skirts of day when Johnny swung his chariot on to the quays confining the river like a pair of lusty arms round a pretty lass. Over to the sou'-west the sky was a vivid green mantle, bordered with gold, a crimson gold that flowered grandly against the green, darkening into a gentle magenta higher up and farther away in the sky; and farther away still, the faint glimmer of the first stars was peeping out from a purple glow of purple gloom. Numerous empty lorries, floats, vans, and drays were flowing quickly past him, each of them, under the magic sky, looking like flaming chariots making for a battle front. He saw golden arrows of the sun shooting up side streets, leading from the quay to God knows where. Here the hard, set, and leering faces of roughs leaning against a corner had changed into sturdy faces of bronze where the sun's shadow lingered, and became darkly golden where the sun's departing beams strayed towards them. The bridges looked like golden pathways, growing grey dauntlessly, turning from pride to get gentleness and peace. He left the crippled handcart by the side of the street, and went over to lean upon the river wall to gaze at Dublin in the grip of God. The old tattered warehouses and shops, bespangled with the dirt of ages, had turned to glory. Children, born into a maze of dirt, their vagrant garments clinging wildly to their spattered bodies, put on new raiment, satinized with the princely rays of the sun, as if she had winced at their ugliness and had thrown her own fair mantle over them all. The great dome of the Four Courts shone like a golden rose in a great bronze cup. The river flowing below was now a purple flood, marbled with gold and crimson ripples. Seagulls flew upward, or went gliding swooning down through thin amber air; white gems palpitating on the river's purple bosom. And far away in the deep blue the stars grew braver, and sat with dignity in their high places, bowing the sun away out of the silken heavens. Johnny bowed his head and closed his eyes, for it was very beautiful, and he felt that his city could catch an hour of loveliness and hold it tightly to her panting breast.

A rippling thrill of emotional ecstasy crept through him, looking at the sky above and at the river beneath; all this beauty and much more, everlasting, to be his and all men's through the life, passion, and death of the wonderful Jesus, when the glare of this poor life slowly darkened into death. He sang softly and fervently, watching the mauve and golden buildings, the crimsoned waters of the river beneath him, the sky like a mantle streaming from the shoulders of God, the Father. Softly and fervently he sang, sang softly to himself and the loveliness around him:

> When our brisk hands build strong where work is done,
> Where steel is forg'd, or gentle silk is spun,
> All work well finish'd, with work that's well begun,
>   Let it praise Thee, let it praise Thee!

> All th' white joy that shines in children's play,
> And th' rich laugh that rings when youth is gay,
> All th' still pleasure in life now turning grey,
>   Let them praise Thee, let them praise Thee!

> Even when horrid poverty and pain
> Darkens th' senses with their stinging stain,
> And human hearts are bow'd beneath the strain,
>   Give us strength, Lord, strength to praise Thee!

> In th' wide streets where th' rich are in full cry,
> In the wide stores where workers serve and sigh,
> In th' dark crannies where th' poorer lie,
>   Give them grace, Lord, grace to seek Thee!

Hearten our city's strife with manners mean;
Blend with our bread the bread of life unseen,
With a gay rose's beauty in between,
    We beseech Thee, we beseech Thee!

He resolved to be strong; to stand out among many; to quit himself like a man; he wouldn't give even a backward look at the withering things that lived by currying favour with stronger things; no busy moving hand to the hat for him. He would enlarge on a spare life, never pausing to pick up a prize that perished as soon as the hand grasped it. His treasures would be simple things, like those gathered together by St MacCua, who had a cock who served his owner by crying lustily at midnight to warn the saint it was time to greet the day with his first devotions; a mouse that saw the saint wasted no more than five hours a day in sleep, nibbling at his master's ear, should he sleep on, till the torment brought the saint to himself, and encouraged him to keep up his devoirs to Almighty God; and a fly that strolled along the lines of the psalter as it was being read aloud by MacCua, settling on the last word murmured when the weary saint rested, remaining there, still as death itself till the saint came back to resume the reading of a canticle declaring penitence or praise. And, O Lord, wasn't it the dark hour for the saint when, one day, his three treasures died, each within a minute of the other, compelling the heart-broken man to write to Colmkille complaining of the great loss these three pets meant to him; getting back a note from the Dove of Iona counselling him not to be cast down, not to wonder at the sudden taking-away of his flock, for their loss was but one more instance of the quick departure of the world's wealth, poor Mac-Cua regarding the Dove's gentle joke as a tender reminder that he shouldn't have been so much attached to the treasures of this fleeting world. So, something like MacCua, he would seek the things that endured; his treasures would be books, bought by the careful gathering of widely, scattered pence. From life he had learned much; and from books he would learn more of the wisdom thought out, and the loveliness imagined, by the wiser and greater brethren of the human family.

He rose up out of his sturdy thinking and his soft singing, went over to the handcart, and began again to push it along the golden road, with the dome of the Four Courts on his left still looking like a great yellow rose in a great bronze cup. At a corner of a street, lower down, a hurdy-gurdy began to play a dance

tune in a violet shadow. He stopped again by the river wall to
listen. The player was robed with the sun as if for a religious
festival. A young woman, dressed in a dark-red bodice and a
black-and-white striped skirt, tapped her feet in the same violet
pool and swung golden arms to the beat of the gay music. Then
she began to dance. Johnny watched her. She laughingly beckoned
to him with a golden hand. He flung off his coat, took a great
red handkerchief from a pocket and bound it round his waist like
a sash. He hurried over, caught in the golden glamour of the
dancer's face, beat time for a moment to the tune, got the swing
of it, and then jumped into the hilarious dance of the young
woman. At a little distance, a group, more soberly clad, for they
stood in the deep shade of a huge building, here and there
flecked with the red rays of the sun, stood and watched and
quietly clapped their hands. The young woman caught Johnny's
hand in her own, and the two of them whirled round in the bonny
madness of a sun-dance, separating then so that she whirled into
a violet shadow, while he danced into a golden pool, dancing
there for a little, then changing places, he to be garbed in the
hue of a purple shadow, and she to be robed in a golden light.

—Grandchildren of kings! he shouted, in the midst of the
dancing; sons and daughters of princes, we are one with the race
of Milesius!

—The finest colours God has in His keeping are round us now,
she panted.

—Th' sword of light is shining!

The violet shades grew darker, the golden light was tinged with
scarlet, but still they danced, and still the player played, waving a
dark hand against a green plane in the sky, and beating lustily to
the time of the tune with an excited foot in a purple pool. Then
they tired, their movements slackened, went slower, waned faster,
and finally came to an end with their arms round each other, while
the dusky figures in the watching group clapped their hands softly,
murmuring that it was well done and was worth the doing. He gave
the hurdy-gurdy man his last sixpence and kissed the girl goodbye.

—You're lovely staying still, he said, and brimming over with a
wilder beauty in the sprightly dance; may you marry well, and
bring up children fair as Emer was, and fine as Oscar's son; and
may they be young when Ireland's free, when Spanish ale foams
high on every table, and wine from the royal Pope's a common
dhrink!

He shoved his handcart along again under the motley dome of the sky, tired, but joyous, praising God for His brightness and the will towards joy in the breasts of men, the swiftness of leg and foot in the heart of a dance, for the gift of song and laughter, for the sense of victory, and the dream that God's right hand held firm. The green, the scarlet, the gold, and the purple – what were they but the glow from the wings of the angels pathrolling the streets of the city.

But the glory of the angels was departing, for the jubilant colours dimmed into darkness, save where, in the distant horizon, a crimson streak showed where the curtains of night had not yet been pulled together. God's shadow was still there, for every church he passed had floods of people pouring into them. He lingered by one of them, and watched the flood going in by the main door, tributaries flowing more gently in by doors on the side, paying a minimum sixpence there, and, at the main gateway, anything above a penny to the Confraternity man standing in the porch, holding a long-handled box, with a wide slit cut in the top to receive the coins, hopping swiftly about, shaking the box encouragingly before those ready to give, and shaking it threateningly under the nose of those who tried to slip in without paying their due. A poster on a gothically-topped board told all that a Mission was being given by a Dominican who was to preach on Hell and the Many Roads that Lead There; and Johnny felt a whiff of brimstone as he looked through the wide-open door. Thoughts of a frightful form and hue hurried through his mind, and harried him, for he saw himself fixed in, and frozen fast in fire eternal; fire keener in its thrust than tusks of steel, while whirlwinds of icy winds and smoky storms, suffocating the burning air, raged all around him, plunging his soul from the deepest misery to a misery deeper still; with senses tuned by immortality to their highest pitch, impaled by justice to endure them all; buried in a screaming pain, yet rushing pell-mell to a fiercer, biting woe; ever shrieking for a chance, that died ten thousand years ago, to come to life again; a shriek, once uttered, sunk to silence by the malice-mongering laughter of hardened devils tossed to hell in heaven's first battle with an evil power. O Lord most mighty, O holy and most merciful Saviour, he murmured, deliver me not into the bitter pains of eternal death. He looked through the wide-open door again and saw, up at the far end of the nave, the shining altar, surrounded with carpeted steps, gay with glittering lights, glowing on a great gilt crucifix, hanging behind, and in its centre some sacred vessel, covered by a pure white veil.

A holy city's our city of Dublin, thought Johnny; more ancient than Athens; more sacred than Rome; as holy as Zion. From every window, if one had only eyes to see, flew a banner that was a red, brown, white, or blue scapular, each with some holy words of the Lord, or one of His saints, embroidered across its field; and from every pillar and every wall hung festoons of rosary beads, the precious jewels of a poor people. Night and day the air was alive with an everlasting murmur of Pater Nosters and Hail Marys, Sé do bheatha, a Mhuire dhílis, he murmured, atá lán de grása; 'tá an Tighearna leat (God thy life, O sweet Mary, who art full of grace; the Lord is with thee). Other lands might boast of their lions and unicorns, their double-headed eagles, or the fleur-de-lis; but here we had the Sacred Heart, sliced with the wound the lance made, and duplicates of the massive keys of St Peter, hanging at the girdle of the Pope. There were more saints in Ireland to the square inch than in any other country on the globe. All the people, at a penny a week, were preparing for a good death; all were enlisted in the army of prayer, praying for the holy souls, prostrate in purgatory; snug on many a manly chest, and lying shyly between the breasts of many a fair potential bosom, lay a tiny miraculous medal, warming away the chill of the fear of disaster or death from the souls of them who wore it. St Dominic knew the streets of Dublin as well as those of Cala-horra; his hand, that fell hot and heavy on the Albigenses, lies gently on the heads here; for of his three great rules, poverty and fasting are kept by crowds of people, though the third of silence has yet a long way to come; and St Francis has gathered more pale and scarlet roses from the wretched wrecked streets of this city than he ever gathered from the grove outside of Portincula.

It was dark now; each street lamp hissed as he passed it; all the buildings were dark, grim, and lowering; the passer-by moved jerkily along, and his joints were creaking; all the sparkling dresses of an hour ago were folded up and put away; and Johnny was just pushing a crippled handcart down a sombre street. He came up with an old, heavily-grey-bearded, bent man chanting a hymn mournfully along the kerb-way. He wore a long, old, grey top-coat reaching to his heels. A section of the hem at the back had ripped away and trailed behind him on the cobblestones. His white head was reverentially bare, and he carried his dinged and

faded bowler in a hand behind his back. He walked slowly along
the kennel, his face turned sideways towards the footpath, watching the passers-by to see if any would show a sign of a search for
a coin, ready to bring the hat with a gentle sweep in front of him
to capture any coin that might be offered. On he moved, three
slow steps at a time, then a pause, then another three slow steps
forward. Moving with him, three steps, a pause, then three more
steps, were a group of gaping children, a sad audience to a sadder
song. They stared open-eyed whenever an emotional tear welled
from his eye and trickled down a furrowed cheek. When he came
near, Johnny saw that the old singer was irritated by the staring
kids, saw a wicked light in his moist eye when he happened to
glance at them and a muttered complaint rippled roughly through
the chanting flow of the hymn. Happily plaintive he made the
hymn, and bitter the mutter meant for the children:

To Jesu's heart all burning with fervent love for men –

—G'way, little gapers, keepin' me from doin' justice to meself!

My heart with fondest yearning shall raise the joyful strain –

—Hell an' hot wather to yous, for idle little ruts!

While ages course along, blest be with loudest song,
Th' Sacred Heart o' Jesus by every heart an' tongue!

Johnny pushed on, walking alongside two men, chatting to-
gether, who were going in the same direction.
—That oul' fella's hymn-singin's after givin' me a sudden idea
about the lone picture I have a doubt of, th' one showin' a kinda
deer an' a letther that's half an eff an' half a dee.
—Now isn't that curious, rejoined the other. What was it?
—Th' deer, a hart – see? and the letther a dee or an eff –
Hartford – see?
—Begod you've got it! Though I never hearda Hartford.
—Nor me, either; but it must be right. What the last ten'll be
like, God knows – stiff ones, I'll take me oath. He rubbed his
hands together, and crinkled his face with a smile; but the missus
is doin' a Novena for me, an' if that doesn't bring luck, I don't
know what will. A thousand down, Bill, or two pounds a week
for life. Jasus, if I won! I'd never see a poor day.

Heaven and Harmsworth close together. Goethe's last wish for more light at last fulfilled. A roaring British Buddha. He comes, he comes, he comes o'er the waters to me. Pieoneers, O Pieoneers. A silk umbrella and the handle of a broom. Broomlay, Fumelay, Doomlay, Zoom. The Congo Comes to Canterbury.

Johnny began to hurry home, for an earlier rising lay before him; *Answers*, the Golden One, would be out tomorrow.

PICTURES IN THE HALLWAY

A NEW RECTOR was expected to come soon to the parish of St Burnupus. Strange ministers from different parishes came Sunday after Sunday to conduct matins and evensong, to preach tired-out sermons, and so hold the fort and keep the young flag flying. The few who came to church regularly, whispered that the new rector was a fine preacher; and that was most important, for the pulpit, not the Holy Table, was the important point in a Protestant church. There was waiting for him a tiny world of faint religion, vague, timid of anything a step away from a rare reading of a Bible verse; a happy or tearful belief that God made a call and left a card at baptism, marriage, or the burial of the dead; a faith that felt easy when *Abide With Me* was sung at eveningtide, or, *Now that Daylight Fills the Sky, We Lift our Hearts to God on High*, by whomsoever happened to be in church at half past eleven on a Saturday morning, and *Hark, the Herald Angels Sing*, while the big and small bells rang out on a brisk and bonny Christmas morning. Regular worshippers were few, for here there was small chance of making a good thing out of Christ. The children were kept busy, piling Bible story and Bible verse into their memories, fast and furious, making up for their parents' sang-freud, sleeping long and soberly Sundays, in the warmth of their beds; reading newspapers fattened on stories of battle, murder, and sudden death, or of jangling jingles in the bedrooms of the nicely rich; eating their fancy's fill in the early evening; yawning their way back to bed again when the moon began her gentle dance in the sky. The parish had raised a sleepy head on a reclining arm when Harry Fletcher came, to have a look at him who came in the name of the Lord, had opened its drooping eyes a little wider for a small moment, and had fallen back into a deeper sleep when Harry left. The people had an idea, in a dazed way, that somehow or other God had made a wonderful world, underfoot and overhead; though underfoot was rough, marred with dust, and stony. Their way to heaven was a lifelong journey through never-ending streets of dingy houses, some of the wayfarers stopping now and then for a drink in a gayer house, glass-framed, and painted a shining red or green, and gilded. In the daytime, making a brush at Varian's, pushing a truck in a railway store, handling a pick on the roads, dishing out tea and sugar in a tea store, carrying a hod up a shaking ladder, or filling in invoices stuck all day to a standing-steady desk: there we all were (or, as Johnny was himself, an inspector of public buildings – the name given to an out-of-work in Dublin), amaking atonement with God in the best way that they could for the fall of Adam, the sin of disobedience bringing death into the world and all our woe, the sin that gave room for the more sinister and desperate one of original sin; for as the psalmist hath said, I was born in iniquity, and in sin hath my mother conceived me; a hard lot to live down, thought Johnny, for every pretty girl that passed sent Johnny's heart singing,

> Under th' blossoming mulberry bush
> A girl's undone in a panting hush,
> When th' stars are bright, where th' grass is lush,
>   On a saintly summer evening.

Good-looking girlish faces and shapely legs apart, the hard, beamless, grey, sleety mist of the dourer Protestantism chilled Johnny; and he crept forward out of it into a brighter and more musical conception of the Christian faith. Colour had come to him, had bowed, laughing, and now ran dancing before him. He had saved some of what he got for doing an occasional job, and had bought a tiny box of paints. He had always loved sketching, and had, in younger days, covered every scrap of fair paper coming into the house, as well as the back parts of pictures in books, with his ideas of battles, and, later on, of men and women; but now that colour had come to him, he longed to be a painter, and his very bowels yearned for the power to buy tubes of cobalt blue, red lake, chrome yellow, Chinese white, emerald green, burnt sienna, and a deep black pigment. Long and prayerfully he had looked in at the window of a big shop in Dawson Street that sold these things, his eyes ravished with the water-

colours displayed there; at the brushes, thin and delicate; the
piled-up boxes of paints of every sort and size; the pyramids of
tubes filled with glowing colours; all so near, yet so far, so far
away from the reach of his hand and the further reach of his
longing soul. He would sometimes curse his poverty, and finish
with a soft prayer that means would be provided to let him buy
what would give him a chance to put on paper the wonderful
colours his eyes saw and his heart loved. He was too ragged and
too shy to venture a visit to the portly, pompous, and awe-
spreading National Gallery. He did the next best thing; at second-
hand book barrows he picked up, for a few pence, two books
enshrining pictures by a religious painter called Fra Angelico,
and one showing lovely things his eyes had not yet seen, far away
from Dublin, of wood, lake, pond, and peasants thrown together,
like a sudden burst of music; all by a fellow named Constable.
With all he had learned from the Bible and the prayer-book it was
but an easy jump into the brightly-tinted world of Angelico;
and from the little church of St Burnupus, in its desolate seat
among the dust of the dowdy streets, the cinders of the bottle-
making factory of North Lotts, for ever pouring out its murky
plumes of smoke, the scarred heaps of mouldering bark and
timber chips round Martin's timber yard, the dung of the cattle,
passing in droves down to the quays, the smell of the beer-
soaked sawdust, floating out from the wide-open doors of the
pubs, blending its smell with that of the foul rags of the festering,
fawning poor, Johnny ferried himself safely to the circle of delicate blue showing forth Angelico's golden-haired Saviour clad in
a robe of shimmering creamy grey, a shining orb in a beautiful
left hand, a halo of heavy gold, transversed with a crimson cross,
encircling His heavenly head; or, there He was, standing in a
purple arch of the heavens, staff in hand, looking with love on
two Dominican brothers, one of whose hands timidly touched
the Saviour's, the two of them dressed in robes tenderly cream,
covered with sombre black cloaks cunningly tinged with green,
standing there gazing at Christ with a look that reverently called
God their comrade. Again, with Angelico, he wandered through
clouds of angels, a little stiff with innocence, thronging the skies
like gaily-coloured Milky Ways, crimson or green or blue-gowned,
powdered with stars or roses or golden fleurs-de-lis. Sometimes he
chanted hymns softly to himself, strolling towards heaven through
a field of pinks and roses, meeting often on his way more lovely
angels, blowing with fattened cheeks through golden trumpets, or

stringing delicate white fingers over graceful psalteries or zithers, sounding in honour of the Blessed Virgin, while her Son fixed another gem in her crown of glories.

Again, under the green, sunlit, or dewy trees, planted by Constable's imagination, giving shade and gracefulness to an eager sun, he wandered afield; or looking down where the ripening corn was striding upward to a golden grandeur, he wandered down quiet paths rimmed with vivid green, touched in with lavish blossoms, shyly forcing forward to kiss a greeting to the careless passer-by; while red-brown cattle, drowsing in the field beyond, stood knee-deep in the sappy grass, the honeyed smell of clover brooding delicately over the sleepy meadow, soothing the sweating brows of boatmen poling barges down the placid river full of sunny nooks making the green shades greener; gentle houses peering out from among the stately elms, the plumy poplars, and the proudly-nurtured ash with its sweeping foliage, moving in the wind, like a dancing Fragonard lady, coy with pride, and fancying herself the gem of the world around her; and over all the greying silver and the tender blue of a fresh and beaming sky.

So, through these two men, beauty of colour and form above and beside him came closer; came to his hand; and he began to build a house of vision with them, a house not made with hands, eternal in his imagination, so that the street he lived in was peopled with the sparkling saints and angels of Angelico, and jewelled with the serene loveliness Constable created out of the radiance of uncommon clay. Even when the rooms were bare of fire and scant of food, he sang and wondered that life had so much to give; and he tried to share all these sights with his mother; but he saw they had but a timid and feebly-whispered message for her, sending her more eagerly back to the motherly care of her crimson geranium, her golden musk, and her fuchsia, with its purple bells and white waxy sepals drooping royally over the sadness of the cracked and withering window.

Into this glowing dwelling-place of Johnny's came the new rector, to take up the pastorate of St Burnupus. Quietly he came, introduced by the city's archbishop, who left the smoke, the cinders, the timber chips, the dung, and the hearty smell as quick as he decently could in his carriage and pair, when he had safely dumped down the new rector where he was to work for the salvation of souls. The archbishop left behind a man of middle height, some forty-five years of age, a sweet face, bearded brown, now firmly streaked with silver; eyes that sometimes glowed with a ripe autumnal friendship, and sometimes glittered with a wintry scorn; small, delicate, graceful, and sympathetic hands; a warm, sensitive, and humorous mouth; a fine presence, gracefully rugged, that endorsed the confidence of a broad and scholarly mind. A man among men; few there were that could stand beside him, and when the place was found where these few were, it would be hard to say the best of them was as good as he was.

A great stir came to the parish with Edward Morgan Griffin, son of a Methodist minister, and once one of the secretaries of the Hibernian Bible Society, so that here was one who was surely a hale Protestant after the Orangeman's pattern, and a joy for ever to the simple soul believing that salvation came with the mumbling of a text of scripture. The choir began to sing well, and Johnny sat with them, singing lustily when he was in the mood, the rector telling him not to be afraid to let himself go. Bible classes flourished, and Foreign Mission work was strongly aided, Johnny acting as secretary to this activity. The vestry was enlarged and made warm and comfortable for smaller meetings. The school grew so that it had to have a new wing added; and the religious life of the parish became vigorous, homely, orderly, and genuine under the direction and with the encouragement of the new rector. Orangemen, purplemen, and knights of the grand black chapter, with civil and religious liberty stamped on their stony faces, hemmed him in, smiled at him, and patted him on the back. Cordons of orange and blue and purple were all around him; and, for a time, all new work was born in contentment and charm. The Orangemen were headed by the people's churchwarden, Frank Donaldson, secretary to the Grand Loyal Orange Lodge of Dublin, a man to whom any speck of colour on a church wall or in a window meant popery and *auto-da-fés* of burning Protestants every morning in Rutland Square, and twice a day on Sundays. His pale, pitiless face for ever stared in front of him, seeing nothing but the evil and the danger of a fringe on a church cloth, and a devil's conjuring trick in the sign of the cross; Edward Doosard, Inspector of the Quay Police (doddering old men, in their childhood, watching the warehouses of the Port and Docks Board, showing gold and brass where the real police showed silver, the dockers cursing them, and the carters cutting at them with their whips whenever they got in the way), his ruby face, jowled like Dutch cheeses, his bull-neck forming a circle above a white collar, like a thick rubber hose, a rusty-fleshed fat hand almost always stroking a bristly moustache, and his piggy eyes trying to tell everyone that he was a pillar of Protestantism; and John Glazier, foreman in the Great Western Railway Goods Store; a true-blue, if ever there was one; a man who would be ready to die for his faith, his rugged face carved like a stone creviced by centuries of frost and rain; his jagged teeth showing grimly when he mentioned some taint of ritualism in some Protestant church; his hands twitching as if they were edging towards a pope's throat. His was the hand of the one in the three that Johnny could hold tight; and here, now, they stood on a high bank, a-swing with millions of moon-daisies, looking down over a fair valley, watching – an eye for the green, and an eye for the orange and blue.

THE BUTTLE OF THE BOYNE

Here on this side of the Jordan stretched out the forces of the great, glorious, pious, and immortal King Billy, Brandyburgers, French Hueforgetmenots, Swiss Swingillians, Dutch Blue Guards, Scandalnavians, the Dublin Quay Police, under Inspector Doosard, and the boys from Sandy Row, with orange banners, blue, purple, and black banners; and there on the other side of the river were the Irish, with one green banner bearing the rising sun; these moving to the left, and the others moving to the right so that they would, sooner or later, come with a clash against each other. Over there, on the opposite side, close to Dinmore Church, watching the Irish Army, all dhressed in their jackets green, with spreading white cockhades in their hats, singing in mournful numbers, *Quick! We have not a Second*, King James sat on his horse, facing south, munching his fists in an agony of sufficient for the day is the evil thereof; his wide-brimmed hat, fairily plumed, pulled down over his black brambly brows, crossing himself from right to left and from left to right so as to make no mistake, in sheer bewilderment at the cannon-balls sailing, sailing over from fifty Protestant guns, ever belching orange flame and blue smoke from their snarling muzzles, twitching himself nearly outa the saddle at every shot; green ribbons knotted on his shoulders, and green ribbons flying from his hair, with *Erin Go Brag* stamped on every inch of them to act as a charm; a harper on his right hand playing *Remember the Glories of Brian, the Brave*, for all he was worth, to get heard over the cannon-fire,

be the main strength he used in plucking the strings; and a piper
on his left hand blowing himself daft in the tune of *I'm Asleep and
don't Waken Me* so as to dhrown the thunder of the thousand and
one Protestant dhrums of the stalwarts of Sandy Row and the
Diamond, beatin' out the tune of *Lilly Bullero Bullen a Law*,
facing forward in front of King Billy's army itching to go over
and down the rabble that adored a god of bread, and signposts
carved and coloured; egged on be cowled monks, with ropes
round their bellies, that should, be right, be around their necks;
carrying loads of lumber to be set up in their churches to give
each corner its own miracle; the thought of it all causin' John
Glazier to send a straight spit of disgust out an' over an' into the
Boyne.

—If only Sarsfield would shake himself loose, said Johnny; if
only Sarsfield could come to the front; if only Sarsfield would head
his horsemen, we'd dhrive King Billy an' his bullyballs head-short
back to their downlands an' dykes on the farther side of the
Zideree Zee.

—He can't move, shouted Glazier joyously, for he's bound to
the chain that binds the beast; an' looksee that bright one forbias
us, with a dhrawn sword in his hand: Art thou for us, or for
adversaries? he called out, above the roaring roll of the drums;
and the bright one said, Nay, but as captain of the Lord's host
am I now come; and Glazier shouted, Hail! well met, brother; for
if you stole a big pig, sure, I stole another. There's the Dutch
Blue Blackguards makin' for the river through a broad vale of
golden buttercups; plunge! in they go, up to their middles in
water, holdin' their muskets over their head: keep your balls an'
powder dhry, me boys, an' your hopes high, for there's no Finn
McCool here now to toss a thousand men in a single second an' a
double throw from where he was to the Isle o' Man in the Sea o'
Moyle's seethin' centre; oh, an' look at them three bleatin'
bastards, Redmond, Dillon, and wee Joey Devlin, dodgin'
behint a round tower, with a wolf-dog lyin' down forbye them;
an' up on the highest bough of an oak-three, the oily-faced
Gladstone, watchin' them, with his Home Rule Bill, that would
be Rome rule, in his hip-pocket, nimble for any evil that
would dislocate the onward march of the Protestant cause of
Erin.

—They're driven back, th' Irish are dhrivin' them back!
shouted Johnny; for the green jackets had lepped into the water,
had come on with their pikes outstandin', hurling the Blue

Blackguards head-over-tip back to the bank they'd just jumped down from, on they came tearin' ahead, singin'

> *Hurrah for the sons of the Shamrock,*
> *Who always victorious have been;*
> *And where is the nation can equal*
> *The boys of old Erin, the green!*

while King Billy on his great white horse galloped along the margin of the river where masses of fragrant meadow-sweet were being flattened by the falling bodies of Blue Guard and Black papist, their white cluster cozened to crimson by the oozing away of the last few moments of life left livin', an' he yelling in a tantrum of fear; Where's me Hueforgetmenots, where's me Inniskilleners, where's me Boys from Sandy Row, an' Doosard with his Dublin Quay Police! Stir yourselves, there, or we're in for popery, brass money, and wooden shoes; throw back the rebels, an' save the laygal government, an' bring peace an' Protestantism an' prosperity to the deluded people of Erin!

—Up, Sarsfield! yelled Johnny.

—Up, King Billy! roared Glazier.

And they turned aside and smote each other, so that their noses bled, and their teeth loosened; and they wrestled, the one with the other, on the grassy bank, among the moon-daisies, between the hedges that were a wild wondher of dog-rose and bramble-blossom.

Then the Inniskilleners, in their orange tunics and true-blue trews, headed by Johnston of Ballykilbeg, wavin' a purple flag with the picture of Randolph Churchill on it, holdin' th' torch of truth, all gallous boys, brethren of the Shepherd's Poy, each with the bumpy gallopin' journey on the back of a goat through a wilderness behind him; each had sat on his arse watching the burning bush, and had crossed the Jordan with Joshua; for they, the Orangemen, purplemen, and blackmen, were even as the men of the tribes of Reuben, the men of the tribe of Gad, and half of the tribe of Manasseh, who went armed before their brethren till their brethren should find rest in the land given them be God; so that each man bore on his breast the sacred number of two and a half; close behind them came the Hueforgetmenots, in their black-and-white uniforms, a crimson plume in their heavy helmets, a silver Bible shining on their breasts, cheerin' for love an' learnin', with the young, apple-cheeked Duke o' Skumberg at their head, his pristine Protestant conscience well locked up in steel; and, to the right of the line, the tut-tut-tuttering old Dublin Quay Police, all in shorts, Edward Doosard leading them off, with a hazel wand in his hand to divine where the water was when he came to the river.

—Oh! look at it – the white, young, romish-wrinkled face of that Harry Fletcher peerin' through the cannon smoke, an' a popish biretta on's head, spoutin' th' Athanasian Creed outa him, an' he turnin' towards the east an' prayin' for the pope's intentions! yelled out Glazier, above the rool of the thousand an' one drums, as he broke off from Johnny's attempt to give him a half-nelson; an' there in th' more distant smoke's th' dim face of St Burnupus' rector, devoted to the formularies, an' shilly-shallyin' with the scarlet woman, the whore of Babylon, who's dhrunk with the blood of the saints, hard at it in the midst of the soaring an' falling bumballs, redhot from the cannons' mouths!

—If y'only knew, you poor pitiful ignorant man, the Pope's praying as hard as he can for the success of the Protestant King Billy, an' the defeat of the Catholic James! said Johnny, trying to get a grip on Glazier again.

—It's a lie, a red an' a roarin' lie! yelled Glazier; for the Pope couldn't pray for anything good an' wholesome, an' th' Vatican's kindled a thousand candles to be burnin' all night before a thousand images to bring about th' desthruction of the good King Billy an' the Protestant cause! Till hell with th' Pope, an' God save King Billy! and Glazier caught hold of Johnny's throat.

—Yeh bloody bigot! yelled Johnny, catching hold of his, God save th' Pope, an' to hell with King Billy!

They struggled among the moon-daisies, their hands circling each other's throats, panting, and hot with envy and hatred; while the cannons blazed away with their venom, and the drums rolled out the glory of strife, till Johnny saw the Irish yielding their bodies to the musket-balls, and the points of the pikes, slowly reeling back, slowly giving way, slowly dying for a foreign king; saw King James turn his horse's head and begin a gallop fast and fearful on the rocky road to Dublin, with Sarsfield, head down, riding beside him, filling the air with and fooling the air with the shout of, Change kings, and we'll fight the battle over again!

Johnny flung Glazier aside and crossed the river by a shallow ford, for the tide was ebbing fast. Looking back, he saw Glazier standing in the midst of blue, orange, and purple banners keenin' over the bodies of Johnny Walker, the clergyman, and the apple-cheeked Duke o' Skumberg, now white as a fresh-blown water-lily, bleachin' in the sun. He shook his clenched fist at Glazier, then turned and dashed through the scattered yellow irises and flattened meadow-sweet, leppin' over countless green-jacketed bodies, now part o' the ground they were sthretched on; dim now are all the hopes for the Catholics in the silver Mass-bell; dying away fast is the thought of drinking the red wine and the yellow ale woven in gaudy dhreams of golden jollity; sighing they go, with the crowds of muddied white cockhades they go, forlornly floatin' down the tide.

—Come back, come back! he shouted after the fleeing King; come back, Seumas, a chaca; come back, Seumas, the shit!

But the King, lying forward on his horse's neck, flew on, forward to a narrower cell of life, to be sealed up for ever with tormenting delusion. All round were soldiers, enamelled in dust and sweat, worn out, their tired senses shrinking from sleep, streaming towards Duleek to get quick on the road to Dublin; and far off, in front of them, oreoled in a cloud of dust, ran Redmond, Dillon, and wee Joey Devlin to get away from the flying bumballs and the beat of the Protestant drums. To his right the village of Old-bridge was a big ball of rolling black smoke from which shot scarlet plumes of flame wherever the thatch of the people's houses blazed. Over in the thick shelter of bushy brambles, half hidden there, heedless of the torturing thorns, frightened faces peered out, watching their simple houses turn to a smoky memory. Farther on to the right, where the struggle had been bitther, he thought he saw, as in a glass darkly, the bearded gentle face of Mr Griffin stooping over faintly-stirring forms, here holding the hand of a bluecoat, there the hand of a green-jacket, a look of sorrowing wonder on his sweet face, for nowhere was there a herb to heal this wound, nowhere a prayer potent to absolve a sorrow like unto this sorrow.

Johnny turned and ran off with great speed, catching up with an old officer puffing his way along from capture or killing. His green coat was torn and muddy, his feet squelched in his sodden jackboots, one golden epaulette hung in tattered shreds from a shoulder, and his tired eyes, dull as a long-dead blue flower, stared in front of him as he ran. He had flung away belt and scabbard, but carried his sword, naked, in his hand.

—Why're you runnin' away? shouted Johnny at him. Are the Irish all turned cowards? Why don't you stand your ground?

—Who's running away? puffed the officer. We're not running away, I'd like you to know. This movement's only one with a pre-arranged plan to take up a betther position. We're tempting th' enemy on, boy, whose black soul's fresh from Satan's arms. They may win the battles, but we'll win the war. That bumball fell a little too close, eh? The world's with us. All God-fearing people are on our side. For God and humanity – those are the holy stakes we're playing for, and the battle we've just fought'll go down in history as an epic; for in it was really a defeat for th' dour and bestial, sullen monarch Billy and all his sooty-nurtured crew. He thought and planned to smash us in five minutes; but took them five long and hotly-passing hours to break and batther through, giving us the vital time to prepare to meet him in a betther place.

—I know of no betther place than the one you're runnin' away from, said Johnny.

—If you don't, we do, but we don't tell everyone, and so aid the enemy. If you go on with undermining talk, me boy, you're just as well in an enemy column.

—Isn't me whole nature longin' to see you win? said Johnny.

—Act accordin', then, if it is, the officer panted. He gave his wrinkled face an ugly twist and pressed a hand to the small of his back; th' oul' kidneys are at me again, he moaned. I'm too far gone for this sort of thing.

The two of them were whirled into the little town of Duleek in the midst of a clay-soiled, swearing, sweating crowd of brown-clad foot-soldiers who had come pouring over the fields on to the white road. Swarming in and swarming out of the little cabins they were, and in and out of the few little shops, frantic for food and drink, prising up the floors, plunging their spiked staves into the thatch to see if any food had been hidden there; for the villagers had fled away and were hiding, waiting for the flood of hunger-mad men to ebb off outa their sight and hearing. Quarrels were breaking out between those who had found nothing and those who had found a little. Here on the threshold of a thatched cabin, two breathless men, one armed with an ugly staff shod with heavy iron on one end, the other with a thick-bladed sabre, were defending the place against an attacking group, armed in the same way, out to capture the bitten loaf of bread and the bit of meat they saw inside on a table; unmindful that they, too, when they had downed the two opposing men, would have to turn aside from their hunger and defend the bread and meat from others pressing on behind to seize the treasures. Farther down the narrow rutty street, a little war raged round a small keg of beer; already wounded men were trying to crawl away from the strife, while two forms lay before the keg, stretched out stiff to show that they were dead, and claimed to be left alone in peace. In a corner of a trampled field of corn, a shouting excited group were sticking a squealing, dodging pig with their pikes, and slashing at him with heavy cavalry swords as he ran this way and that, streaming with blood, to escape the death that was so surely coming to him; while in the distance an attentive ear could easily hear the rolling thunder of the Protestant tom-toms beating a triumphal march forward. Many, having wrung the very last drop of movement out of their bodies, lay in a deep stupor on the dirty street, stirring no way, even when heavy feet stamped careless down upon them. Some were holding a shattered arm to their breast with a sound one; many more wore bloodied clouts around their heads; and a few who had gone as far as life could take them, sprawled in the gutter, murmuring mercy out of Mary the Mother o' God for the last time in this world. From an upper window in a higher house, a young officer bellowed an appeal for a little order out of the seething crowd, but the jaded men, stampeding and roaring round for quietness and food, had no ear for him; and left him there, white-faced and agonizing, with a shouting mouth making a dumb appeal for a rally that would face about to fight again for a sacred cause. A strong sun made the smell of blood and sweat seem horrible, while loud cries shot out on every hand, cries of resentment against the bitter thought of the depredations that would surely follow their defeat.

—Where's it goin' to go we are, now? and the questioner held up his staff shod with iron at the end: looka, that's what they gave us to meet the charge of a gallopin' horse; to shove aside a cannon-ball flyin' hot in the air; or th' fall of an invincible sword fashioned at a forge in Toledo, or, maybe, in Damascus itself!

—Th' bastards! cried another; it wouldn't penethrate through cow-shit! Only give us the waypons, an' we'll fight again, an' show them, with no food an' less dhrink to nourish us!

—Twelve cannons against their fifty, an' six taken away be th' flyin' King for company, and th' other six sent to where they warn't wanted, said a third. A reasonable an' a ravin' curse be ever on th' head o' th' dastard wherever he goes; an' if he was standin' before me now, it's a sharp an' sudden look at th' closin' door o' heaven I'd be givin' him; for it's th' shamblin' caution of this King nothin' but in name that has brought to light the gapin' death wounds shown in many a poor riven body today!

Th' poor oul' Boyne, thought Johnny, stepping over a stiff figure that had a rugged little cross, made of hazel twigs, pressed close to a pair of blackened lips; the river that had on it the home of the Dagda, the earth-builder; the river hailed as a friend by Ptolemy; the river of a thousand kings; the river that in its frown of winter and its song of summer must have often flowed in fear, listening to the thundering gallop of the Grey of Macha and the Black Sainglain, once the battlesteeds of the terrible battle-goddess, Morrigu, the Battle-Crow; and the battle-creaking clang of Cuchullin's bronze-poled chariot tearing along its banks, shaking the whole valley as it shook when the waters of the magic well burst forth to chasten Boann, the beautiful daughter of Nechtan, for her contempt of it, bruising her madly, its foaming waves striking at her and chasing her quick to the sea; or the clang of shield on shield and the clash of steel against steel when the Fenians tossed their foes about in battle. No more are you, now, proud river than a poor fancy of your old form, reaching the low level of a charmless holy wather for th' Protestants of Ulsther.

Shoving a slow way through the crowd of excited, swarming soldiers towards a lane at the west side of the town, the officer, pulling Johnny after him, slipped and planked a jackboot on a green-jacketed body squirming about at the end of the lane, turning it over to show a sloppy-red breast, with waxy fingers dabbling in it, and blue lips in a waxy face that murmured in a faint bitterness, Thinka what he's brought on me; God o' th' wondhers, thinka what he's brought on me! The cowardly kindled dastard, with his, Spare me poor English subjects, when he seen me land a larrup on a Sassenach's skull that scatthered his thimble-ful o' brains an' sent them to feed th' minnows o' th' Boyne; checkin' me to a halt so that I got th' musket-ball that would ha' passed by had I moved another half-foot forward!

—Look, said the officer agitatedly, pointing a hand to the north, there go the tips of their orange-and-blue banners rising over the slopes beyond! If we stop much longer, we're done. Let these curs become captives – they'll soon find that even th' little they have here'll be less still when the orange lily blossoms where the river Shannon flows. Oh! this ache in the kidneys! Like the stab from the beak of the Morrigu! I go for a fond sleep to a little grey house in the west, to a friend at Yellow Furze, for a fond sleep and a sad sleep.

—An' leave the flag, an' leave your men, and throw away the white cockhade! said Johnny, dismayed, for he could now plainly see the rugged face of Glazier, with its flapping ears, grinning at him and making a mock of him, thumb to nose, on the summit of a hill looking down on Duleek.

—I'm leaving nothing! answered the officer angrily. I still stand for the fight in defence of our Christian inheritance. This is going to be a fluid war; and I can give vital help where I'm going. Whoever holds out the longest'll win in the end; and we'll do that; but I must have sleep, and a long rest to let the kidneys settle themselves. You cut across the fields and get to the road farther down, and hurry off to Dublin. I go to my little grey home in the west, little grey home in the west, under a spreading chestnut tree, and roses round the door, for a simple sleep for a few hundred years or so; and then we'll show them there's one more river to cross, and that our indominus indominant people are prepared to live or die for altar and throne. So goodbye, young friend; remember we're one at heart if you be Ireland's friend, there are but two great parties in the end; only two in the end, so goodbye for the present, and away he faded, faded into the smoke of the cannons; and Johnny turned and ran, too, away, away from the rabble of hungry and disconcerted soldiers making a merit of disorder and uproar in the narrow street of the town of Duleek; and just in time, for as he ran he was followed by a mocking shout from Glazier, and looking back, he saw coming over the smoky hill beyound the town, the boul' boy, followed be Inspector Doosard, leading on the tut-tut-tuttering fogeys of the Dublin Quay Police, stepping like deers prancing over the mountain heather, headed by their fife and dhrum band shrilling out the tune of *The South Down Militia* composed be Colonel Blacker of Sandy Row and Downing Street. On, on he ran, closing his eyes, and stopping his ears while passing by the siege of Athlone and Limerick and the desolation of Aughrim; opening his eyes for a second when he saw, in the core of a flash of lightning, Sarsfield galloping out of Limerick, in the wind and rain, at the head of half a thousand horsemen, fast galloping, faster still, a hard, fast, head-bent gallop to fall on the Williamites at Ballyneety; galloping through them, shouting when a sentry called out for the password, Sarsfield's the word, and Sarsfield's the man, through them, over them, past them, wheel, and a hard, fast, sword-slashing gallop back again, through them, and over them, Galloping O'Hogan, knee to knee with Sarsfield, his face alight with joy in the darkness; then down

PICTURES IN THE HALLWAY   237

with a lep, to blow, as high as halfway up to heaven, the great
siege guns gathered together to batther in the walls of Limerick,
and the long mighty tin pontoons, built to span the Shannon, to
blow them up with a bursting roar in a sheet of flame and a rending
thunder of smashing steel flying far that was a shout from Ireland,
and she on a hill, deafening the yellow-faced loons, and dazzling
them, flying all ways to shake themselves free from the biting
swords of Sarsfield's men, showing what Sarsfield could ha' done
had Sarsfield had his way, giving the shock of hope to Ireland, and
encouraging the people to call their sons, not Patrick, after the
saint, but Patrick, after the soldier; till after the red lightning-
flash and the long, long journey, Johnny stood now on the lawn in
front of the church of St Burnupus, engaged in a fight to see
whether the Orangemen could be shifted by the votes of the
Vestrymen from the Select Vestry of the parish. They, through the
Select Vestry, where they had the majority, ruled the parish, and
had harassed the rector for a long time, turning turk on him
because they thought they saw a romish gleam in the white of his
eye; because he had refused to admit that their institution had had
a divine origin; and because he had refused to become a chaplain;
because he had even opposed the loan of the church for an annual
Orange Service, when the Orangemen came in orange, purple, and
black sashes, heavy and hanging with silver regalias of King
Billies crossing the Boyne, open Bibles, crowns and anchors, an'
God knows god wot; with their dames hooked to their arms,
wearing bunches of orange lilies in their bosoms. When they'd
settled themselves, they sang suitable hymns, such as, *Tramp,
Tramp, Tramp, th' Boys are Marchin'*, *Sound th' Loud Thrumpet
an' Tickle th' Dhrum*; read suitable verses from the one and only;
and had a suitable sermon preached by a suitable cleric from a
suitable text; the rector holding that a church was the place for
the worship of God, and not a place for the veneration of any
King Billy, however noble, good, or wise a king or man he
might have been; adding that they could hardly blame the
Catholics for their doulia veneration of the saints, their hyper-
doulia veneration of the Blessed Virgin, when the Orange Brethren seemed to give a fuller and more gorgeous veneration to the
Prince of Orange, to the Rev Mr Walker, and to the defenders of
the Walls o' Durry; and because they thought, on account of the
rector's reverence for the sixth chapter of the gospel according to
St John, he seemed to hint at the real presence of Jesus in the
sacrament of the Lord's Supper. They disliked, too, the idea of

him showing such favour to Johnny, poverty stricken and ill-kept; asking him to his house, discussing all kinds of questions with him, welcoming him every Sunday to the vestry before the service began when the rector was to preach, to sing a hymn with him, or recite a prayer that the rector's words might be blessed and bear fruit in the minds of his hearers. All this, in spite of the warning that Johnny was a Fenian, a few of them saying that his mind was swelling with every sort of caustic comment on England's hold of Ireland; and that he had even tried, in their hearing and in front of their very eyes, to confound the plain warrant of Holy Scripture with the falsifying fables of the Fathers and the popery-drenched pamphlets of the Puseyites on the In-vocation of Saints and Angels, Regeneration in Baptism, and Prayers for the Dead; for Johnny often opposed even his own beliefs to heighten an argument. Because of these things, the Orangemen had opposed most of the plans of the rector, making everything he tried to do unhappy and uncertain, so that those who liked him were constrained to interfere, and use their votes to banish this unruly and unreasonable opposition; and Johnny led them on, visiting their houses, and persuading them to come and take their part in the activities of the parish. A good few of the workers were working late, and the time for voting had been extended to eleven o'clock. Such a thing, and such intense diversity, had rarely been seen in any parish before, and all was silent and determined excitement. So here was Johnny standing on the lawn, near the schoolhouse door, doing the part of a sentry to see that no disentitled or unentitled person came to cast a vote. An April night it was, with a fine moon out in the sky, and the buzz of spring in the cool nippy air. There she was like a golden disc in the breast of a blue-mantled angel, showing herself off to everything coming within her silvery circle, making the bloated spire of St Damnaman's look like a gleaming dagger held up in the huge hand of a blackman; and giving the few shabby shrubs on the lawn a mantle lovelier than the finest ever woven for the kingly back of Solomon. It was a quarter before eleven now; Johnny knew from his list that all his friends were present; that a few doubtful ones, and some who had shouted their devotion to true-blue Protestantism, hadn't yet shown themselves, and he wished that the clock would go quicker. When the first chime of the hour was struck by the clock inside, Johnny saw that the door was made fast and tight against all newcomers, and then strolled into the crowded room where the scrutineers were already making ready to count the votes. Up at the top, beside them, sat the rector, close to his eldest son, a bright and genial youth of fifteen years. Dotted here and there were the Orangemen whom Johnny knew, and he saw the yellow head and genial pugface of Georgie Middleton stuck between the bulbous one of Doosard and the lean and hungry-looking one of Donaldson: his old pal of the school had crossed the Jordan to come under the orange-and-blue banner of the House of Nassau; had become one of the half-tribe Manasseh, or a warrior of the tribe of Reuben or of Gad.

An hour of whispering passed while the votes were counted, selecting twelve good and true men to help the rector in the work of the parish. Then in a sudden silence, the result was handed to the rector's churchwarden to be read out to the Vestrymen; and Johnny saw by the grim smile on Walmsley's face that the blue-and-orange banner was low in the dust. Again he saw the flowing river and the blue sky over the yellow irises; he again scented the presence of the river-banked mass of meadow-sweet; heard the diminished sound of the Protestant drum; saw from the midst of the moon-daisies the gathering of the Irish, with James, a chaca, left behind, and Sarsfield at their head.

Not a single name of the Orange party's choice appeared on the list of elected members, and a great clapping of hands sounded a *feu de joie* for the Orangemen, who stood up, and went out in silence and an angry shame. When Georgie Middleton was passing by, Johnny held out a hand to him, but Middleton struck it down and passed by and went out. Glazier halted for a moment before Johnny and stared him hard in the face.

—I never thought I'd live, he said bitterly, to see a Jesuitical manifestation in this parish! But, looksee, all of ye, we are prepared to fight to the last man, and die on our own doorsteps if need be, for a Protestant althar and a Protestant throne! And he and his friends passed out to walk under the wonders of the moon.

The Vestrymen, their work done and battle won, filed out, murmuring good wishes into the rector's ear. Coming over to Johnny, he shook his hand warmly, saying, Thanks, John, for all you did. It's a pity it had to be done, he added with a sigh, for even minor disunity is far from desirable.

—It has, at least, placed you among friends, said Johnny.

—I deeply wish you were one of them John.

—I can be one without being on the vestry, said Johnny, embarrassed, but pleased. Better men than I have been selected.

—They didn't think of you, said the rector; had I been of them, your name, John, would have been thrust forward. He placed a hand affectionately on Johnny's shoulder. You are a remarkable soul in many ways, and your presence would have been a great encouragement to me.

—The mother'll be glad you won; she sent her best wishes.

—Thank her for me, John. A dear and intelligent woman – she always reminds me of my own mother, and a soft light shot into his keen eyes. I suppose we must call it a victory, John, though I had rather there had risen no need for a fight; and that we Christians were content to hold the faith in unity of spirit, and in the bond of peace. Goodnight, dear friend, and God be with you. He shook John's hand again and went his way, with his son, to walk under the wonder of the moon.

When all were gone, and the lights out, and the door shut, Johnny went his way home, the midnight moon laying down a silvery carpet under his passing feet, slow to move towards sleep, and end the day. By his help, the orange banner had been replaced by the green flag, or the blue, with the sunburst awake in its centre. Whatever its colour or symbol might be, how well it would look flying from the turrets of the church, like a rare jewel entrusted to hold together the silvery mantle of the shining moon.

He shook himself. He was staying too long in the Hallway looking at the pictures. All done by others. Very beautiful and strong, but all done by others. He'd have to start now doing things for himself. Create things out of his own life. He'd begin to make pictures himself; ay, pictures, too, that would be worth hanging in the Hallway for other people to see.